THE FA[LL]

of the

UNITED STATES

How prophetic end-time events bring down the world's greatest superpower & ignite WWIII

RONALD WEINLAND

Copyright © 2022 by the-end.com, inc.
All rights reserved. Published April 15, 2022
Printed in the United States of America

the-end.com, inc., P.O. Box 14447, Cincinnati, OH 45250
Visit our website at **falloftheus.com**

Library of Congress Cataloging-in-Publication Data
Weinland, Ronald.
  Fall of the United States
  ISBN: 978-0-9753240-2-8

CONTENTS

Chapter 1   1
IS THE WORLD GOING MAD?

Chapter 2   19
MAJOR ATTACKS AGAINST THE U.S.

Chapter 3   49
END-TIME DESTRUCTION

Chapter 4   82
TURMOIL WITHIN RELIGION

Chapter 5   122
END-TIME DESTRUCTION IN TWO CHRISTIANITIES

Chapter 6   154
GOD'S CHURCH IN THE END-TIME

Chapter 7   179
THE SEVEN THUNDERS—A PRELUDE TO WWIII

Chapter 8   197
GOD'S HOLY DAYS REVEAL HIS PLAN

Chapter 1
IS THE WORLD GOING MAD?

HAVE YOU EVER FELT that the world is going mad? People can no longer coexist with one another. Corporations are trying to make money at the expense of others. Nations are edging closer and closer to war. The world is increasingly becoming more chaotic and peace seems to be so far-off. The ability to work together to resolve differences has all but disappeared.

Drama has taken on new meaning as conflict is being acted out in people's lives with rapidly increasing tension, stress, frustration, misery, and unhappiness. Drama is becoming a way of life as dissension is being stirred up and conversations consist of an apparent need to "share" one's misery and dissatisfaction in life with others.

Much of this very negative effect on human life is the result of an accelerating dependency on technology. The ability to quickly and widely disperse the spread of information and ideas is growing out of control. In turn, this has enabled the escalation of drama that is more easily and more readily finding its way into people's lives. Many find the result to be overwhelming and they are unable to cope with the impact that it's wreaking on their daily lives.

Few seem to grasp how these things are changing society in a way that is taking peace and calm out of our lives. These rapid changes taking place in society are a direct result of mankind's inability to adjust to such fast growth in the advancement of technology.

Since this technology is new, we do not have any precedent for how to use it properly. Little thought about our health and wellbeing is considered with its development. This in turn is having a very negative impact on human life—one that is not being readily recognized for the depth of danger that actually exists.

Slaves to Technology?
For thousands of years, mankind moved forward slowly in its understanding of science and of the world itself, as well as the life that is on it. It hasn't been until the last one hundred and fifty years that real accelerated growth in the mastery of mathematics, engineering, physics, astronomy, and chemistry have begun to truly take hold. This has had a huge impact on human life.

Especially over the past seventy years, technology has consistently been increasing in its momentum and is having a larger impact on the way we live. Technology has produced a very positive impact on the quality of human life. But along with this, the misuse of technology has also been thrusting its way forward and it is having a very negative impact on society.

The rate at which these changes occur has been growing so rapidly that society is finding that it cannot keep up. As a result, the ability to adequately address technology's negative impact on people's lives is sorely lacking.

Just pause and consider how so many are seemingly becoming slaves to technology. The use and often misuse of cell phones is a perfect example. The Internet and apps allow for an endless array of ways to control every aspect of life. The "need" for this constant contact is becoming addictive. This should come as no surprise as software developers are constantly manipulating people's behaviors to keep us glued to their products for the longest time possible, and in return, they make more money.

Addicted users can easily be spotted as they walk around like zombies, unable to look away from their phones. Some cross in front of traffic because they cannot see the car or truck heading toward them. Others can be spotted behind the wheel of a car, unable to move forward when the traffic light turns green because the urge to engage with their phone is just too strong. Sadly, entire families have also been transformed into tech junkies. They can easily be observed in just about any restaurant, sitting in complete silence as each member dives deep into their own hole in cyberspace.

Through Facebook, WhatsApp, Twitter, Instagram, TikTok, Reddit, and many other venues for social media, drama is being shared on levels never remotely experienced in ages past. People's lives are becoming captive to these seductive creations of modern technology. As a result, the diminishing exchange of shared life experiences, in live face-to-face contact, is creating a need for the dependency of the human mind to be fed with steady flows of information. This is actually robbing people of rewarding life experiences and of the potential for a far more meaningful and enjoyable social life.

The sharing of life through technology is not the same as learning and experiencing how to live life through sharing with others on a personal plane through face-to-face relationships. There is a great difference between the two. Those who develop a dependency on such media find a growing dissatisfaction with life. Hopefully, the COVID-19 pandemic has helped more people to appreciate the difference.

This dependency can easily begin to cause individuals to become less sensitive and caring toward others. It can create a numbness and an inconsiderate mindset toward others. This inward retreat into oneself produces greater selfishness and drama in life and the ways of calm and peace become more obscure.

These distinctions are clearly escaping the attention and understanding of these tech addicts, most of whom do not even realize the extent of their usage. The result is producing a world where not just individuals, but communities, organizations, and even nations are turning inward. This only produces accelerating divisiveness, contention, disagreement, and social unrest between people.

The result is **drama** on a level that has never remotely been experienced before, and the world isn't able to deal with it. It has spiraled out of control, and indeed, the world is going mad!

Today, the concepts of mutual compromise, making concessions, searching for agreeable middle ground, give-and-take, or finding a happy medium seem nearly foreign. It is as though these concepts have become a lost art. Yet it is through such learned practices that people can grow closer together and thereby work out differences that can then produce rewarding results in life.

Reaping What We Sow

If life wasn't confusing enough, now we have terms like "woke," "cancel culture," and "cultural appropriation" that we must familiarize ourselves with for fear of otherwise offending others, perhaps being rejected, or of even being attacked. We find we are being increasingly pressured to fit into a specific mold of how to act and what to speak about or not speak about.

An environment that pressures others to be in agreement or disagreement with them tends to only widen the gap that works to alienate and divide society even more. Peaceful or calm conversation with others who hold different ideas or opinions is becoming rare.

Instead, society and nations are rapidly moving inward into a spirit of heightened selfishness and egotistical behavior. Too many want their own way and will slander, demean, ridicule, resist, mock, fight, tear down, fiercely debate, and attack anyone or anything that gets in the way of what it is they want. What others want is simply dismissed and not even considered.

Since COVID-19 struck, a downward spiral has sped up this negative process that is producing division and discontent throughout every nation. This has also produced an even greater dependency on social media. The exceedingly bad news is that this is only going to get worse—much, much worse before it will begin to change.

Just over the last year, there has been a dramatic shift away from what anyone could truly classify as peace. Instead, we see rapidly rising discontent, disagreement, division, chaos, lawlessness, crime, suicide, murder, drug addiction, abuse and misuse of power, oppression, etc. Yes, the world is moving toward madness!

This rapidly veering shift away from peace in the world is being witnessed by change that is clearly moving the thinking and actions of many toward extremism. Moderation is needed to bring opposing sides together in order to more effectively work out differences. However, the news today only reports on the extremes of both sides because that is what causes people to react and respond emotionally. This in turn results in people's emotions controlling them, therefore, they tend to move farther into the extreme right, extreme left, or the extreme on whatever position is being taken.

Algorithms used by social media further intensify this push to the extremes by uniting people with similar views and excluding those with opposing views. When people are only exposed to a one-sided conversation, the potential **balancing benefit** of different views and ideas is eliminated. This tends to polarize society and create further extremism on both sides.

As a result, more people are being unwittingly moved into a position of choosing sides. Once this happens the natural inclination is to not back down. This too is exactly what is happening on an international scale between nations, which is then producing an environment of confrontation between nations that is creating a new era of saber-rattling.

It is not possible to close your eyes and hope everything changes soon or that it will simply just go away. Instead, we need to understand that there is a cause for all that is going on and it is affecting everyone. No one can hide, even though some may try. The world is beginning to reap what it has sown over the past few decades.

Due to the growing misuse of ever-evolving technology, we are witnessing a dangerous change in society that is leading the world into a horrifying war.

Warned for Over 70 Years!

What the world is now witnessing and experiencing is a rapid movement toward a **prophesied third world war**. There are few in the world today who are actually aware of world events and news that affect trends, thinking, world trade, economies, international relations, and the steady movement toward a world war.

For over 70 years now, there have been forewarnings of very specific end-time events that would come to pass which would lead into a third world war. Many of these pronouncements were about major events to occur in Europe and they have been taking place exactly as one man foretold.

Let's consider what began to be said about this coming war back in early 1950. Right after WWII, it was perfectly predicted how there would be four major events that would occur in Western Europe, which would lead up to the beginning of WWIII. Three have come to pass and the construct of the last one has now been recently reported in European news.

It was stated that Germany would rise in world power as the leading nation of the united European nations. This seemed totally ludicrous – nonsensical – to so many who heard it, especially considering the devastation that had just been wrecked upon Germany by the allied forces.

Yet this man explained how **(1)** Europe, with Germany at its helm, would rise up again in a union of nations that would have **(2)** a common government, **(3)** a common currency, and **(4)** a final military union that would consist of exactly 10 European nations.

Think of how absurd it must have appeared to so many at that time, when right after WWII a man was saying that Germany – a nation reduced to rubble – was going to rise again and be at the forefront of a united Europe. This seemed so preposterous that this individual was indeed highly ridiculed and dismissed by most who heard these predictions.

How could anyone be taken seriously by proclaiming such things back at that time after such a horrible war had just been fought between the Allies and the Axis powers of Germany, Italy, and Japan? Millions had lost their lives.

Yet, after these things were predicted to come to pass, it was seven years later, in March of 1957, that France, West Germany, Italy, the Netherlands, Belgium, and Luxembourg signed the Treaty of Rome to establish the European Economic Community (EEC), also known as the Common Market. This eventually transformed into the development of the European Union that exists today.

This man stated that these forewarnings were **end-time prophecies** that God had revealed to him. So again, the question should be asked, "How could a person predict something so seemingly incredulous that has now proven to be so absolutely true?"

Although many people mocked and ridiculed what he claimed were end-time events that would lead up to WWIII, these events he predicted continued to come to pass as he said they would. Although he did see Europe come together in a cooperative governmental structure in 1957, it wasn't until 13 years after his death that Europe introduced the currency of the euro to the world in 1999. This European Union grew to be 28 nations, and only recently has Great Britain opted out of that union. So far, 19 of the 27 member states of the European Union have adopted the euro as their official currency.

Then, 32 years after his death, in 2018, Europe entered into a unified military agreement among **10 nations** - which is the exact number he also foretold would come to pass.

The following are excerpts from *THE WEEK* magazine dated 8 November 2018 in the article entitled, "Emmanuel Macron unveils European defense coalition."

> A coalition of ten European militaries ready to defend the continent's borders has been unveiled in Paris, just days after Emmanuel Macron called for a "real European army". [...]
>
> *Reuters* reports that the European Intervention Initiative took official shape in Paris "after months of negotiations with

Germany, who France wants at the centre of the force".

The imminent departure from the EU of Britain, long opposed to EU military collaboration outside Nato, has revived talk of defence cooperation - as have concerns that Trump might prove less willing than his predecessors to come to Europe's defence in the face of a newly assertive Russia.

Macron's push to bring together a core 10-nation coalition of the willing "was born out of French impatience with the EU's efforts at defence co-operation", known as Permanent Structured Co-operation (Pesco) says *The Economist*. [...]

Coming just days after Macron called for a "real European army" to reduce dependence on the United States, and with the vocal support of senior figures in Brussels, the coalition agreement will once again be raising the spectre of a European Army.[1]

This final major prediction concerning a uniting military force within Europe has much to do with other future events since much of what will come to pass centers around Europe's involvement in this last great war.

But before proceeding, it needs to be asked, "How could anyone make such predictions *that* early on that seemed so ludicrous to most people? How could anyone give such forewarnings that were so exact concerning what would come to pass in Europe?" This in itself should cause people to stand up and take notice because it was explained that after these events would come to pass that the next thing to follow is... a nuclear war. So now, just how close is that war?

The predictions of those four major events for Europe have actually proven to be true and have come to pass over a period of nearly 70 years now. But what is even more important is the matter of how people have responded.

That response has much to do with the purpose of why this book is being written. And although those prognostications have occurred exactly as they were given, there are many more warnings concerning predictions that are now coming to pass and even escalating.

Prophecies About Europe Given 2500 Years Ago
In the Bible, the prophet known as Daniel had prophetic revelations given to him that are directly tied to what was revealed to this man nearly 70 years ago about Europe.

It was nearly **2500 years** ago, after the nation of Judah was conquered and the people were taken into captivity in Babylon, that Daniel began to have many prophetic things revealed to him that have come to pass in the rise and fall of kingdoms and nations ever since. The coming together of these final ten nations of Europe actually began to be revealed when Daniel was given to interpret a troublesome dream of Nebuchadnezzar, the king of Babylon.

The dream was about a great statue that was constructed of different metals throughout. Only Daniel was found who could tell him what his dream was and what it meant.

It was on this occasion when Nebuchadnezzar had called upon Daniel to interpret the dream, Daniel replied by letting him know that there was no one who had any such ability to reveal what his dream was about, not even him.

"*Daniel answered in the presence of the king and said, 'The secret which the king has demanded cannot be declared to the king by the wise men, astrologers, magicians, or the soothsayers. But there is a God in heaven who reveals secrets, and He has made known to king Nebuchadnezzar what will be* **in the latter days.** *Your dream, and the visions of your head upon your bed, were these...*'" (Daniel 2:27-28).

God used this dream to reveal through Daniel all the major kingdoms of the world that would lead up to the latter day, up to the very end-time. The following verses explain that passage of time as Daniel began by telling the king what he saw.

"You, O king, were watching; and behold, a great image! This great image, whose splendor was excellent, stood before you, and its form was awesome. This image's head was of fine gold, its chest and arms of silver, its stomach and hips of bronze, its legs of iron, and its feet partly of iron and partly of clay. You watched while a stone was cut out without hands, which struck the image on its feet of iron and clay, and broke them in pieces. Then the iron, the clay, the bronze, the silver, and the gold were crushed into dust, and it became like chaff from the summer threshing floors, and the wind carried them away so that no trace of them could be found. Then the stone that struck the image became a great mountain and filled the whole earth" (Daniel 2:31-35).

In a condensed explanation, as one moves from the top of the statue to the bottom, one is moving through time until the end-time when the toes are reached. The first part of the image of gold was about the Chaldean-Babylonian Empire of which Nebuchadnezzar was king in that present kingdom of Babylon. This was followed by the portion made of silver which represented the Medo-Persian Empire, and after that, the bronze, being the Greco-Macedonian Empire that followed.

The interpretation of the dream began with the description of the statue's head of gold being the present kingdom of Babylon under Nebuchadnezzar, and it went on about the rise and fall of major kingdoms (empires) through time. It ended with the fourth portion of the statue, which was uniquely described as being legs of iron with feet of both iron and clay. This represented the last great kingdom that would go through several revivals in Europe.

A statue with feet of iron and clay is not a good mixture for supporting such a large figure. Yet the legs of iron and the feet of iron mixed with clay describe so very well the struggle that has gone on for hundreds of years in Europe. Much of its pertinent history carried the identity of the Roman Empire, and later, the Holy Roman Empire. Its history fits succinctly into prophecy that describes it in several places of scripture.

Daniel was given to know that the lower part of this statue was about a future kingdom that would lead up to events that would change this world in "the latter days." Although it was revealed to Daniel that this statue was about future kingdoms that would rule, the identity of those kingdoms was not yet known.

The knowledge of who those kingdoms were throughout history and the knowledge of how modern-day Europe is identified in this statue was, in turn, **revealed** to this man who foretold these events that have now come to pass. This man knew these things because of these and other prophetic warnings that he came to see and believe concerning the **end-time**—events that were **revealed to him by God**. There is no other way to know AND predict the things he said – so accurately – so perfectly – other than the fact that it had to come from God. Just as Daniel stated to Nebuchadnezzar, "NO human has such ability."

So Who Was This Man?
The man who began warning about a third world war and of those specific events that would transpire in Europe was Herbert W. Armstrong. Before his death in 1986, he had been responsible for publishing tens of millions of books, booklets, and magazines that contained much information about the end-time. *The Plain Truth* magazine alone was being published in seven languages with a monthly circulation of over 8.2 million copies. At that time, by comparison, the well-known and highly circulated *Time* magazine only had a circulation of 5.9 million.

His weekly television program *The World Tomorrow*, along with his radio broadcasts, blanketed the United States and large portions of the rest of the world. The reach and scope of this coverage was far more than any other religious organization had ever done or has done since.

It is interesting to see how others in the world recognized that there was something unique and meaningful in what he was saying. However, he was treated far differently in the United States where he lived and worked than how he was by many other nations.

His recognition from people in other areas of the world primarily began when he received a very unique award from King Leopold

III of Belgium. It was a watch made from a cannonball taken from a battlefield in World War I by Leopold's father, King Albert I. King Albert had the cannonball cast into four watch cases with the desire that they would be presented to the four individuals that he felt had made **the most significant contribution to world peace.** King Albert never found anyone he felt worthy to receive the fourth watch, and so, he passed it on to his son, who was moved to give it to Herbert Armstrong in 1970.

From that time forward, recognition of Herbert Armstrong from other world leaders grew and he became known to many as an "ambassador without portfolio for world peace." He carried his message to Prince Mikasa and a number of the members of the Japanese Diet. Emperor Hirohito conferred upon Herbert Armstrong the Order of the Sacred Treasure, Second Class—one of the highest decorations that can be presented to a non-Japanese. During a period that covered two decades, seven successive Japanese Prime Ministers counted Herbert Armstrong as a personal friend and counselor. Some members of the Japanese Diet even referred to themselves as being his Japanese sons. Although these leaders showed great admiration for Hebert Armstrong, none of them acted upon the end-time warnings he proclaimed.

Herbert Armstrong was endeared in friendship with King Hussein of Jordan, King Bhumibol Adulyadej and Queen Sirikit of Thailand, and Prime Ministers of Israel, including Golda Meir and Menachem Begin. Others who counted him as a personal friend were Egyptian President, Anwar Sadat; Jomo Kenyatta, Founder and first President of Kenya; Emperor Haile Selassie of Ethiopia; Mayor Teddy Kollek of Jerusalem; and longtime friend, Nagendra Singh, who was a Justice at the World Court in The Hague, Netherlands.

Herbert Armstrong also had personal meetings with leaders like Prime Minister Margaret Thatcher of the United Kingdom; Juan Carlos, the King of Spain; Egyptian President, Hosni Mubarak; and Indian Prime Minister, Indira Gandhi. Yet again, of all of these world leaders, none acted upon the message he carried.

President Ferdinand Marcos of the Philippines decorated Mr. Armstrong with the Presidential Merit Medal "for his moral presence and compelling influence in moving people toward the creation of a just and peaceful world order." He received the decoration of "Commander of Our Most Nobel Order of the Crown of Thailand." Once again, neither of these leaders nor their people acted upon the warnings he carried.

Other leaders with whom Herbert Armstrong met included President Allende of Chile; President Suharto of Indonesia; South Vietnam's president, Nguyen Van Thieu; and he was invited to Romania by President Nicolae Ceausescu.

Herbert Armstrong also met with Deng Xiaoping of the People's Republic of China and was the first recognized Christian leader to officially visit leaders inside China, yet this went unreported in the world. In this unprecedented visit, he addressed officials from 76 nations in the People's Great Hall in Beijing. He spoke concerning the way to real peace and why humanity fails to achieve it. No other religious leader has ever been invited to such an event in China, yet the world has known nothing of this.

Herbert Armstrong received numerous other honors and visited many other world leaders, but it went fully unnoticed by the western world to whom Herbert Armstrong said that God had sent him to proclaim His message.

End-Time Prophecies About the U.S.A.
Herbert Armstrong not only foretold of specific events that have now been fulfilled by the European Union, but he also gave specific prognostications concerning more notable modern- day nations.

The nation that has received the greatest warnings over the longest period of time is the very nation that will be the first that is prophesied to fall. Major predictions were covered in his most widely published book, *The United States and Britain In Prophecy*. Yet it is within the United States that Herbert Armstrong was looked down upon the most as he was maligned, falsely and maliciously lied about, hated, and even persecuted by his own government.

Even after more than three and a half decades since his death, there is still much hatred and lying reflected in those things written about him. This is not at all unlike what happened to Christ who was also deeply hated by others because of the message he was sent to give mankind. It is far more about the "message" than it is about any individual who delivers it.

Throughout history, mankind has been consistent about not wanting God to meddle in its affairs. And how is that going? It is God who has created all things and given us this incredible planet to live upon, but look at what we are doing to it, especially now through the technology that has been developed. This earth has been polluted far more over the past couple of decades than it has over the preceding several thousand years put together.

With ever-burgeoning populations and such massive misuse of technology, mankind is only proving what God has said about what would happen if we continue to ignore Him. We will simply continue to destroy this creation itself. God has revealed that if He did not intervene to stop us that we would finally end up annihilating ourselves.

This ability to destroy the planet has not been possible until this present age with its explosion in technology. It is through the misuse of technology and what it can produce that mankind can destroy itself and this earth.

The truth about end-time events has permeated the United States for decades and people have not seemed to care. It needs to be stated again that Herbert Armstrong began warning of final end-time events directly after WWII. That warning went out with great power to the United States, but the people and their leaders did not show much concern about it. **They did not listen.**

That trend of not caring and of **not listening to those warnings** has only worsened over the years since Herbert Armstrong died in 1986. This type of apathy has been fueled by and speeded up by rapidly growing technology that has now actually led the rest of the nations of the world into this same kind of spirit that has been permeating the United States for some time now.

That spirit that produces a willing deafness toward warnings about a nuclear war for this end-time is the very purpose for writing this fifth book. Four books precede this one that focus on the cataclysmic warnings of WWIII that are about to engulf this world.

The first book was *The Prophesied End-Time*, which was published in June of 2004. Additional prophecies beyond what Herbert Armstrong foretold about the European Union were addressed, and they explain the truth about the end-time events in Revelation, known as the **"Four Horsemen of the Apocalypse."** Each of those events that traditional Christianity has misunderstood about the end-time and are still looking to be fulfilled have already taken place. Their fulfillment began to emerge on the world scene in 1994.

Then the second book followed which was published in 2006 and it was entitled, *2008—God's Final Witness*. This covered additional prophetic prognostications about two witnesses, described in the Book of Revelation, who will come on the world scene in a very active manner once catastrophic end-time events have actually begun. This book further describes what the **Seven Thunders of Revelation** are all about. The first great event of those Thunders actually began with the **9/11 attacks** (11th of September 2001).

This book also included a strong warning of a coming economic collapse, which did strike the world in 2008. Even today, economists continue to compare what is happening now to the trends of what occurred in 2008.

The third book published ten years later in 2016 was entitled, *Prophesy Against the Nations*. It focused upon a message given by God for the end-time once cataclysmic events begin: if any nation would listen to Him, then He, in turn, would listen to them.

When the Countdown Ends was the fourth book which was published by May 2020. That book thoroughly outlined a very specific timeline of events that have been occurring since 1994, which outline a prophesied countdown to WWIII. Once this book was written, it then became glaringly obvious how quickly the world had become so much worse since the second book was published in 2006. This too is a great sign of how close that final war is.

When that fourth book concerning a specific countdown to the end of this age was published, it was rare to find any article in the news that reflected concern of a coming world war. Now, for those who do a little searching for such news around the globe, such articles can be found on a regular basis. Yet people don't seem to take notice, and they certainly don't show any deep concern or worry about it as they should.

Similarly, as it was before WWII, people are mostly asleep concerning the threat of another world war. Only in this past year have some begun to show a few signs that they see movement toward such a war. It is like awakening out of a deep sleep and still being very groggy. However, people will find that it is too late at this stage to address such matters on any national level because the majority will remain asleep. Only the war itself will begin to awaken people, and with a nuclear war, that is just too late!

Nuclear War Is the Ultimate Madness
Throughout the centuries, wars have come and gone. But, over the past century, war has become increasingly devastating due to the rapid development of technology. Toward the end of WWII, the world was sobered when the first two atomic bombs were dropped on Japan. It only took two of these new bombs to kill nearly 200,000 people.

Those two bombs were actually very small compared to what mankind has developed since. Nuclear weapons have now been made that are nearly 4,000 times more powerful. That is very difficult to grasp, let alone to imagine the destructive capacity they contain.

The first two atomic bombs sent up a mushroom cloud, each to about 25,000 feet (over 4.7 miles) or 7,600 meters. In 1961, the Russians set off the Tsar Bomba (RDS-220) that sent up a mushroom cloud over 37 miles high or 60 kilometers and sent shockwaves around the globe nearly three times over. Such power is nearly unimaginable. The flash of that detonation was seen some 620 miles away (1,000 km). An uninhabited village 34 miles (55 km) away from ground zero was leveled, and buildings were damaged as far away as 100 miles (160 km). Such a device could nearly level the entire city of Los Angeles or New York City.

The ability to annihilate all life on earth has not existed until the development of nuclear weapons. The world is now inching closer to using them, and mankind has always used the invention of weapons of war.

Although it would seem unthinkable, nations will begin to use nuclear weapons once the first ones are unleashed upon the United States.

The ultimate madness of this present age is about to manifest itself in the ultimate insanity of human thinking as this world is plunged into a nuclear nightmare.

Back in August 1945, when those two atomic bombs exploded in Japan, the world entered a new age. It was the beginning of an age that revealed what God long ago declared would eventually come to pass. It involves much prophecy that God foretold would happen in the end-time—not of the end of mankind, but the end of one age and the dawning of a new one.

More Prognostications for Our Time NOW
God gave evidence to support His warning that when specific events would come to pass in Europe, then a final world war would soon follow. Herbert Armstrong gave those warnings about what would be fulfilled in Europe before that war would begin.

In addition to those preliminary end-time prophecies that have now been fulfilled, the fulfilling of several other prophecies are now to quickly follow, and some have already begun. Prophetic events that have not been recognized by this world include such things as 9/11, the economic collapse of 2008, and even the COVID-19 pandemic.

These kinds of events will intensify in frequency and magnitude of their impact upon every nation on earth. Knowing that there are future events still to come which are prophesied to take place can help give much-needed strength to make it through what is now in front of us.

We must first focus on some of the horrific events that are destined to come to pass and to learn more about how God is revealing them at this time. These events are even more specifically identified and outlined than those Herbert Armstrong gave concerning the rise of the European Union.

The reality is that we are living in extremely volatile times. Catastrophic events are soon going to begin erupting throughout this world, regardless of what anyone thinks, believes, or does. They are going to happen just as the events concerning Europe have now come to pass.

Although these prophetic events are highly unpleasant to consider, it must be understood why they must be allowed to happen before a far better world can finally emerge.

Indeed, the world is in a decline and getting much worse. Revolutions and wars come and go, but nothing changes. Leaders come in and out of office, but no great changes occur that dramatically improve life. People want meaningful change but can't seem to attain it.

So why has God allowed the world to continue as it has, generation after generation? Why would He now allow for over 1/3 of all life to be erased from existence? Why would God allow for such destruction that is prophesied to happen in our time? What is the purpose?

If this final war is not the end of mankind, then what is to follow? These are important questions that have astonishing answers. And there is good news about what is to follow!

Footnotes

[1] "Emmanuel Macron unveils European defense coalition." The Week, 8 November 2018, www.theweek.co.uk/97636/emmanuel-macron-unveils-european-defence-coalition.

Chapter 2

MAJOR ATTACKS AGAINST THE U.S.

AS STATED BEFORE, Herbert Armstrong perfectly predicted four great events that pertained to Europe rising once again with Germany as the predominant leader. He began to give these predictions in earnest starting in 1950. However, it took 68 years for them to all come to pass.

More recent prognostications have been given about other specific end-time events. These events have already been leading up to and include what will soon transpire in the final war—WWIII. These prophetic events for the end-time have been accelerating in their fulfillment, especially since 9/11.

A perfect example is given in the Bible concerning this accelerated process that is now happening. God gave an analogy to show how the process for final events would come to pass. It is likened to a woman in labor before giving birth. In the beginning, the contractions tend to be further apart, and with less intensity and suffering. But over the complete time of labor, the contractions begin to occur more frequently, and the intensity and suffering also increase.

Although the labor in childbirth is usually spread out over several hours, the final fulfillment for end-time events is spread out over many years. While something that comes to pass in a short period of time, as in hours, is easy to understand, the ability to clearly see something that is happening over a few decades is much more difficult. Nevertheless, final events are accelerating in frequency, as well as in intensity.

End-Time Events Sealed Until Now!
Through only a few verses in the Book of Daniel and the Book of Revelation, it was revealed to Herbert Armstrong the meaning of events concerning Europe's rise just before a final world war would begin. But there are many verses in the Book of Revelation that expand on this and numerous other events that will be fulfilled in this last period of the end-time.

John, who was both a prophet and an apostle, wrote the Book of Revelation because he was told to record what was shown to him while he was imprisoned on the Isle of Patmos by the Roman government. Although it was revealed to him what he was to write, it was not revealed to him what these things meant. God made it clear that these things were not to have their meaning revealed until the latter days in the end-time.

Although many prophetic things concerning our time now were given to both Daniel and John, as well as to many other prophets, they were not given understanding of these things. Daniel wanted to know the meaning of those prophetic things he had written concerning the "latter days," and he asked, "When will the end of these things be?" Then he was given a very direct answer:

"*Go your way, Daniel, for the words are* **closed up** *and* **sealed** *until the* **time of the end**" (Daniel 12:9).

The Seals of Revelation were also to remain closed up and sealed until this end-time. We are now very close to having final catastrophic events come to pass because the reality is that all Seven Seals have already been opened and have all had their meaning revealed. There are no **more Seals to be opened**, and this in itself loudly cries out of how close WWIII actually is.

It was stated earlier how traditional Christianity has misunderstood the events known as the Four Horsemen of the Apocalypse and that they are still looking for these prophesies to be fulfilled. These Four Horsemen are what are being described in the first four Seals of Revelation.

The reason some in traditional Christianity believe the end-time is so much farther away is because they are still looking for the First Seal to be opened since they believe these Four Horsemen are about catastrophic events that will come upon this world. Yet that Seal was opened on the 17th of December 1994. Traditional Christianity has not recognized what happened on that day because these were about events which took place in God's Church and not on the world scene.

The Omen of 9/11

Destructive and even cataclysmic end-time events that are prophesied for this world to experience began with the opening of the **Sixth Seal** of Revelation. That opening occurred on the 11th of September 2001, the day of the First Thunder of Revelation.

In addition to the Seven Seals in Revelation, there are seven specific Thunders that reveal end-time events that are to take place until WWIII is over.

The events of 9/11 were the revelation that the First Thunder was now starting. That Thunder is about the beginning "terror of war" for the end-time. This was the FIRST physical event that not only served to fulfill a small beginning for end-time tribulation that had **just begun**, but it also served as a **prophetic sign** of what would follow that would thrust the world into a third world war—a nuclear war.

The prophetic sign fulfilled by the events of 9/11 serves as a kind of omen—a prophetic glimpse—of a foreboding that will culminate in the complete collapse of the United States as a nation. Although this was a terrorist attack, it foreshadows major attacks that will come from nations that possess nuclear weapons.

Consider what happened on that prophetic day. From the vantage point of all nations of the world, there could have been no greater symbol for the great wealth, might, and stature of the United States than that of the World Trade Center towers in New York.

Seven buildings were destroyed which in itself carries great prophetic significance. God uses this number often to symbolize "that which is complete." God declares that He established the seven-day week at creation. He also established seven annual Holy Days that he gave Israel to observe, with each in itself being prophetic in nature.

Seven is also used extensively in the Book of Revelation. There are, of course, the Seven Seals of Revelation, and the Seventh Seal itself is divided into seven specific segments that describe WWIII and how it is brought to an end. These are revealed by the announcements of the Seven Trumpets of the Seventh Seal.

Even the Sixth Seal is divided into seven segments that reveal the Seven Thunders.

While the World Trade Center was best known for its iconic 110-story Twin Towers, it was actually comprised of seven towers in total. All of the original buildings of the complex were destroyed in the September 11, 2001 attacks. Towers One and Two collapsed, and the others (numbers 3, 4, 5, & 6) were damaged beyond repair and later demolished. Building Seven collapsed in the late afternoon on the day of the attacks.

The meaning of a world trade center and its symbolism for Wall Street and a worldwide economic system should not be lost on anyone. The first event that will soon occur has to do with worldwide trade, as a major global economic implosion first destroys the economy of the U.S. above all others. The **complete** destruction of these seven buildings is prophetically symbolic of the complete destruction that will come upon the wealthiest nation the world has ever known.

Even the jet that struck the Pentagon is a prophetic foreboding of what will happen once the first four Trumpets of the Seventh Seal are unleashed upon the United States. This will be seen first and foremost with the downfall of the world's greatest military power.

The Next Attack on the United States Will Be Nuclear

The events of the first five Trumpets will fulfill what the attack on 9/11 portended. This fulfillment is about the complete collapse and demise of the United States through the use of nuclear weapons.

It is necessary to first review what is described by these Trumpet announcements that reveal the events that start WWIII. Afterward, it will be important to show how these events describe nuclear attacks upon the United States.

The first four Trumpets of the Seventh Seal are about the first major attack that is made upon the United States of America. She has been the greatest single nation in the end-time, and the events of these four Trumpets are structured to cripple her world dominance, influence, and power. She is the first of all nations to be humbled by God because she has been given the most by Him and has been given the greatest opportunity to listen but has not. This humbling process that will be poured out upon the United States will be very strong against her.

The impact of these four Trumpets will also be felt by the United Kingdom, Canada, Australia, and New Zealand, and they will suffer mightily as well. However, the extent of their suffering fully depends upon how each country responds once the impact from the First Trumpet is realized. If they do not respond correctly, as the full force of each Trumpet begins to be unleashed, then they will only multiply their own suffering.

The world was shocked by what happened to the United States on 9/11. However, that shock is nothing compared to the shock and fear that will grip the world once the events of these four Trumpets begin to take place. The destruction from these events unfolds quickly, just as the events of 9/11 unfolded in one day.

WWIII will begin as these events develop, and the greatest exchange of weapons in an all-out nuclear war will begin soon after this.

Revelation 8 shows in very prophetic language the events that will lead to the fall of the United States as the first nation to be brought down.

"The first angel sounded, and hail and fire followed mingled with blood, and they were cast upon the earth, and a third part of trees were burned up, and all green grass was burned up" (Revelation 8:7).

This First Trumpet event begins with what John could only describe from this vision as being "great fire being cast to the earth" and becoming mixed with blood. He tried to describe in the best way he could what he saw concerning the weaponry of today and its destructiveness.

This is indeed about modern weaponry that can appear as bright fire coming out of the sky and engulfing life in its path. It not only kills humans and animals in its immediate path, but it also reaches far beyond, causing massive destruction on all forms of vegetation.

It needs to be understood that it does not say this happens across the entirety of the nation since this is not about an all-out nuclear attack. These first events are only about the beginning of what takes place that will end up fully crippling the U.S. That which is being described by this verse only concerns the areas of the country in which this takes place.

It does not reveal where this attack comes from and prophecy does not specifically declare who is behind it, but it will happen. It will happen to the most powerful nation the world has ever known.

That which is described next by the Second Trumpet is not something that happens much later. Through the prophetic language being used, it reveals that this is something that can happen simultaneously with the first.

John next describes what he saw happening in a port city, yet this could be about more than one port city. A number is simply not revealed.

"Then the second angel sounded, and something that looked like a great mountain burning with fire was cast into the sea, and the third of the sea became like blood. A third of the living creatures in the sea died, and a third of the ships were destroyed" (Revelation 8:8-9).

How do you think a person living nearly 2,000 years ago would describe a vision of such catastrophic events in which the most powerful weapons that are of this modern age were being used? If one is describing such a thing occurring in a port city today, it could be seen to be like a mountain on fire that was cast into the sea.

Many ships will be destroyed and that carries a dual fulfillment. One is a destructive strike against any future global commerce. The other is a massive strike against a powerful naval force.

It states that this fire killed a third part of all the life that was in and on the sea, and that then the water became like blood, which is symbolic of the massive amount of human and animal casualties that occur in these port cities.

John continues by describing the event from the sounding of the Third Trumpet.

"The third angel sounded, and there fell a great star from the sky, burning like a torch, and it fell upon a third of the rivers, and upon the springs of water. The name of the star is called Wormwood. A third of the waters became wormwood, and many people died from the water, because it was made bitter" (Revelation 8:10-11).

Again, in each case, John is describing as best as he can what these events looked like as he saw them. His description of a star was describing something that appeared as a bright light falling from the sky that had flames like a torch.

In the specific areas of the country in which this occurs, it destroys life in rivers and spreads a deadly contamination in a third of all water in that region. The description of these events is simply a continuing accumulation of an overall condition of destruction being multiplied. Each Trumpet focuses upon specific destruction, yet they are all connected to the same overall event as the Fourth Trumpet reveals more fully.

"Then the fourth angel sounded, and a third of the sun was struck, and a third of the moon, and a third of the stars, so that a third of them were darkened. So the sun did not shine for a third of the day, and likewise the night. Then I looked, and I heard an angel flying through the midst of heaven, saying with a loud voice, 'Woe, woe, woe, to the inhabitants of the earth because of the trumpet blasts from the three angels who are yet to sound!'" (Revelation 8:12-13).

The Fourth Trumpet blast is a culmination of the effects from the first three Trumpet blasts, and it warns of more destruction to follow. Whereas the first three Trumpets detail destruction that occurs in specific regions, the Fourth Trumpet reveals that in these same areas the normal levels of sunshine will be temporarily reduced by one-third. For a time, even weather patterns will be affected by the events of these Trumpets.

The knowledge of the devastation caused by these Trumpet events will immediately begin to affect other nations around the world and food hoarding will begin to take place when it becomes known that there will be a vast reduction in food supplies. The destruction that takes place from this attack will result in the immediate beginning of famine in many nations of the world. Many depend upon what is produced in the United States. The worldwide effects that will follow from the Fourth Trumpet blast will eventually result in widespread death—even into the millions.

Nuclear EMP Attacks
The prophetic significance of the first four Trumpets is that the United States will become fully crippled and totally vulnerable as a nation. Today, just the use of two or three EMP (electromagnetic pulse) weapons is in itself enough to completely incapacitate the U.S. for months.

These events from the first four Trumpets do not contain a description of EMP weapons that John could see and then describe. Nevertheless, it has been revealed that this first major attack upon the United States will include the use of nuclear EMP weapons. With all the devastation caused by nuclear weapons in a few major cities, including certain port cities, the addition of an EMP attack would prove to be paralyzing for a very long time.

Scientists have tried to calculate the kind of effect an exploding nuclear EMP device over the central part of the U.S. could have. Since such a weapon exploding high in the atmosphere over a populated region has never been used, the known effects are not certain, but it would be absolutely devastating in the light of such widespread modern technology being used within the U.S.

A few excerpts from the September 2020 issue of the publication *MITRE* should help illustrate the kind of vulnerability the U.S. has to such an attack. The MITRE Corporation states that it is an organization that is federally funded as well as having public-private partner relationships. Its federally funded research and development centers "assist the United States government with scientific research and analysis; development and acquisition; and systems engineering and integration." They also operate an independent research program "that explores new and expanded uses of technologies to solve sponsors' problems."

The following are quotes that come from a publication entitled, "Electromagnetic Pulse: The Dangerous But Overlooked Threat."

> There's a threat to national and homeland security that could bring the U.S. power grid to a dangerous standstill for weeks, months, or even years. And this often-overlooked threat requires only a limited number of nuclear weapons to carry it out. [...]
>
> A nuclear electromagnetic pulse (EMP) could wipe out the U.S. power grid—and along with it satellite ground stations, financial markets, healthcare systems, transportation networks, military command and control systems, and the technologies Americans rely on. [...]
>
> Some claim, and past reports and studies indicate, that an EMP event could disrupt key activities like banking, shopping for groceries, buying gas for generators, and even driving a car. Clean water could become scarce. Hospital generators could run out of power, with outages lasting several weeks or more. Public panic and, ultimately, loss of life could follow. [1]

Although there are many articles written on the devastating effects of an EMP attack upon the U.S., the following excerpts in a *Euronews* article on October 17, 2017, are quite sobering.

> At a recent US Homeland Security hearing, two experts warned officials that an electromagnetic pulse (EMP) attack by North Korea posed "the biggest threat" to the United States and that the government was largely ignoring the danger.
>
> William Graham and Peter Vincent Pry said that an EMP bomb exploded at high altitude above the US could "shut down the electric power grid for an indefinite period, leading to the death within a year of up to 90% of all Americans." [...]
>
> Speculative scenarios suggest such an event would wipe out critical infrastructure – no refrigeration for food and medicine, water processing plants grinding to a halt, the total disruption of communication systems and planes falling from the sky.
>
> Graham and Pry, who previously headed up the Congressional Commission to Assess the Threat to the United States from Electromagnetic Pulse, claim the weapons currently being developed and tested by the rogue state make a catastrophic EMP attack a real possibility. [2]

Then there is a very telling report that is contained in a publication of the FDD (Foundation for Defense of Democracies). The following excerpts are from an article entitled, "Heading Toward an EMP Catastrophe" that is dated July 22, 2015.

> For over a decade now, since the Congressional EMP Commission delivered its first report to Congress eleven years ago in July of 2004, various Senate and House committees have heard from numerous scientific and strategic experts the consensus view

that natural and manmade electromagnetic pulse (EMP) is an existential threat to the survival of the American people, that EMP is a clear and present danger, and that something must be done to protect the electric grid and other life sustaining critical infrastructures–immediately.

Yet this counsel and the cost-effective solutions proposed to the looming EMP threat have been ignored. Continued inaction by Washington will make inevitable a natural or manmade EMP catastrophe that, as the Congressional EMP Commission warned, could kill up to 90 percent of the national population through starvation, disease, and societal collapse. [...]

The EMP threat is as real as nuclear threats from Russia, China, North Korea, and Iran. Nuclear EMP attack is part of the military doctrines, plans and exercises of all of these nations for a revolutionary new way of warfare that focuses on attacking electric grids and civilian critical infrastructures–what they call Total Information Warfare or No Contact Wars, and what some western analysts call Cybergeddon or Blackout Wars.

The nuclear EMP threat is as real as North Korea's KMS-3 satellite, that regularly orbits over the U.S. on the optimum trajectory and altitude to evade our National Missile Defenses and, if the KMS-3 were a nuclear warhead, to place an EMP field over all 48 contiguous United States. [3]

Indeed, these threats are real, and they have largely been ignored as elected leaders and even the population as a whole shows no real interest. Yet ever since 9/11, efforts have been stepped up to address this threat by experts and scholars from backgrounds in academia, military, intelligence, and the private sector.

The ability to coordinate an EMP attack is not a difficult thing to do in this age. Today, there are hypersonic missiles, submarines that can launch missiles close to major cities so that there is no time for a response, and even nuclear weapons can be launched from satellites that can circle above any nation and then be used to strike at any moment.

Regardless of the exact way and timing for when these events occur, the result of the first four Trumpets will be that the United States will be crippled by a relatively small nuclear first strike.

A Second Major Attack, Fatal Upon the U.S.
In addition to Herbert Armstrong's prediction that 10 nations would rise in Europe to form a final military alliance, he also predicted how they would use their combined power. He foretold how these ten countries would unite to attack the United States and defeat it in a massive military strike.

Now, consider again how preposterous it was to those who, directly after WWII, heard Herbert Armstrong foretell how Europe was going to rise again, with Germany leading the way. For people today, the prospect of **Europe attacking the U.S.** with nuclear weapons is even far more preposterous! Yet, that is exactly what is prophesied to happen in the fulfillment of the Fifth Trumpet event that follows the first four which cripple the U.S.

Just before this Fifth Trumpet event, nations will be in deep shock over the devastation caused in the U.S. by the first four Trumpets and they will be quite fearful because of the uncertainty of what will follow next.

Many areas of the world that have been held at bay by the domineering influence of the United States and her closest allies will now be determined to accomplish their own will. Just consider the nations that have had long-lasting border and territorial disputes, as well as nations who have religious and political disputes which have never been resolved. Now they are no longer held back!

THE FALL OF THE UNITED STATES   31

Although it was given to Herbert Armstrong to foreknow that Europe would rise as a world power one last time, it was not revealed to him how all this would come to pass. This brings us to **current prognostications** that God has been revealing more fully over the past two decades.

The Fifth Trumpet has already been largely explained in the book that precedes this one. So instead of going into great detail, it will simply be explained what these verses in Revelation are prophesying. These verses also speak of the last revival in Europe of the old prophetic European empire, which would consist of 10 nations uniting in military power. That which is being revealed in Revelation is about their primary role in this last revival to fulfill precise prophetic timing that powerfully escalates into an all-out nuclear confrontation between nations.

"Then I looked, and I heard an angel flying through the midst of heaven, saying with a loud voice, 'Woe, Woe, Woe, to the inhabitants of the earth because of the trumpet blasts from the three angels who are yet to sound!'" (Revelation 8:13).

This verse describes incredibly dire warnings being given to the world. Yet these warnings will not be received until after the U.S. has been crippled and **the attention of the world** has become keenly focused on what has just happened. This verse is now warning of far greater catastrophic events that will follow because there are three Trumpet events that have yet to take place, as there are seven Trumpets in total.

These last three Trumpet events are being further described as three **Woes** that are yet to come upon mankind. These will make the first four Trumpet events seem quite small in comparison.

It's disheartening to realize that it isn't until this moment in time when people have become so horrified, shocked, and scared, that **some will then begin to listen** to the **One** who has forewarned of this time for over 2,500 years.

Those events that Herbert Armstrong spoke of concerning Europe, that have now been perfectly fulfilled, were true because it was **God** who gave this to him. It is God who revealed the meaning of prophetic writings to him. But the world has not listened, just as God also said would happen. It has always been that way, even as the prophet Jeremiah was given to speak:

"'They have not listened to my words,' says the Eternal, 'which I sent unto them by my servants the prophets. Even by starting early and sending them, yet they would not listen,' says the Eternal" (Jeremiah 29:19).

God began early on to send His servant Herbert Armstrong to warn this present age about end-time events that would lead up to WWIII. The truth is, this message has been going out into the world for the past 70 years and the intensity and urgency of the warnings have only increased, but indeed, who has listened?

The Fifth Trumpet: The First Woe!
The devastation that follows the first four Trumpet events results in unimaginable destruction across the U.S., along with the death of tens of thousands of people and potentially much more; however, the verse in Revelation 8, about the three Woes, gives a warning of far worse events that will quickly follow. Once nuclear weapons are used against any major nation, it is certain that a far greater use of nuclear weapons will follow, and that is what will begin to happen at this juncture.

The event of this Fifth Trumpet—the 1st Woe—is the beginning of an all-out thermonuclear war—a full-scale WWIII. In reality, that war began when the U.S. was first attacked, but what happened then is exceedingly small compared to what happens next.

This Trumpet is expressed in unique terms in order to stress the amplification of the kind of destruction that will begin to take place on earth. This is far beyond the destruction that will have first come upon the U.S. as a result of the events of the first four Trumpets.

"Then the fifth angel sounded, and I saw a star fall from heaven to the earth, and to him was given the key of the bottomless pit. He opened the bottomless pit, and there arose smoke out of the pit like the smoke from a great furnace, and the sun and the sky were darkened because

of the smoke of the pit. Out of the smoke there came locusts upon the earth, and they were given power like scorpions of the earth have power" (Revelation 9:1-3).

Once again, John is describing in the simplest ways he can what he had seen in a vision. That which he saw was the escalation of nuclear weapons in war. This event is so massive that it now describes how everything is being darkened by it, much more so than in the previous events.

Prophetically, the locusts are about vast armies and of their power to conquer. The description of scorpions is about the power they possess to strike quickly when they attack. Today, because of modern technology, such military power can use just a few weapons to destroy millions of people in only minutes.

Remember, this Fifth Trumpet is about an all-out thermonuclear strike against the United States that will quickly bring an end to her existence as a functioning nation. Most people in the U.S. may think the mention of such a thing is ludicrous, but that doesn't slow down or prevent what is coming.

From this point forward, there is no other way to adequately explain these events than to tell what they mean in terms that God has revealed.

Once more, it is understood that people will not begin to give measurable credibility to these warnings until after they witness the devastation caused by the first four Trumpets. Then at that time, the possibility of what has been forewarned about this next attack will begin to be seen as being fearfully feasible.

Indeed, it is difficult for people to regard and contemplate what is being stated about the kind of destruction that will come as a result of this cataclysmic event. It becomes even harder to believe as this portion of Revelation 9 begins to be explained. That is because these verses are speaking of Satan being released from a spiritual restraint that he has been placed in since the end of WWII.

In today's world, the likelihood that God "exists" is in question by an ever-increasing number of people. However, the possibility that there is a being who exists on earth who is identified as Satan is even far more unbelievable and doubtful in the thinking of most.

Yet, there is a real being—a spirit being—who is known as Satan. Before the creation of mankind, God had created an angelic realm composed of spirit beings called angels. It is recorded that one of the three archangels who had been created, rebelled against God. The name he was first given was Lucifer, which means "shining one," or "light-bearer."

Long before the creation of mankind, this archangel turned against God and persuaded a third of the angelic realm to follow in his evil ways. When God revealed to the angelic realm that He was going to create mankind and His purpose for doing so, Lucifer changed and began to become envious of mankind. He began to resist and work against what God was going to do, and once mankind was created, he became relentless in his pursuit to taint the thinking of mankind and to cause as much destruction and misery as he could.

After his rebellion against God, he then became known as Satan (meaning "adversary") and the Devil (meaning "false accuser"). These names describe the kind of evil that reflects his perverted thinking and actions that work against all that is good. He uses the power he has to influence mankind to exercise his same kind of thinking that moves people to be false accusers of others and to become adversarial toward one another.

Yet he is also called by another name that reflects the use of his power that he has exerted for thousands of years in order to bring mankind to engage in great battles. That name is Apollyon which means "destroyer." Satan has been the primary force, in a spirit realm, who has led people into destructive wars over the millennia.

Satan's Power for War
Satan is also referred to by other names in the Book of Revelation, and indeed, he is described as having great power to lead nations into war. He is identified prophetically as a dragon and as a beast having seven heads and ten horns. The description of the "beast" is symbolic

of Satan's actual power to dominate multiple periods of European conquest and government supremacy, which are also represented by the legs and feet of Nebuchadnezzar's statue.

As previously covered, it was the bottom portion of Nebuchadnezzar's statue that symbolized the longest enduring kingdom of all the prophetic kingdoms being represented. This bottom portion depicts the different nations in Europe with their varying degrees of strength and weakness, loosely bonded, that come together and lead up to the time of mankind's final war. Throughout most of its history, this kingdom has been known as the Roman Empire. That empire is also spoken of prophetically in Revelation through symbolism. In the following verses it is described as the beast with seven heads and ten horns:

"Then I stood on the sand of the sea, and saw a beast rising up out of the sea, having seven heads and ten horns, and on his horns ten crowns, and on his heads a blasphemous name. Now the beast which I saw was like a leopard, his feet were like the feet of a bear, and his mouth like the mouth of a lion. The dragon gave him his power, his throne, and great authority. So I saw one of his heads as if it had been mortally wounded, and his deadly wound was healed, then the whole world marveled and followed the beast" (Revelation 13:1-3).

These verses are about Satan having the power **to give power** to the various prophesied governments that have reigned with great might over the people of Europe. The "sand of the sea" is prophetically symbolic for the masses of humanity that have lived throughout the reign of this long-lasting empire. The Roman Empire began in 31 BC and continued until it fell in 476 AD, which was the time it was "mortally wounded."

The head that received a "deadly wound and then was healed" is about what happened to the Roman Empire once it fell. This old empire experienced a kind of revival when Justinian came into power in 554 AD. This prophecy is revealing that this first revival would be one of seven revivals, which is described as the beast having seven heads. The seven heads are about seven distinct periods of time when this beast would exercise its power over those whom it would govern. Each revival would be led by one primary leader—one head over each revival.

The fifth revival was under Napoleon. The reign of five revivals is described in the verses that follow those described in Revelation 13. In addition, Napoleon's reign ended exactly within the timeframe that God said it would.

"So they worshiped the dragon who gave authority to the beast, and they worshiped the beast, saying, 'Who is like the beast? Who is able to make war with him?' And he was given a mouth speaking great things and blasphemies, and he was given authority to continue for forty-two months" (Revelation 13:4-5).

The first five verses of Revelation 13 are describing seven revivals of powerful rule in Europe—power that has always been associated with war and the ability to conquer. Verses 4-5 describe a specific phase of this European rule that lasted for exactly 1260 years. This tells how long this power would be able to be exerted over these revivals in Europe and over their leaders. It is stated that it was for a prophetic forty-two months. There are 1260 days in a prophetic period of 42 months—with each day representing a prophetic year.

This period began with the rise of Justinian's reign that began in 554 AD and it ended with the fall of Napoleon in 1814, exactly 1260 years later. This prophetic interval covered the span of time known as the Holy Roman Empire. It saw the rise and fall of five prophesied leaders within that period. It carried this description as being a "Holy" Roman Empire because of the influence the great church of Europe had over the people and upon those leaders.

These verses speak of the dragon—Satan—as being the one who gave these revivals authority (power) and each rule is described as a beast, which is a reflection of where their power to rule and conquer came from.

Two Revivals Remaining

After the fall of Napoleon, Europe struggled with its identity as several of its rising national powers were vying for power. The great church of Europe was no longer able to exercise the kind of authority over these rising nations of Europe as it had experienced for centuries before. This now brings us to a volatile time for Europe when there was a great surge forward in invention and technology.

Although they had grown in power and influence, the individual nations of Europe were not cohesive at all. They were largely divided. Hence, the accurate description of the feet being of iron mingled with clay.

The movement toward a sixth revival of a European Empire, depicted by the feet of clay and iron (not the toes), occurred with the outbreak of WWI. That war involved an alliance of Germany, Austria-Hungary, Bulgaria, and the Ottoman Empire. They were known as the "Central Powers." It was the first war that broadly involved other nations around the world. The Central Powers fought against Great Britain, France, Russia, Italy, Romania, Japan, and the United States. These were known as the Allied Powers.

After nearly 5,900 years of mankind, those involved in this war were the first to experience the use of vastly superior weaponry in a rapidly growing period of scientific knowledge, invention, and technology unlike all the millennia before.

This war brought about great social upheaval as millions of women entered the workforce to support men who had gone to war and also replaced those who never came back. The war itself resulted in the death of some 9 million soldiers and 10 million civilians. In addition, this war helped to spread the world's first pandemic—the Spanish flu of 1918, which killed an estimated 30 to 50 million people.

This first world war was only the beginning of the sixth revival of the prophetic European Empire, as it only set the stage for a far more massive resurgence under Hitler. This resurgence and attempt to conquer Europe reveals the mind that was actually behind it, as it is the same one behind all the revivals of the last prophetic European Empire. Since Satan was not able to work through a great church to influence revivals in Europe as he had before, he now worked directly through one man as he exerted powerful spirit influence upon the mind and thinking of Hitler.

Hitler was determined to establish a Third Reich. The translation of the German word "Reich" is "Empire or Kingdom." This reveals the desire and affinity he had to again raise up the old Roman Empire in Europe, but under the German name and German leadership.

The "Third Reich" became the most popular term to describe this historical period, although it was Hitler's desire that it be known as "Großdeutsches Reich" (Greater German Reich). Another term he used was "Tausendjähriges Reich" (Thousand-Year Reich).

Hitler wanted to transform Berlin, to make it the capital of a Greater German "World Empire"—one greater than the Roman Empire. He declared at a rally in Nuremberg that "…in the next thousand years there will be no other revolution in Germany."

Even in this, Satan was seeking to mock God's truth, as there is only one Millennium, which is about a prophetic period of time for when God has declared He will establish a just and righteous government to rule the world. It is declared that in God's Kingdom that there will be no more revolution—no more wars.

Satan has resisted and fought against God from the beginning of the creation of mankind. He wasted no time in leading the first two created people, Adam and Eve, into sin and rebellion against God. He even tried to have Christ killed as a young child, and he has worked against God's prophets and apostles over the past 6,000 years, primarily by having them imprisoned and/or killed. He is also responsible for leading a devastating attack against God's own Church in this end-time that resulted in the Apostasy prophesied by the apostle, Paul.

Hitler's reign was the completion of the sixth revival of a prophesied European power depicted by the sixth head of the beast. One more revival yet remains.

A Unique Moment in Time
As it has been described, it was revealed to Herbert Armstrong there would be ten nations that would become united in military power within Europe in the end-time. Those ten nations were seen as being

depicted by the ten toes of the statue in Nebuchadnezzar's dream. The scriptures just covered in Revelation 13 concerning the ten horns with ten crowns represent the same prophecy.

Then, the same ten nations are further spoken of in Revelation 17. Although there is much more that will yet be explained about the verses of this chapter, for now, there is only a need to cover what concerns the seven revivals of Europe and those final ten nations.

Revelation 17 speaks of a woman that is sitting on a scarlet beast with seven heads and ten horns. So once again, there is another unique prophetic description of seven heads (seven revivals of a prophesied European Empire) and of the ten horns, which are about the ten nations that comprise the last revival.

"Here is the mind which has wisdom. The seven heads are seven mountains, on which the woman sits" (Rev. 17:9).

First, wisdom is being spoken of here, since this verse begins to explain the meaning of what was being described in the earlier verses. This wording is used, stressing "the mind which has wisdom," because it is to be understood that the revelation of anything prophetic comes only from God. Mankind has no such wisdom—no such ability to know the meaning of recorded prophecy.

Here, God was giving His wisdom to Herbert Armstrong so that he could understand that these verses applied to the seven revivals of Europe and that they lead up to the events of the end-time.

Herbert Armstrong was given to understand that God uses "mountains" as metaphors to prophetically speak of larger nations or kingdoms. In this verse, it was clearly revealing that a woman, being a metaphor that represented that great church in Europe, was "on" each of these beasts during their revivals.

This "woman," after the fifth revival under Napoleon which ended the Holy Roman Empire, no longer had the same kind of power and sway she had enjoyed and exerted since the time of Justinian. Nevertheless, her presence and influence throughout those periods of time are still what has molded Europe into being what it is today.

The next verse then begins to address the two revivals that remain.

"*There are seven kings, five are fallen, and one is, and the other is not yet, and when it comes, it must continue a short time* [a little season]" (Revelation 17:10).

This verse is uniquely written. It was recorded in such a manner that it could only be **understood** for what it was saying **at the very specific moment** in time that **it was actually occurring.**

Once again, the seven revivals of Europe are being addressed. It says that "five had fallen," which became the case after the fall of Napoleon who was the head of the fifth revival. But then it states that one "**is**," meaning, that at the time this verse would be understood, would be when "one revival" was currently in existence. Herbert Armstrong was being given to "see" this when WWII was coming to an end, while the reign of Hitler—the one "is"— was still ongoing.

After that time, Herbert Armstrong began to warn the world that there would be one more revival because he was given to understand that "the other is not yet" was about the seventh and last revival. Thankfully, when that last one comes, it will only exist for a short period of time. The nuclear war that is coming will be short-lived, or else mankind would annihilate itself, just as God has declared.

The First Woe!
We have now come full circle back to the event of the Fifth Trumpet. This is when the seventh and last prophesied revival within Europe will take place. It is when a final ten nations in Europe become united in military agreement to engage in a nuclear attack upon the United States.

This is the first of three Woes that are prophesied to come upon mankind, and they portend massive destruction on earth, including the deaths of a vast number of people around the world. This Woe itself is described in terms of killing tens of millions of people.

Prophetically, this event can now happen in a number of different ways, as the interaction between nations is exceptionally fluid and ever-changing at a fast pace. Nevertheless, this **will happen** in the manner that is outlined in these prophecies.

But what would lead Europe to attack the U.S. in the first place?

In recent years, the attitude of Europe toward the U.S. has been rapidly changing. Not only Europe, but much of the world, has been growing in bitterness and disdain for how the U.S. has consistently worked to manipulate its own will and purpose over them.

Threats and practices involving sanctions, the heavy-handedness of control over the petrodollar, and restrictive worldwide banking policies have been pushing nations into an eventual showdown with the U.S. Nations also experience other forms of what they consider bullying from what they see as invasive military practices or the practice of militaristic bribery for guarantees of protection and/or the purchase of weapons.

Most all of Europe is fully fed up with the kinds of pressuring done by the U.S. to insert itself into their business and governmental affairs. They are tired of being told what they should do. Much of Europe has been thankful in the past for how the U.S. intervened to help liberate them from the destructive Nazi regime during WWII. But the ongoing expectations from the U.S. have added a heavy toll upon their relationship, which is becoming more burdensome, making it harder for them to bear.

Over the past few years, French President Macron has been pushing for a "real European army." The countries of Europe feel as though they are in a kind of vise that is being squeezed, with NATO being used as a hammer to beat them into submission. Because of this, they want their own military that is independent of such pressures.

They are sick and tired of the U.S. trying to pull their strings as though they are some kind of puppet that is expected to do the will of their former liberators to whom they should "evidently" forever be indebted.

In November 2018, French President, Emmanuel Macron, unknowingly made a rather ominous statement that few could possibly understand because it fits precisely into a prophetic narrative. He stated, "We have to protect ourselves with respect to China, Russia, and even the United States." This is far more ominous than anyone can imagine, as this last and seventh revival of a European empire will be at the forefront of an eventual confrontation with all three of those nations Macron mentioned.

More and more, Europeans are expressing their disdain for the United States interfering in their affairs. An article earlier this year in the New York Times expresses quite well the growing animosity that is building in Europe toward the U.S. The article was entitled "Europe Struggles to Defend Itself Against a Weaponized Dollar."

A few quotes will help illustrate the kind of resentment that is rapidly developing which will soon lead into the fulfillment of the most dangerous prophetic events the world has ever experienced.

> BRUSSELS — The new Biden administration is making nice with the European Union, talking of renewed cooperation and suspending retaliatory tariffs stemming from an old dispute between Airbus and Boeing.
>
> But despite the warm words and efforts at rebuilding trust, the American willingness to punish its European allies and impose sanctions on them in pursuit of foreign-policy goals continues to rankle.
>
> It is an underlying tension, a ready reminder of the asymmetric power of the United States. That is especially so when it comes to what are known as secondary sanctions. While Iran and Russia, for example, may be the primary target of sanctions, the secondary sanctions punish other countries and companies — very often European — that do business with them as well. [...]
>
> Secondary sanctions cut off access to the American banking system, an effective threat because of the centrality of that system and the global reach of the dollar.

The weaponization of the American dollar and the Treasury is a marked vulnerability for Europe, which depends on open markets. It has prompted serious discussions of how to defend Europe and the euro from Washington's whims, and it has become a central part of the argument about how to create "strategic autonomy," so Europe can protect its own interests.

Last month, the European Union announced efforts to strengthen an "anti-coercion instrument" against "unfair trading practices." The main sources of them are China and Europe's self-professed ally and partner, the United States.

While Europe favors using multilateral institutions on trade disputes, "we cannot afford to stand defenseless in the meantime," said Valdis Dombrovskis, the European Union's commissioner for trade. The European Union must be able to defend itself "from those trying to take advantage of our openness," he said. [...]

European resentment about American secondary sanctions "is linked to an awareness of our own internal and economic fragility," said Nathalie Tocci, director of Italy's International Affairs Institute and adviser to Mr. Borrell. [4]

Similar statements and concerns from a number of other leaders reflect a rapidly growing indignation that is sweeping across Europe. The momentum of this negative sentiment and the frustration associated with it is quickly moving Europe toward acting upon the unthinkable.

The speed at which prophetic events are moving should be seen as happening at an alarming pace. That which may seem far off, is not!

Upon hearing what is being said about this First Woe upon mankind, the inclination of too many would be that they would take solace in the secure feeling that no such thing could ever happen as long as NATO exists. That would be a huge mistake and would reflect a very false sense of security. Europe is bent on having the self-determination of their own military operations apart from any influence and control from NATO, which is what prophecy reveals will happen.

NATO has already established the ability for this prophecy to become fulfilled simply by putting weapons in place that can easily come under Europe's sole control. Europe already has great power at its fingertips if it chooses to use it. France has a large stockpile of nuclear weapons in Europe and NATO has positioned a very large number of nuclear weapons throughout Europe. The day is soon coming that they are going to use them! *That* is the prophecy for the fulfillment of the Fifth Trumpet.

Why Is the U.S. the First Nation to Fall?
As it has been stated, the first five Trumpets are first and foremost about the complete collapse of the United States as a nation. But one may ask, "Why?"

Part of the answer to this has already been touched upon. The primary reason is that it is a matter of God's judgment against her because she has not listened to Him. That too has much to do with the very reason this book is being written.

Earlier a quote from Jeremiah was given that spoke of how God has always sent warnings early on before destruction would come. Yet the tendency of mankind has been to simply ignore God and not listen to Him. Then over time, as a result of not listening, God allows destruction to come upon them for not responding. This foolish proclivity of mankind is addressed more fully toward the beginning of the Book of Jeremiah.

"Since the day that your fathers came out of the land of Egypt until this day, I have even sent to you all My servants the prophets, even by starting early and sending them, yet they would not listen, nor incline

their ear, but stiffened their neck. They did worse than their fathers. Therefore you shall speak all these words to them, but they will not listen to you. You shall also proclaim to them [context— 'proclaim His words'], *but they will not respond. So you shall say to them, 'This is a nation that does not listen to the voice of the Eternal their God, nor receive* [His] *instruction. Truth has perished and has been cut off from their mouth"* (Jeremiah 7:25-28).

In this end-time, God has revealed that these verses are first and foremost prophetically directed toward the United States. This book specifically has been written to proclaim God's very words that were written by Jeremiah nearly 2650 years ago.

God is directing that what He had recorded in these verses is to now be said first and foremost to the United States. Then, it is also to be directed to every nation of the world, since their response to Him has been the same. These are His words to each nation: **"This is a nation that does not listen to the voice of the Eternal their God, nor receive His instruction."**

The greatest obstacle in the way of hearing this message is human pride.

Beginning early in 1950, God began to give end-time warnings to the U.S. through Herbert Armstrong. A warning began to be given about an attack from Europe that would crush the United States if it did not listen to what God was saying.

In addition, if the world did not listen, then even far greater destruction would follow, and it would be worldwide. Obviously, the world has not listened, so cataclysmic worldwide destruction will come upon mankind from the Second and Third Woe.

Although Herbert Armstrong worked tirelessly to warn the U.S. and the rest of the world, the response he received is in itself another prophetic fulfillment that has now come to pass concerning this end-time. It is that even after many years and all the millions of dollars spent on a vast number of publications, radio and television programs, and personal appearances, the result has been the same. The general population, including its leaders, has not listened to God's warnings.

Therefore, knowing far in advance that this would be the response of nations around the world, God established judgment that would be allowed to come upon the world, beginning first against the United States.

This book and the four that have preceded it are about these same warnings that Herbert Armstrong gave. Those books have contained even more revelation given by God. But once again, the general population and its leaders still will not listen. Even as this book is being written, it is understood that this condition will not change until after the first five Trumpet events that bring down the United States as a nation.

Nevertheless, this book is still being written because God has revealed that what Jeremiah wrote in these verses was to be stated one more time, just before these events begin to come to pass.

The reason that the U.S. is the first to fall is because it has been given the greatest opportunity over the past 70 years, above all other nations, to hear God's warnings concerning what He reveals will be an end to mankind's self-rule on earth.

In his book, *The United States and Britain In Prophecy,* Herbert Armstrong revealed how God had prophesied He would make the U.S. the single greatest nation the world has ever known. It would be given the greatest wealth and strongest military above all nations that have ever existed. It is God who gave this to the United States.

Yet rather than acknowledging it was God who gave all this to them as a nation, people and their leaders have taken the credit for such greatness to themselves. God declares that it is a nation that has become filled with pride and arrogance, and that **He** will humble it. That humbling will occur through the first five Trumpet events that are now about to begin. The reason for such emphasis on these five events is because God reveals it will take that much to destroy the pride of such a great nation before humility can begin to be produced.

The more the United States holds to her pride, the more she will suffer until she is humbled. This is a matter of God's judgment and what He has determined concerning how it should be humbled.

This humbling process is similar to how God dealt with Pharaoh and Egypt in the time of Moses. God humbled Egypt in order to deliver Israel out from under her, but it was at great cost to Egypt and to all her people due to their **pride**. Most of Egypt's agriculture was totally destroyed along with most of its livestock. Many people died from the plagues, including all the firstborn of Egypt. Lastly, Pharaoh and his military were destroyed in the Red Sea. Pride is a great evil, and it is a stubborn foe to sound reason.

Today, government and its many agencies are deeply embedded in pride. The same is true of massive corporations, financial and educational institutions, etc. It is pride that is leading the U.S. up to the brink of a massive economic collapse—one that is steadily moving toward a complete global collapse. This is the very thing that is at the forefront that will trigger the first four Trumpet events.

Over the past 6,000 years, every great nation and empire in the world has fallen. It is prophetic for our time now that the single greatest, most powerful and wealthy nation the world has ever known is about to fall as well.

Not only will the U.S. experience horrific suffering due to the first five Trumpet events, it is revealed in the Book of Revelation that it will also experience plagues and devastation from events that are called Thunders. These too will escalate against her unless or until she begins to listen to God.

The more the United States holds to her pride, the more she will suffer until she is humbled. This is a matter of God's judgment and what He has determined toward the U.S.

Footnotes

[1] "Electromagnetic Pulse: The Dangerous but Overlooked Threat." The MITRE Corporation, 27 Apr. 2021, www.mitre.org/publications/project-stories/electromagnetic-pulse-the-dangerous-but overlooked-threat.

[2] Euronews. "North Korea EMP Attack 'Could Kill 90% of Americans.'" Euronews, 17 Oct. 2017, www.euronews.com/2017/10/17/north-korea-emp-attack-warning.

[3] Barnes, Abigail, "Heading Toward An EMP Catastrophe." FDD, 24 Oct. 2018, www.fdd.org/analysis/2015/07/22/heading-toward-an-emp-catastrophe.

[4] Erlanger, Steven. "Europe Struggles to Defend Itself Against a Weaponized Dollar." The New York Times, 12 Mar.2021, www.nytimes.com/2021/03/12/world/europe/europe-us-sanctions.html.

Chapter 3
END-TIME DESTRUCTION

THROUGHOUT THE AGES, new weapons have continuously been invented that have enabled mankind to have greater power to destroy, kill, and conquer others in war. This is most evident in nuclear weapons. In WWII, just two atomic bombs used against Japan killed nearly 200,000 people. This was an act that shocked and horrified the world.

In the years that followed there was a rush to make even greater and more destructive weapons. This insanely maddening quest has led to the creation of nuclear weapons that are now hundreds of times more powerful! Yet, that is the way of mankind. Now, the potential use of one large nuclear weapon has the power to destroy any of the largest cities in the world.

It is inevitable that nuclear weapons will eventually be used in all-out war. This is what God has revealed is prophesied to happen in the first two Woes.

The Sixth Trumpet—A Second Woe!
By the time the effects of the Fifth Trumpet—the First Woe—have ended, massive destruction will have taken place across the United States. The level of nuclear devastation from the events of this Fifth Trumpet is prophetically revealed to destroy a third of the U.S., which also means the death of over one hundred million people.

"One Woe is past, and behold, there are two more Woes coming after this" (Revelation 9:12).

It is at this juncture that the world is warned of even far greater destruction that will follow.

"Then the sixth angel sounded, and I heard a voice from the four horns of the golden altar, which is before God, saying to the sixth angel who had the trumpet, 'Release the four angels which are bound in the great river Euphrates.' The four angels were released, who had been prepared for the hour, day, month, and year, **to kill a third of mankind***. I heard the number of the horsemen to be two hundred million"* (Revelation 9:13-16).

This **Second Woe** is about the destruction that will come from the event that has been announced by the **Sixth Trumpet**. This Trumpet refers to a massive escalation in WWIII as other nations feel they too must become engaged in it. Armies of the world will be quickly drawn into this horrific war, and as it is noted in the scripture above, the multitude assembled will be two hundred million.

In addition to the great military powers that already exist at this time, most all nations quickly work to enlarge their military might. It is seen as a matter of their very survival since the whole world becomes drawn into this final war—and they know this is an all-out war that has come to them!

There are two powerful nations that are identified in this Second Woe that cause the greatest ruin worldwide once they begin to unleash their nuclear weapons. These are prophetically revealed to be Russia and China.

This Second Woe is many times greater in its destructiveness than the First Woe. There is not much to be said about this Sixth Trumpet event because this prophecy is given to simply reveal the magnitude of destruction that will come from it. It means exactly what it says. This cataclysmic **Woe** will result in **one-third of all mankind** being destroyed. This alone will account for the death of over **2.5 billion people**! This is unimaginable, but it is soon going to come to pass.

Although it is God who foretold these events that will destroy so much of mankind and this world, it is **not God** who is doing this to mankind. It is of **mankind's** own doing—the result of its own choices. God has simply given prophecy that reveals what would be inevitable and what mankind would eventually do once it had the kind of technology that now exists.

Furthermore, for mankind to finally begin to listen to its Creator, there needs to be a shift in the thinking of the pride-filled and self-reliant ways of mankind. Therefore, God is going to allow mankind to come to this level of self-destruction and death because there is no other way to achieve this. It will be the result of mankind's own decisions that this level of massive destruction comes to pass. God reveals that once mankind has come to this measure of worldwide destruction that He will then intervene to stop it. **He will prevent mankind from annihilating itself.**

At the point that God intervenes, there will still be massive arsenals of nuclear weapons that can be used. The level of destruction that will have occurred up to this point in time will be accomplished by only a fraction of the complete arsenal that exists among the nations. God declares that if He did not intervene at this precise moment, the use of nuclear weapons would then rapidly escalate and end up destroying every living thing on earth.

The World Still Refuses to Listen

At the time God intervenes to put an end to WWIII, before mankind continues with war and annihilates itself, up to 3 billion people will have died. This is unthinkable, but it will happen. Nations will be filled with anger, fear, vengeance, and every other kind of emotion that totally obscures soundness of mind that might otherwise be able to lead to the end of the war.

Nations with nuclear power in their control come to believe that they can no longer put any trust in others to stop using their nuclear weapons. Therefore, they determine to use theirs first. It is at this point that God must intervene.

Pride runs very deep in human nature. Even after everything that has happened to this moment in time, the majority of mankind will still continue to resist God and will not listen to why these things are happening and where it is all leading—to total annihilation.

Although there will be several million around the world who will begin to cry out to God and to listen at this time, the overwhelmingly vast majority will still refuse to consider anything God says. This is what is being spoken of in the verses that follow the description of the vast militaristic state of the world:

"But the rest of mankind, who were not killed by these plagues, still would not repent of the works of their hands, that they should not worship demons, and idols of gold, silver, brass, stone, and of wood, which neither can see, nor hear, nor walk. Neither would they repent of their killing, nor of their sorceries, nor of their fornication, nor of their theft" (Revelation 9:20-21).

This expression about the "rest of mankind" does not mean this is about every person, but rather it reflects the spirit and attitude of the vast majority. There will be some few million who have been repenting and crying out to God for His intervention and deliverance.

The destruction is unimaginably massive by this time, as over a third of everything has been destroyed. Most of the stronger nations who still have much power in their control are filled with obstinate pride. They believe they can still survive, come out on top in all of this, and reestablish themselves as great again. They still believe in **their own ability** to win this war and to solve all the problems caused by it. The last thing on their mind would be to look to God or repent of "their own ways."

Unless humbled, mankind will not listen to God. So, that is exactly what God is going to do—He will humble the resisting powers that remain. If He doesn't, they will blindly and stubbornly destroy themselves and all life on earth. This haughtiness and pride of mankind runs exceedingly deep. It is the real obstacle to cooperation and peace.

The Seventh Trumpet

It is a matter of God's judgment that this world has been given more than enough time and information to know and to understand what is about to come upon it in the form of a final war. The simple truth is that people do not want to hear what God has to say. They do not want anyone, including God, to tell them how they should live.

Over the past 70 years, the world has established a record—a witness—of its actual concern for end-time warnings. People may not want to hear about a third world war that is nearly upon us, nevertheless, **they will experience it**.

"The Second Woe is past, and behold, the **Third Woe** *is coming quickly. Then the seventh angel sounded, and there were great voices in heaven, saying, 'The kingdoms of this world have now become the kingdoms of our Lord, even of His Christ, and He shall reign from now and forever more'"* (Revelation 11:14-15).

This event is about an interval in time when God begins to reveal how He is going to intervene in the affairs of mankind to end this catastrophic war. This Third Woe that is coming will now **come from God**. It has the likelihood of being far more destructive against mankind than the two previous Woes. The word "likelihood" is stated because it wouldn't have to be this way if mankind would listen to God and begin putting an end to this heinous war. But what is the likelihood of that? The nature and predictability of mankind's actions reveal the certainty that this Woe will be much greater than the one before.

The language being used in these verses about a Third Woe that "is coming quickly" has baffled both scholars and teachers of traditional Christianity. They cannot remotely begin to grasp what God is saying about the kingdoms of this world becoming the kingdoms of Christ.

The reason for such lack of insight is because these same people do not begin to grasp and understand what is meant by the name "Christ."

Knowing and understanding what is being said here has everything to do with the very existence of mankind. Few in the world have ever known or heard the truth of God's purpose for creating human life. Few have ever known that God has a preset plan for human life and how He is systematically accomplishing that plan and purpose to bring mankind to a much higher level of existence.

God has clearly established cyclical periods of time for mankind. He gave the seven-day week to mankind wherein the seventh day was to be a reminder that He is our Creator and the Creator of all things. God gave the seven-day week to prophetically symbolize His 7,000-year plan for accomplishing His purpose in the creation of all mankind.

Very few have ever known the purpose of God revealing to the prophets, throughout time, about a Messiah whom He would send to rule over mankind. The words **Messiah** and **Christ** mean exactly the same thing— "the anointed One." But anointed for what? It means anointed to be a king, just as so many kings in Old Testament times were anointed.

The Israelites and Jewish nation, up to the time of Christ, knew that the scriptures speaking about a Messiah were about God sending a king to reign in His Kingdom, but they did not fully understand what that really meant.

Even the disciples struggled with what Christ was telling them about himself. They believed he was the prophesied Messiah—the Christ—and that God was going to establish him as that king and thereby free them from the Roman occupation of that time. But they did not understand that he had not come, at that time, to be that king. Christ further confirmed this by the answer he gave when being questioned by Pilate.

"My kingdom is not of this world. If my kingdom were of this world, then my servants would fight, so that I would not be delivered to the Jews. But my kingdom is not from here." (John 18:36).

The word translated as "world" is actually the Greek word "kosmos," which means "order, ordered system, arrangement." He was telling them that his kingdom was not of this system of mankind, but that it was for another time that the Kingdom of God would be established at his second coming. He will be King in the ordered system that God establishes after ending WWIII.

The Kingdom of God Will Rule Over Mankind

Revelation 11 is revealing a major change in government on earth. It is about a change from a worldly system governed by mankind to one being governed by God.

"Then the seventh angel sounded, and there were great voices in heaven, saying, 'The kingdoms of this world have now become the kingdoms of our Lord, even of His Christ, and He shall reign from now and forever more'" (Revelation 11:15).

Even as Christ was coming into Jerusalem on the last week of his physical life, thousands of people cried out to him and praised him as the Messiah, the son (descendant) of David, the one whom God was sending to be their King over His Kingdom on earth.

Christ stated many times to the disciples that he had not, at that time, come to fulfill the role of the Messiah, but instead, that of the Passover. But they could not understand the spiritual meaning of his words and his explanation until they received of God's spirit after his death. That was on the day of Pentecost in 31 AD when God's Church became established. It was at that time, as recorded in the Book of Acts, that they then knew he was indeed the King of God's Kingdom that would in time reign on earth, but that he had first come to fulfill the meaning and purpose revealed in the annual observance of Passover.

Christ came first as the Lamb of God so that he could suffer death in order to become the Passover for all mankind. But he is coming again as the one the disciples were looking for in their time. He is about to return, this time coming to fulfill the role of the **Lion of God** who will reign over all nations of the earth as the King of all kings in God's Kingdom.

The Kingdom of God is not in heaven as many believe, nor is it in the hearts of men as others believe. It is a Kingdom that will reign over its subjects and those subjects are those who will live on into a new era of mankind that follows this last war—**WWIII**.

Just as the seven-day week was established by God, so is the period of the 7,000 years it prophetically symbolizes. God gave the first six days of the week to mankind to focus on their own work, but God established the seventh day—the weekly Sabbath—as a time mankind was to focus upon His work, His instruction, and His truth.

So in like manner, that symbolism is prophetically revealed in the 7,000 years God has established for mankind. We are nearing the end of 6,000 years of mankind's self-rule.

Mankind has been allowed to live "its own ways" for that period of time, and those ways are leading to complete annihilation if God were not to intervene. God has given mankind 6,000 years of self-rule to practice every form of government imaginable. How has that worked out?

But in the next 1,000 years—in the Millennium—mankind will learn to live God's ways as it comes under **His government** that will rule all nations of the world during that time. It will be a time of peace and fullness for human life. There will be no more wars. WWIII is mankind's last war!

Once that 1,000-year reign begins, only one government will rule on the earth. God will not allow any government of mankind to exist ever again. There will be no dictators, no politics and no political parties, no voting, no government of mankind ever again. That is what the "good news" (gospel) of God's truth is all about.

In addition, there will only be one church—God's Church. There will be no other church organizations and no other religions allowed to be practiced. The mass confusion that exists in different religions today will be no more.

This Seventh Trumpet event begins with the announcement that man's reign over the past 6,000 years is finally being brought to an end, and now, God will intervene and begin His reign on earth in His Kingdom, with Christ at its head. It is here that Christ finally becomes the King of kings over all the earth.

So when it is announced that the Third Woe is coming quickly, it is then declared first that the kingdoms of this world have now become the kingdoms of Christ and that he will begin to rule. These same verses go on to tell that this is now the time that God will take rule over the earth.

*"Then the twenty-four elders, who sat before God on their thrones, fell on their faces and worshipped God, saying, 'We give you thanks, O Lord God Almighty, who is, and was, and is yet to come, because **you have taken to yourself your great power,** and will now reign'"* (Rev. 11:16-17).

By God sending His Son to reign in His Kingdom over the nations of the world, He is taking to Himself that which He has not done over the previous 6,000 years. Instead, God has allowed mankind to exercise its own kind of rule in order for it to learn the ultimate lesson—that it cannot rule itself.

It is at this moment in time that God takes control of that which is His anyway and sends His own Son to rule over His Kingdom. It is only in this way that a new era for mankind can begin. It is the only way that peace can be assured throughout the Millennium of Christ's reign. It is the only means by which mankind can begin experiencing an advanced level of maturity, the opportunity for equitable prosperity, and the exercise of the right use of highly advanced technology far beyond what is even known today.

The final chapters of Revelation reveal this second coming of the Messiah to become the King of kings. He is the one who is the Passover **and** Christ of mankind. He is the literal Son of God, whose Father is the One Eternal Almighty God. He is the one who came into existence once born into physical life from his mother Mary.

Christ and His Army

Christ is not returning as a Lamb like he did the first time when he humbled himself and did not resist when he was beaten and then killed in order to become the Passover for all mankind.

This time he is returning as a great King and he will begin his reign by attacking and conquering those who will not cease from their destruction of mankind and of all life God created to live on earth.

However, he is not returning alone. Over the past 6,000 years, God has been preparing some who have lived and died who would then be resurrected at Christ's return in order to reign with him. It is a very specific number who will return with him as part of his army.

"*Then I looked, and behold, a Lamb* [Christ] *was standing on Mount Zion, and <u>with him</u> were* **one hundred and forty-four thousand**, *having His Father's name <u>written on their foreheads</u>* [not literally, but metaphorically, which is about them becoming part of Elohim]" (Revelation 14:1).

These are further described in scripture as being the **firstfruits of God's plan** of salvation, with Christ described as being the first of the firstfruits. This is about the first phase of God's plan when His government is to become established. It is about those who will be the first to become part of what is described in the Old Testament as Elohim—the God Family.

The 144,000 will come with Christ to rule with him in the Kingdom of God over mankind. Before that Kingdom is fully established to reign on earth, they will first fight alongside Christ as a mighty army. They will bring the Third Woe upon mankind that puts an end to WWIII, as they engage in a great battle to end the war. The first two Woes are initiated by mankind, but this Third Woe will be initiated by Christ and the 144,000. This is actually about the very means by which God is going to put a stop to mankind's ruinous rampage that is leading to annihilation.

"*Now I saw heaven opened, and behold, a white horse. He who sat on it was called Faithful and True, and in righteousness he judges and <u>makes war</u>* [Gk. – **wages war**]. *His eyes are like a flame of fire, and on his head <u>many crowns</u>* [figuratively—**now to rule over all nations**]. *He had a name written that no one knew except himself, and he was clothed with a robe dipped in blood, and his name is called The Word of God* [**who is Christ, who spilled his blood as our Passover**]. *The armies* [**the 144,000**] *in <u>heaven</u>* [the heaven of the atmosphere above the earth (in the sky)], *clothed in fine linen, white and pure, followed him on white horses. Now out of his mouth went a sharp sword, that with it* **he will strike the nations**, *and he will rule them with a rod of iron. He treads the winepress of the fierceness and wrath of Almighty God, and he has on a robe and on his thigh a name written:* **King of kings** *and Lord of lords*" (Revelation 19:11-16).

The wrath of God being spoken of is not what most believe it to be. This is speaking of an "execution of judgment" that comes from God. It is that which God has deemed just and right. It is about those who come in God's righteousness to execute judgment by waging war against those who are warring on this earth. If Christ and his army did not intervene to stop it, then the earth would be completely destroyed. This righteous execution of judgment that is waged by Christ and the 144,000 is the war that will end all wars for all time.

It was earlier quoted that at the first event of the Seventh Trumpet twenty-four elders declared to God at that moment in time that "*...you have **taken to yourself your great power**, and will now reign.*" Then the next verse records that they went on to say the nations were angry and that the time for God's wrath [His judgment] had come and it was now time to **destroy those who are destroying the earth**.

Yes, the nations become filled with anger and engage in a nuclear war. Now the time has come to put an end to it, or everything would be in ruin with no life remaining. It is at this time that the next event of the Seventh Trumpet is declared, and it concerns this great army that returns with Christ. They will engage in war and *"destroy those who are destroying the earth."* This is the Third Woe upon mankind. Each Woe becomes more destructive upon human life and this one is more powerful than the Second Woe which killed a third of all mankind.

Although God does not give an exact number, it should again be understood that "likely" well over another third of mankind will be destroyed by this great army. Those who are to be destroyed will not cease from warring and they still will not listen to God. Therefore, Christ and his army will use greater power, such power never experienced by mankind, to begin destroying those who refuse to stop their fighting. They will be stopped!

Once Christ and the 144,000 have brought an end to mankind's war, then the first part or first phase of the Third Woe's destruction of mankind will be over. There will yet be a second phase to the complete fulfillment of the Third Woe, but that will not occur for another 1,100 years.

An End to Satan's Presence

The next great event spoken of, within the fulfillment of the Seventh Trumpet, concerns Satan and the demonic spirit realm.

"Then I saw an angel come down from heaven, having the key of the bottomless pit and a great chain in his hand. He laid hold on the dragon, that old serpent, who is the Devil, and Satan, and bound him a thousand years, and cast him into the bottomless pit, and shut him up, and <u>set a seal</u> upon him, that he should no more deceive the nations, until the thousand years <u>should be fulfilled</u>, and <u>after that</u> he must be let loose a little while" (Revelation 20:1-3).

This addresses how Satan will be put back into a "bottomless pit" which is the prophetic description of the place of spirit restraint. This is a restraint that he has been put in several times before as described earlier concerning the different revivals of the European empire. However, something new is now added. It makes it clear that he is not only put back into that spirit restraint, but that this time, **a seal** is being set upon him so that he has **no power whatsoever to deceive the nations** while in this final restraint.

Before this, Satan was only restrained from having power to be able to bring nations to war, but he was still able to influence and deceive people. When this event takes place, he won't have any power. He will not be able to be in any presence of mankind.

This final restraint will extend just beyond the Millennium, lasting for 1,100 years. During this time, Satan cannot interfere in any way with what God will work to accomplish during the time His Kingdom is reigning over mankind. The Millennium will be a far superior time for humanity with the fact alone that Satan and the demons cannot work to deceive and stir mankind to evil as they have been for the past 6,000 years.

The Millennial Reign of God's Kingdom Established

Once WWIII has been brought to an end by Christ and his army and Satan and the demonic realm being placed in spirit restraint, then the Millennial reign of God's Kingdom on earth will begin.

Finally, after 6,000 years of constant failure with mankind's systems and governments, a new world can be established—one that cannot fail. There will only be one government that is truly of God—one that is without human interference.

There will be only one religious practice that will be overseen through one true Church—God's Church, over which some of the 144,000 will be given to administer all that is right and true from God. Consider the peace that will come when only **one** Church exists throughout the earth—the one that is true. There will be no more division, fighting, hatred, and jealousy between religious groups. Teachers who reflect or promote self-righteousness, judgmental attitudes, piety, false doctrines and teachings, and so much more will no longer prevail.

The Millennium will be without terrorism, wars, gangs, and cartels. There will be no need for armies or armaments. Large police forces, legal firms, insurance institutions, and complex banking systems will all be downsized dramatically, if not made obsolete over time. This is only the beginning in addressing the many kinds of changes that will take place.

There will be no government agencies that conduct central or foreign intelligence gathering or federal investigations. There will be no more oppressive tax collection agencies or the high taxation that is everywhere today.

The determination of justice will be quick, impartial, without political influence, with no bias, and with no juries. There will be no false imprisonments ever again and no life sentences or excessively long sentences in prisons. The entire system will be changed from top to bottom. That is something that mankind cannot begin to do. Six thousand years of archaic, cruel, dehumanizing, and immoral practices of human "justice" will be brought to an end.

Homelessness, disease epidemics, human trafficking, drug addiction, illicit drugs, rampant crime, and so much more will become things of the past from a corrupt, selfish, and out-of-control age of mankind and its failed rule of itself.

Can you begin to see the differences that God's government over mankind can make? Doesn't this sound almost as though it is far too good to possibly be true? That is the point! That has been God's message to mankind over the past 6,000 years—that mankind needs His government in their lives, and that without it, there is only needless suffering, injustice, frustration of life, confusion, evil, drama, killing, and wars.

This new era that is about to be ushered in will be **a time of healing for mankind and healing for the earth itself.** It is then that the earth will begin to become renewed and cleansed from all that mankind has so polluted and destroyed. God reveals that even the deserts will begin to be productive. Mankind will begin to reverse the destruction it started thousands of years ago, which has caused the creation and expansion of so many deserts and uninhabitable areas on earth.

Over the millennia, God has been telling mankind of a better world that is coming—one governed by His Kingdom. That message throughout the ages has been one that is called the "good news." It is the **good news of God's government** that is now about to be established on earth under the reign of Christ.

This "good news" is the meaning of what is translated in the New Testament as the "gospel." Christ said much about that good news, however, the world did not understand it, as it was yet neither the time to fully reveal it nor for it to be fulfilled.

This is just a glimpse into what the Millennium will be like. This new era for mankind would not be possible without God's intervention through the Third Woe that ends WWIII and the establishment of His Kingdom under Christ.

Why Such Ignorance About God's Kingdom?
So why aren't people aware of this government that God is going to establish? Why don't teachers of religion talk about the 1,000-year reign of Christ as the King of kings? It is in their Bibles, but they refuse to teach about it. Why? This needs to be answered!

THE FALL OF THE UNITED STATES 63

Much more will need to be addressed, but the quick answer to this question is that what is stated in scripture does not agree with their doctrines. It doesn't fit in with their teachings. But why not?

Earlier in this chapter, verses were quoted that speak of the time Christ will return in what is described as him riding upon a white horse with an army coming with him. What ministers in traditional Christianity teach that Christ will return and come with an army? Why don't they teach about the 144,000 who are plainly identified in scripture? Why don't they speak of a 1,000-year reign that is also clearly spoken of in Revelation? Does anyone teach about Christ coming to strike the nations and then proceeding to rule over them with strength?

*"Now out of his mouth went a sharp sword, that with it **he will strike the nations**, and he will rule them with a rod of iron. He treads the winepress of the fierceness and wrath of Almighty God, and he has on a robe and on his thigh a name written: **King of kings** and Lord of lords"* (Revelation 19:15-16).

Besides Christ, who else could be spoken of in the previous verses that describe this King as wearing a robe dipped in blood and his name being "The Word of God"? Christ is clearly identified by this name in John 1 as being "the Word of God made flesh." He was born into physical life from his mother, Mary, but his father was God.

The first three verses of the following chapter were quoted earlier where it spoke of Satan being placed back into his place of spirit restraint (the bottomless pit). It then goes on to address those who came with Christ, in his army. It tells how these have thrones because they are made kings who are to reign with Christ in God's newly established government over mankind. This is the Kingdom of God that will reign throughout the Millennium.

*"Then I saw **thrones**, and they who sat upon them, and judgment was given unto them [**to the 144,000 who will then reign with Christ**], and I saw the lives of those [the same] who had been cut-off for the witness of Joshua [**cut-off from the world**], and for the word of God, those who had not worshipped the beast, neither his image, neither had*

*received his mark in their foreheads, or in their hands, and they lived and **reigned with Christ a thousand years**. But the rest of the dead did not live again until the thousand years were finished. This is the first resurrection"* (Revelation 20:4-5).

From this point forward there is no way to explain all that is **TRUE** and from God except to also clearly state the plain truth about all that is false in traditional Christianity. The best way to accomplish this at this stage is to simply focus on what **is being said** in these verses that are being covered. Then it will begin to become clear why teachers of traditional Christianity **don't teach** about them.

It is so much easier for people to come to understand what John is writing in Revelation when they know the context. The first few chapters give a summary of instructions for God's Church. The following chapters of the book quickly move into the description of events that are to be fulfilled in the end-time. Then toward the very end of the book, John writes about events that will follow once God has established His Kingdom.

In the verses just quoted, a unique group of people is being described. These individuals are introduced beginning in Revelation 5. They are those who through time have been redeemed through the blood of Christ. This tells of how Christ has been working with them to become kings and priests unto God.

Then Chapter 7 goes on to reveal the number of those, whom as it states, "have washed their robes and made them white in the blood of the Lamb." Wearing white robes is symbolic language for becoming changed by repentance through the blood of Christ and now being clothed in righteousness.

This same chapter also reveals the number as being 144,000 who have been redeemed over time (throughout 6,000 years) then becoming clothed in the white robes. In these verses, it is revealing that they then become part of God's Family, as they are then being described as spirit beings.

Then it was already quoted in Revelation 14 how Christ (as the Lamb of God) was standing on Mt. Zion and the 144,000 were with him.

As the context through these chapters of Revelation is showing, the 144,000 who come with Christ as his army are those who have been redeemed through time. Then, in Revelation 20, it states that these will reign with Christ for 1,000 years. It also states that this is all about the first resurrection. But who within traditional Christianity teaches about a first resurrection?

A First Resurrection of Mankind
If God had redeemed these throughout time and this event is spoken of as being a first resurrection, then why does traditional Christianity teach that all people who become redeemed by the blood of Christ go immediately to heaven upon death? What need would there be of a resurrection of so many if they have already gone to heaven? These teachers cannot give answers to this because it contradicts their doctrine.

In God's plan of salvation, the truth is, that after death, there are different resurrections to life. Upon death, no one goes to either heaven or hell.

The teaching of anyone going to a place called hell is false. Numerous scriptures have mistranslations in which the word "hell" is used, wherein the word "hell" carries the meaning of "a place of eternal punishment."

The vast majority of these mistranslations come from the Hebrew word "sheol" and the Greek word "hades" which mean the same thing. The correct translation and meaning of both of these words is "grave" or simply "a hole in the ground." This is where most people's bodies end up after death—in the grave. Once a person is dead, there is nothing. There is no life there and no life again until God gives it in a resurrection from the dead.

There are a couple of other Greek words that are also translated as "hell," but they are not about a place of eternal torment or punishment for those who live evil lives. One word that is used is simply a reference to a place of restraint.

The other mistranslation is from the Greek word "Gehenna," which is a reference to a valley in the area of Jerusalem. This word in scripture usually has the Greek word for "fire" connected to it. Some believe that hell is a place of great heat and fire that is associated with eternal torment and punishment the damned receive upon death. These two words used together in this manner are indeed about a final punishment that ends physical life from which a person can never receive life again—never to be resurrected to life again. It is about a punishment that lasts forever because the person can never live again, but it is not about being eternally punished.

Indeed, upon death, no one goes to hell and upon death, no one goes to heaven.

On the Day of Pentecost, when God started His Church in 31 AD, Peter made some rather pointed statements to the Jews. He quoted some of the prophecies that David wrote about the Messiah and explained how those things had now become fulfilled in Christ. Those prophecies were not about David as some thought.

The Jews of that time had strayed far from the teaching God had delivered to them through Moses. Many of them did not understand what David wrote because they thought certain verses in Psalms were about David himself, but they were not. One statement is very telling for those who hold to the concept that upon death the faithful go to heaven. If this were true, then most certainly David would be there, as he is spoken of as being a prophet and one whom God said was "a man after His own heart."

"Men and brethren, let me speak freely to you about the patriarch David, that he is both dead and buried, and his tomb is with us to this day. Therefore, being a prophet, and knowing that God had sworn with an oath to him that of the fruit of his body, according to the flesh, He would raise up the Christ to sit on His throne; he [David], *foreseeing this before, spoke concerning the resurrection of Christ, that his soul* [life] *was not left in* hell [**Gk.— "hades" meaning the grave**], *nor did his flesh see corruption. This Joshua, God has raised up, of which we are all witnesses"* (Acts 2:29-32).

It is stating at the end of these verses that Christ's body would not see corruption (decay), and it did not since he was only in the tomb for three days and three nights. It is making it clear here that these verses being quoted from the Psalms were about Christ who would be resurrected before his body would decay. Peter also made it clear that this was not about David because his body did see corruption (decay), as Peter clearly stated that his body was buried and in the tomb to that day, many hundreds of years later. David did not go to heaven, but instead will be one of those resurrected at Christ's coming and will reign with him.

Only one person over the past 6,000 years has been resurrected to everlasting life and he is the only one who has gone to heaven to be with God his Father, and that is Christ.

Since traditional Christianity does not believe in future resurrections, they steer clear of these verses from Revelation 20. How could they reconcile their beliefs with what these verses are saying? How could they possibly make sense of them when it contradicts their own beliefs?

These verses also address another incredible subject that is never spoken of—a subject that is exceedingly encouraging concerning God's plan and purpose for all who have died and remain dead. It is part of the true gospel—good news from God!

The verses of Revelation 20 speak of the time for the Millennium (1,000 years) when the 144,000 reign with Christ over the nations of this earth. Then after mentioning all those resurrected to reign for that 1,000 years, it states: "But the rest of the dead lived not again until the thousand years were finished."

Who are the rest of the dead? That should be self-explanatory. They are the people who have lived and died throughout the past 6,000 years who were not part of the first resurrection of the 144,000. They are the "rest of the dead."

For now, all who have lived and died have returned to the dust of the earth just as God said would happen (Eccl. 3:20), but there comes a time in God's plan when these people will have the opportunity to be resurrected to life once again. Going on in this verse, it shows when they will be resurrected. It states that they will "not live again until the 1,000 years are finished." Notice what else is stated in those verses of Revelation 20.

"But the rest of the dead did not live again until the thousand years were finished. This is the first resurrection [of the 144,000 being spoken of]. *Blessed and holy is he who has part in the first resurrection, because on such the **second death** has no power, but they shall be priests of God and of Christ, and shall reign with him a thousand years"* (Rev. 20:5-6).

After stating that the rest of the dead did not live again until after the Millennium, it then refers back to the 144,000 who were resurrected to come with Christ. It says that they are blessed who are part of this first resurrection "because on such the **second death** has no power" over them. That is because they are not given a second physical life, but are instead created as spirit beings in the God Family, just as their elder brother Christ. They can never die.

The Fulfillment of the Seventh Trumpet

There is another vital element concerning God's plan that will be completed during this period of Christ's reign over the next 1,100 years.

That last verse refers back to the 144,000 who will come with Christ and reign with him for 1,000 years and it states that those who come with him are of the **first resurrection**. God has revealed that following this there will be other resurrections, at different times, as He continues to complete His plan for salvation.

As stated earlier, upon death people do not immediately go to a heaven or hell. They remain dead until God resurrects them. This is a great truth that is part of what is referred to as the **"mystery of God"** that will be revealed throughout the following 1,100 years. It is a **"mystery"** to mankind because they have not known about it and it remains a mystery until it is revealed to them.

Traditional Christianity would have people believe that upon death people go immediately to heaven or hell because they believe that people have an immortal soul—a form of immortal life that is in them. That is not true. Only God Almighty has immortality inherent in Himself. Even after Christ had been dead in the tomb for three days and three nights, God had to resurrect him from the dead and then give him a new body—one that was of spirit. Yet Christ was able to physically manifest himself as he did in the presence of his disciples during those 40 days after his resurrection.

Christ did not have an immortal soul and he remained dead until God resurrected him. Then after those 40 days, he ascended into heaven and has remained there and will continue to be there until he returns to be the King of kings in the Kingdom of God that will reign on earth.

Establishing the Final 100 Years
There is an incredibly great event that takes place just before the resurrection to a **second** physical life for **"the rest of the dead."** Before those who have lived and died over the first 6,000 years are resurrected to a second physical life, another resurrection to spirit life in the Family of God takes place first.

Just before this final 100 years begins, there is a **resurrection** that takes place that is **similar to the first one of the 144,000, but this time, it is much, much larger.** This is a resurrection for those who have lived and died during the Millennium and have had the opportunity to learn God's way of life. Those who have made the choice to faithfully live His way will now be resurrected into spirit life—into the Family of God as spirit beings just like the 144,000 had been.

God has great purpose for this resurrection to take place at this time, rather than at the end of the 100 years. It is for the purpose of the massive job that lies ahead in the governing, teaching, and aiding of all the billions who are about to be resurrected to a second physical life.

After this second great resurrection into the God Family, the final hundred years will begin—the final years of mankind's existence. God refers to this period as the **Last Great Day.** It is the time when billions will be resurrected to a second physical life. This time period is also known as the **Great White Throne Judgment**. This descriptive title is used to identify this period as a time of final judgment upon mankind.

"Then I saw a great white throne and He who sat on it, from whose face the earth and the heaven fled away [Gk. – escaped or fled away from] *and no place was found for them as I saw the dead, small and great, standing before God, and books being opened. Also another book was opened, which is of life. Then the dead were judged according to their works, by the things which were written in the books"* (Revelation 20:11-12).

This is about the resurrection of billions to a second physical life, those referred to in Revelation 20:5 as **"the rest of the dead."** It is a time when these billions will now come into a period of judgment for how they choose to live their second physical life. In their first life, they did not know the truth of God. It was not His purpose to reveal His truth to them at that time. Instead, the only ones to whom He revealed His truth were the ones who were being prepared to become part of His government—part of the 144,000.

All these will be resurrected to physical life once again in order to be taught what is true from God. This will be their time to choose how they want to live—by the ways of God or by their own ways as they had lived before. Babies and children will be resurrected whole and complete—healthy and without handicaps of any kind. People who died of old age will be resurrected to whole and healthy bodies as well—in bodies that are not of old age, but middle-aged.

In this resurrection, it needs to be understood that God has given the first 7,000 years for the reproduction and growth of mankind. After the 7,000 years have ended, which is when the Millennium comes to an end, there will be no more reproduction. When this final 100 years is established, and there is a great resurrection to physical life once again, God will have removed from mankind the ability to reproduce human life. Women will not have the ability to become pregnant and no children will be born during this time.

God makes it clear that when He calls someone and then gives them the ability to see His truth, then at that time they begin to come under judgment. It is during that period that they must, according to their own will, choose between God's way or the way of self (the way of the world, Satan, and/or others). When all are resurrected to a second physical life, they are able to then come to know God's truth. It is then that they will have to begin to choose between God's way or their own way.

John's description of a **great white throne** is symbolic of a time of judgment before God. It states that the heaven and earth had fled away or escaped. It is showing that until this moment, this mass of people had not come under the judgment of God but had, in a manner, escaped it during their first life. They will be resurrected in a much better world where the potential for choosing God's way of life is now much easier to do. They will now live in a world where Satan and the demonic world are no longer present, and in a world where deception, lies, and false religions no longer exist.

It is in this final age of mankind that people will begin to experience righteous government and justice. During the previous 1,000 years, the Kingdom of God will have reigned over the earth and the world will have changed in ways that are difficult to envision. Science and technology will take a massive leap forward. These things will all work together in such a manner as to increase productivity and prosperity in human life, far, far beyond what one is able to imagine.

It is in this resurrection to physical life again that God's judgment finally comes upon all the rest of humanity. All who are a part of this great resurrection are given life in a new world that is governed and taught by God's Son and all those who are now in the Family of God. It is showing in these verses that all people through time, the small and great of their time, are now resurrected before God to receive His truth through His word that is clearly opened (the books being opened) to their understanding.

In addition, it refers to another book being opened to them—the Book of Life. They will have the opportunity to have their names (their life) added to those who are in the Family of God and living into everlasting life. These too must go through a process of **choosing** whether to live by the Word of God in how they live their life. Will they **work** to live by God's way or not?

The following verse is a summary of the final 100 years of mankind. It begins with describing a great resurrection of all who have died. Notice what is stated about the judgment after these 100 years are completed.

"The sea gave up the dead who were in it, and death and the grave [some use the actual Greek word 'hades,' and others use 'hell'] *delivered up the dead who were in it. Everyone was judged according to their works. Then death and the grave were cast into the lake of fire. This is the **second death**. Anyone not found written in the Book of Life was cast into the lake of fire"* (Revelation 20:13-15).

Then upon being given a second life and the ability to know God's truth, people are then judged according to their free choices and the works in their life that reflect those choices.

Finally, the end comes when those who have chosen to live God's way are judged to be received into His Family in everlasting life. However, those who chose to live other than God's way are judged to receive **a second death**—death for all time.

A Second Death

Is a second death taught in traditional Christianity? No! It is clearly in scripture, but ministers and teachers steer clear of saying anything about it because it conflicts mightily with what they believe. They cannot begin to grasp how anyone could die twice because that would mean that they have to live twice.

Although many will have chosen to live God's way of life during that 100 years, there will be those who just do not want to live that kind of life and will instead choose to live how they want—just as they did in their first life, which is the way of self—the way of selfishness—the way of the world. God has allotted 100 years during this time period for people to make a choice as to which way of life they want to live.

Those who choose their own ways—the ways of their previous life—are free to do so, but they will not be given life beyond that 100-year period of the Great White Throne Judgment. Instead, their judgment will be one of eternal death, not one of eternal punishment—of being punished forever.

God's way is not one of having any be tortured or punished for eternity for not choosing His way of life. God is not vindictive or cruel as so many have made Him out to be. He does not want to see people live in torture and torment for everlasting life for not obeying Him. That would indeed be a sick mind to place such a punishment on anyone. Thankfully, God is nothing like that! He is not the type of God that traditional Christianity has portrayed Him to be by their perverted teaching of hell and hellfire.

The Choice of Life
The period of the Last Great Day is all about the choices people will make during that final 100 years. It is a time to choose life, or not. It would seem a simple choice, but it will not be so.

Things are much different in the lives of mankind during that final 100 years. This second chance for physical life takes place in a world that is vastly different from the world they encountered previously. What remains the same, however, is the same human nature that molded them into what they became in their first life.

Obviously, babies and children who are resurrected to a second life will not have the bad experiences of sin-filled choices that teens and adults have had. But for those who are older and who were more fully set in their own ways upon death, many things that they have previously lived have of course not been in agreement with God's way of life. Those ways are not easy to change. Even after God has provided so much to those resurrected to a second physical life, there will be vast numbers who will simply choose not to change. They will still want their old ways and not God's.

Such people will still prefer to live a way that produces drama, including such things as unfaithfulness in marriage, theft, corruption, politics, drunkenness, drug addiction, sexual perversion, unrestrained reveling, hatred and jealousy of others, self-recognition above others, lust of power and wealth, and all other ways that are produced by the choice of living by selfish human nature—by what self **wants**.

Although billions will be resurrected to a second physical life, not all will want to change. All will not want the way of God that is shown to them at that time. Instead, they will resist that way. Many will simply conform because of the kind of society that is being governed by the Kingdom of God reigning over the nations, but they will not agree with it and will not want it.

Only those who actually choose and want God's way of life will be able to make the kind of changes in their life that are required in order to grow to a spiritual level that God will receive them into His Family. God does not owe anything to anyone. He has already given us everything that we have. If it comes down to a person simply choosing that they want their own way of life and not God's, then that is their choice. God's way cannot and will not be forced upon anyone. His way must be **freely chosen**.

So at the end of that 100 years, it will be clear to God who those are that will become part of His Family into everlasting life. It will also be clear who those are that have chosen their own ways and not God's.

By that time there will be billions who will have chosen to live God's way of life. They will have chosen life. They will have taken hold of the opportunity God placed before them to become part of His Family in everlasting spirit life.

However, there will potentially be billions who will not have accepted God and His way by the end of that 100 years. Instead, they will have chosen their own ways just as the archangel Lucifer did vast millennia before.

It was Lucifer who first rebelled against God and then became known as Satan the Devil, as well as the Beast and False Prophet. He led a **third of the angelic realm** with him in his way of selfishness and pride in order to get more of what he wanted in wealth and power for himself. Those who rebelled with him became known as demons, and they too have opposed and fought against God ever since their rebellion.

If such a great number of spirit created angelic beings could make such a choice over a vast period of time and turn away from what God had offered them, it should not be difficult to understand how great numbers of carnal, selfish human beings will do the same thing over a short period of time.

God's Plan Nears Completion
After the last 100 years of mankind has come to an end, there is a space of time that follows which God has not yet shown the exact duration, but it is short. It is a time for the final judgment of God to be administered to mankind. This will conclude the Great White Throne Judgment of God.

The exact sequence of all the events that follow has not yet been shown by God, but He has clearly given what will come of all who have chosen His way of life and those who have rejected it.

It is an incredible story of how all this transpires and concludes the age of mankind. God has shown how he finishes this age and the process whereby He administers final judgment to all who have refused Him through time.

In Revelation 20, when Satan has a seal set upon him, it is stated that he should be confined there "until the thousand years should be fulfilled, and after that he must be let loose a little while" (verse 3). It does not specify the exact moment he is released after the 1,000 years are completed, but in other verses, the context shows that it cannot be until the end of the 100 years that follow the Millennium. Then it goes on to show what happens when he is released.

"Then when the thousand years have ended, Satan shall be let loose out of his prison, and shall go out to deceive the nations which are in the four quarters of the earth, Gog and Magog, to gather them together for battle, and their number is as the sand of the sea" (Revelation 20:7-8).

Satan must be released from his confinement one last time in order to help bring a completion to God's plan for all mankind and an end to mankind's existence. Satan will fulfill what he is best at accomplishing, by the way of deception and destruction, just as one of his names signifies: The Destroyer.

Satan has always served to help speed the process of bringing nations to war. Throughout history, nations over time have always built up to war. War between nations has always been inevitable, an absolute. It is the way of mankind. But as part of God's plan, the destructive nature of that being has often worked to bring the certainty of eventual war between peoples and nations to a quicker conclusion so that the amount of suffering and evil that would otherwise come from longer wars could be lessened.

With mankind, wars are the inevitable result of selfish human nature. They are certain to come to pass because of the inability of mankind, of itself, to live the way that produces peace. Experiencing peace can only come from choosing to receive the help of God's spirit in order to live God's way of life. During the Millennium and the Great White Throne Judgment periods, mankind will have the opportunity to choose and learn that way. God will not allow conditions to come to a point where anyone will have the ability to engage in war. The rule of God's government will ensure peace between nations.

However, once Satan is released, all his effort will be used once again to lead mankind to engage in great war—a war that will be stopped before it even begins.

Satan is easily able to influence those who have now lived twice and have not chosen God's way of life. Those who choose to live in a different manner than what God has revealed as true and right are living in sin. That is the definition of sin—to live against what God has shown is right.

As Satan is released to go out into all the world, the expressions of "Gog and Magog" are used as prophetic symbolisms for the masses and kinds of people who have refused God's way of life. It is further described that the number of these people are as the sand of the sea. Considering the population of mankind throughout its thousands of years of history, the number of those who actually refuse God and His way of life will be several billion.

One cannot fully grasp the thinking of an unsound mind. It is difficult to grasp what Satan is doing except to know that his hatred for God's plan and his hatred for mankind is so deep that he simply wants to cause and see as much destruction of God's creation as possible.

Although Satan has consistently fought against God and tried to destroy all that he can, he has never remotely come close to thwarting anything that God has purposed, but still, he tries. Just the same, in this final period at the end of 100 years, he will still work to unite as much of mankind as possible to fight against God's Family, even though there is no way they can possibly succeed. Satan must, in some manner, deceive billions into believing they can succeed. God has simply not revealed how such a thing can transpire, but it is recorded what they will attempt to do.

"They went up over the breadth of the earth and surrounded the stronghold of the saints, even the beloved city, and fire came down from God out of heaven and devoured them" (Rev. 20:9).

This verse shows how these vast numbers of people who are led by Satan will come up against God's people with the purpose of warring against them. God's people are referred to in many different ways prophetically, and here it states that they comprise the beloved city. It is not the actual physical city of Jerusalem, but the spiritual one of God's people.

It then shows that God stops Satan and those who have followed him from starting a war. Even though their purpose will be to war, God will not allow a war to start, but will simply destroy Satan and that army. This will be the second phase of the Third Woe upon mankind

There are verses that describe seven angels that have seven vials (of seven plagues) that are to be poured out upon mankind. It is shown that one of these seven angels is present during this time period at the end of the 100 years. Although these seven plagues that are to be poured out upon mankind are not yet understood, it is shown by this that this is the Third Woe spoken of that is to take place during the fulfillment of the Seventh Trumpet. It takes just over 1,100 years for the events of the Seventh Trumpet to become completely fulfilled.

The events of the Seventh Trumpet begin at Christ's coming with the 144,000 as an army that will fulfill the first phase of the Third Woe, which is to put an end to WWIII and destroy those who are destroying the earth. It is then that Satan and the demonic world are placed into a spirit restraint and a seal is set upon them so they cannot be around mankind. Then they are released for a short time at the end of the 100 years.

As Satan and the demonic world strive against mankind and work to bring about another great war, God prevents it. This will be the second and last phase of the Third Woe which will be fulfilled by those seven angels pouring out their vials upon the earth.

This is the final Woe upon mankind. It brings an end to the existence of mankind. It is powerful and it is swift. It brings an end to Satan's feeble attempts to fight against what is God's.

Indeed, God's plan includes the ultimate destruction of Satan and the demonic world, which must be accomplished in order for God's plan for mankind to be fulfilled. This is addressed in the very next verse.

"Then the devil who had deceived them was thrown into the lake of fire and brimstone wherein this beast and false prophet shall be tormented day and night forever and ever" (Rev. 20:10).

Many have believed that since God created Lucifer as an archangel, a spirit creation, that he, therefore, had eternal life. But that is not true. He was a created being. Only God has immortal self-sustaining life inherent in Himself for all eternity. The angels do not have such self-sustaining life in themselves and were simply created as spirit beings. Physical life or spirit life, which God has created, can also be taken away or ended by God.

It is that knowledge that torments Satan about his future fate. This being has existed as a false teacher (false prophet) and he has always lied about God and God's purpose for His creation. Satan is the one who has deceived mankind with all his false teachings and false doctrines that so many have accepted as being true about God and the one whom they call Jesus.

So indeed, Satan is "the" false prophet and also the beast. That beast is the one who raised up the prophesied revivals of the European empire. His power as the beast and his deception as the false prophet will carry over into the Great White Throne period of that final 100 years. This is because a vast number of people lived their first life when Satan had great influence, and they will still have those memories of that time when they are resurrected to a second life. Many of them preferred the life of that deception they had embraced back then, and therefore, they still do not want the truth that God has placed before them.

The reality is, many will still choose the way of Babylon, the false beliefs and practices, the deceitful practices of past governments, and all the false ways of life people lived before. They prefer that life above God's. Those false ways are symbolized in the expressions that identify Satan's work of both a beast and the false prophet. Those ways can only be fully destroyed when those who have embraced those ways are fully destroyed.

Before this, those false ways will begin to be destroyed through the work that takes place during the Millennium, although they will be brought right back to the forefront when all the people who had practiced them all their life are then resurrected to a second physical life. Many will choose to reject that former life and receive what God has revealed, but many will not.

In the verse above, it states that Satan "shall be tormented." He is tormented with the knowledge of his demise. The expression translated as being tormented forever and ever does not mean into everlasting time but is used in the Greek language as a span of time that continues as long as specific conditions last. If the end to an age comes to pass, then so do the conditions that surround it.

Once Satan is thrown into the kind of fire that God is describing (not something that is physical), then that age of his existence comes to an end, but until then he is constantly tormented by the knowledge of what is yet to come.

God's Plan Fulfilled
At some point during these final events that have just been addressed, all who have chosen and faithfully lived God's way of life are changed—resurrected—to spirit life in God's Family, Elohim.

This is a time that marks the complete fulfillment of God's plan and purpose for having created mankind. Then, the spiritual Family of God is complete. God explains this time in many different ways.

"*I also saw a new heaven and a new earth because the first heaven and the first earth had passed away, and there was no more sea*" (Rev. 21:1).

In this verse, John is explaining how a great change has now taken place on earth and nothing is as it was before. Everything was being made new and different.

The expression about there being "no more sea" is not literal concerning the seas and oceans of the world. It is a prophetic symbolism for the fact that there is no more "sea" of humanity as has existed over the previous 7,100 years. The age of mankind and God's purpose for the creation of mankind has now been accomplished—it is complete—the mystery of God is fulfilled and there is no more human life.

"*Then I, John, saw the holy city, new Jerusalem, coming down out of heaven* [the heaven above the earth—the sky] *from God, prepared as a bride adorned for her husband. I also heard a loud voice from heaven saying, 'Behold, the tabernacle of God is with men, and He will dwell with them, and they shall be His people. God Himself will be with them. God will even wipe away every tear from their eyes. There shall be no more death, nor sorrow, nor crying. There shall be no more pain, for the former things have passed away'*" (Rev. 21:2-4).

Those who are resurrected are now added to what is described as the new Jerusalem, which is a spiritual dwelling together of God's people who have entered into His Family. These verses show that since they are now delivered from death, sorrow, pain, and tears that existed in their physical lives, they will no longer experience such things since they are born into a spirit creation—composed of spirit. Then a great declaration follows once these have all been delivered from among mankind to be in the God Family.

*"Then He who sat on the throne said, 'Look, I make all things new.' He also said to me, 'Write, for these words are true and faithful.' Then He said to me, **'It has been done!** I am the Alpha and the Omega, the beginning and the end. I will give to him who is thirsty of the fountain of the water of life freely'"* (Rev. 21:5-6).

It is at the time when the purpose of the Great White Throne period is accomplished and all existence of mankind has ended, by either receiving of a second death or of being resurrected into everlasting spirit life, that God declares He has now made "all things new" and that **"it has been done!"** The mystery of God—His plan and purpose for the creation of mankind—has been fully revealed and completed. The events of the Seventh Trumpet have ended.

After God has declared what He will fulfill, He continues on with a final warning to mankind.

"'Those who overcome shall inherit all things, and I will be their God and they shall be my children. But the cowardly, unbelieving, abominable, murderers, sexually immoral, sorcerers, idolaters, and all liars shall have their part in the lake which burns with fire and brimstone, which is the second death.' There came unto me one of the seven angels who have the seven bowls filled with the seven last plagues and he spoke with me, saying, 'Come, I will show you the bride of the Lamb—the wife.' Then he carried me away in the spirit to a great and high mountain, and showed me the great city, holy Jerusalem, descending out of the sky from God" (Rev. 21:7-10).

Toward the end of all His written word, God has once again stressed the importance of choices that people are free to make, and that with wrong choices there are consequences. There are those at the end of the final 100-year period of mankind's existence who will experience a second death, and then there are those who will become God's children into everlasting life.

Chapter 4
TURMOIL WITHIN RELIGION

Have you ever considered why there are so many different religions in the world? Or why people believe what they do? The reality is that most people simply continue with the same beliefs into which they were born.

If one were to delve deeper into the many different religions that exist, it would become obvious that there are vast differences, discrepancies, and disagreements. This has created incredible confusion for mankind and has led to great divisiveness and even wars.

The largest religion in the world, which accounts for nearly 1/3 of all mankind, is Christianity. There are three broad divisions within Christianity, one of them being Protestantism. It is estimated that there are over 45,000 different denominations alone in this faith worldwide. Add to this that non-denominational churches are gaining in popularity, and the real number of these different Protestant groups, each with different ideas, is even much greater.

Is it any wonder that there is so much confusion and division in the world since these various groups all have differing beliefs? All of this has only led to greater variance, divisiveness, discord, conflict, and rivalry between organizations within traditional Christianity. This is the very reason why so many people question and even doubt whether there is absolute **truth** that even exists.

A large part of the problem is that few within traditional Christianity have any knowledge whatsoever of when or how the specific teachings of the church they adhere to came into existence. This issue is compounded by the fact that most have no knowledge of where the doctrines and teachings of their church have come from. It is taken for granted that all which they are taught and believe has come from scripture.

This is why so much of the world has been blinded from the real truth. Their religious assumptions and unwillingness to challenge their own long-held beliefs have stopped them from listening and heeding end-time prophecies that have been accurately foretelling events that are leading up to mankind's final war. This in turn reveals the true attitude of mankind toward God. It also reflects the level of apathy that exists in traditional Christianity. This is why God is going to expose it as being false.

Truth does exist and God is about to make this abundantly clear to mankind when he sends His Son, along with the 144,000, to establish His Kingdom (government) and one true Church on earth.

You can wait until Christ's return to learn what is true, or you can begin to know it now.

The Origin of the Church of God
So when did God's Church actually begin? The first mention of people being added to the Church was directly after the Pentecost of 31AD when God began to pour out His holy spirit upon his disciples, just as He had promised. Then immediately following Pentecost and the miraculous events that happened on that day, the disciples remained in the area of Jerusalem for a time as they began teaching about all that Christ had fulfilled.

"Then day by day they were of one mind to continue in the temple [**teaching**], *and broke bread from house to house, as they would eat their food with gladness and singleness of heart, while praising God and receiving favor with all the people. Then the Lord added to the Church*

daily such as should be saved" (Acts 2:46-47).

So God began adding to the Church those whom He was calling to receive salvation. Then later in the Book of Acts, Paul makes it clear whose Church this was.

*"So now, look. I have known that all of you, among whom I have gone preaching the Kingdom of God, will not see my face again. Therefore I have called you to witness this day, that I am clear from the blood of any. For I have not held back from declaring unto you all the counsel of God. Therefore take heed unto yourselves, and to all the flock, over which the holy spirit has made you overseers, to feed the **Church of God**, which He has purchased with His own blood* [the blood of His Son]" (Acts 20:25-28).

This instruction being given by Paul to the ministry is the first account that clearly identifies the Church as being God's Church, and it is referred to in this manner in scriptures that follow. The Church is never referred to in any other manner in scripture as belonging to anyone else, not even to Christ, although he is identified as the head of the Church. Nowhere in scripture is **God's Church** referred to as being Roman Catholic.

These are important distinctions because it shows two vastly different churches, God's Church, and the Roman Catholic Church, each calling themselves Christian up until the latter part of the Middle Ages. This is when some began to organize into other groups and break away from the Roman Catholic Church, which was the beginning of Protestant churches.

The first Church calling itself Christian is the one that began on Pentecost in 31 AD. However, it is recorded that it did not take long before others began to misrepresent themselves by impersonating the disciples. This was done in order to gain a following for the purpose of recognition, stature, and generally with the goal of receiving wealth from others. Some of these people are spoken of and some are even listed by name in several of the books of the New Testament.

Few today know that the first church within today's "traditional Christianity" began in 325 AD. That church formed the Roman Catholic religion. It had a beginning that is not hard to trace and identify. However, the first church organization calling itself Christian actually began in 31 AD—the Church of God. To make it clear, the Church of God was not established by the Romans, but by God. Nevertheless, the Roman Catholic Church claims that the teachings of Jesus were passed along to them.

The Origin of the Roman Catholic Church

By the time the Roman Catholic Church became established in 325 AD, it was the only other established organization calling itself Christian that was able to continue through the centuries that followed, other than the Church of God that became established in 31 AD.

As true Christianity began to slowly grow and move into other regions of the Roman Empire, it received great resistance from that government especially, but also from others in the world. This happened in the same manner as Christ's own words were resisted and rejected by the majority, which led to him being sentenced to death by that government. That kind of resistance against God's Church hasn't changed much throughout the centuries.

Following Christ's death and the establishment of God's Church, ideas about Christ and his teaching began to creep into the Roman-dominated world. There were priests and teachers of other deities who liked and adopted the stories about God and His Son. They exploited these stories as a way to sway and influence people with their ideas and beliefs of their own deities, mixing the true history of the past with their own false beliefs and teachings.

Indeed, the ancient Romans were noted for the great number of deities they honored, and they attributed their success as a world power to their collective piety or pietas (their religious devotion, duty, and loyalty) through their efforts of keeping good relations with the gods. The Romans conquered many nations and used the practice of assimilating many of those conquered people's religious beliefs and practices into their own. This is simply a matter of written history.

Ancient Roman religion was centered more upon knowledge of the correct practice of prayer and ritual rather than upon faith in what was believed. When God's Church began after 31 AD and the teaching of Christianity began to spread, the priests and teachers of the Roman deities found it easy to assimilate those practices and teachings about God and Christ into their own. This practice and movement proved so successful that they too adopted the name "Christian" to identify themselves.

By 325 AD, this movement among these priests of the Roman Empire, who were calling themselves Christian, had grown in such influence and power that Emperor Constantine himself stepped in to consolidate the teachings of this new kind of Christianity. History records that he did this because there were divisive influences among these widely scattered priests who had organized into different groups. He set out to unify them and create a new state religion.

Constantine wanted to bring the priests into agreement with a newly established and unified set of beliefs. Not only that, but he also set out to eradicate and outlaw a sect of Christianity, which to most Romans was too closely associated with Judaism. Jews had long been hated within the Roman world. They were even used as slaves to build the great Colosseum in Rome.

The Roman Emperor Constantine called for a conference in which all matters about Christendom were to become established and united within the Roman Empire. He called together what became known as the **Council of Nicaea in 325 AD** and he also participated in its decision-making process.

It is here that the Nicene Creed became established, which is a statement of belief that included the creation of the Trinity doctrine. In historical accounts, it is recorded that much of Constantine's motivation for bringing the primary leaders of Roman priests together was because of the divisive teaching of one of these Roman priests named Arius. In the view of Constantine and the larger group of Roman priests, Arius was holding too closely with the teachings of those Jews who were going throughout the Roman Empire teaching about Christ.

THE FALL OF THE UNITED STATES 87

There was great dispute among the Roman priests about the nature of Christ. Arius taught that he, the son of God, was created and his life only came into existence after his birth from Mary his mother. The vastly more popular group, who had the ear and agreement of Constantine, believed that Christ was also God and had eternally existed.

These matters can easily be looked up and read on the Internet. To make a long story short, the Trinity became established as one of many doctrines at that time, which then became established as one of the primary teachings of this new Roman Church. Constantine was creating the official religion for all the Roman Empire.

Arius became labeled as a heretic and was exiled. Although he did agree with many of the other teachings of those priests who had gathered in Rome, he would not change his stance in his belief that Christ did not exist before being born of his mother Mary. His divisive stand with those priests of Rome did spur them to consolidate their belief in a Trinity doctrine and the belief of Christ's eternal existence. This controversy set the way for a different church, one other than the original Church, to emerge on the world scene, which greatly grew due to it being backed and supported by the Roman government of that time. Then, nearly 1,100 years later, other churches calling themselves Christian broke away from the government of that Roman Church and became the foundation for Protestant churches and what can best be described as "traditional Christianity."

Not only did the doctrine of the Trinity become established at that time in 325 AD, but Easter was also officially adopted. Because the springtime observance of Easter was in direct opposition and teaching to the annual springtime observance of Passover, Passover became outlawed in the Roman Empire.

Even the observance of the weekly Sabbath on the 7th day of the week became outlawed. This new Roman Christianity used the story of Easter as their authority for changing the seventh-day observance of the Sabbath to the first day of the week—Sunday. This change was justified, not by scripture, but by them, by teaching that Christ was resurrected on a Sunday morning, which he was not! When they came to the tomb of Christ on that Sunday morning following his death, the angel declared that he had already risen. But it did not say he rose Sunday morning.

Furthermore, the Catholic Encyclopedia acknowledges that there is no authoritative scripture giving authority to change the 7th day Sabbath to the 1st day of the week on Sunday, rather they declare that it is by the authority that they claim was given to the Catholic Church and its popes. Therefore, they are basically stating that all Protestant churches have no authority in scripture for observing the 1st day of the week on Sunday as their Sabbath, but instead, they have accepted the authority of the Catholic Church for doing so.

Although persecuted over the centuries, the original Church of 31 AD has continued to this day in the annual observance of Passover, despite it being outlawed very early by the Roman Empire. It is clear that Christ himself instituted the new ceremony for the observance of Passover in the Book of John, chapter 13. The apostle, Paul, also taught and commanded the Church to observe that same ceremony in its observance of Passover (1 Cor. 11:23-28 & 1 Cor. 5:1-8).

So which is true? Is Passover or Easter to be observed by those calling themselves after the name of Christ? These are decisions one must make as to what they choose to believe and what they choose to disbelieve.

The world is so very confused as to who God really is and what God truly says. The purpose for pointing out these misconceptions and false stories about God and Christ has everything to do with whether you can begin to recognize and believe **the warnings given for the end-time**, in order to properly prepare for a **third world war**.

Two Opposing Teachings About Christ

Due to its support by the dominant world power of that time, the Roman Church that Emperor Constantine established over the Roman Empire quickly grew in great popularity, power, and size. It continued its growth in popularity, influence, and power over the centuries that followed and became recognized as "Christianity," while God's own Church became oppressed and suppressed and seen only as a dangerous sect.

So the truth is, the Christianity that began in 31 AD is not the same "Christianity" that developed and grew large in the Roman Empire and the world after 325 AD.

The ability to honestly face and address vast differences in two opposing teachings about Christianity can begin by simply looking back at childhood. At some point, children raised in traditional Christianity learn that they have not been told the truth about some very basic things. They learn that there is no Easter bunny, and they face the truth that there is no such thing as Santa Claus who lives in the North Pole and takes presents to children all over the world on the same night. That is a view largely promoted within the United States and adopted by many throughout the world. But there are similar associations with the observance of Christmas that include some different customs and names for Santa Claus. The story of Santa Claus originated from the British figure Father Christmas, and the Dutch Sinterklaas. In other places in the world, he is also known as St. Nick or St. Nicholas.

The next logical step should be to ask where Christmas actually came from in the first place. It isn't out of scripture—none of it. Most teachers within traditional Christianity have now come to recognize and acknowledge that Christ was not born anywhere around December 25th—and not in winter at all. The historical account in scripture reveals that he was born in the early fall.

It has actually only been within the past few decades that teachers of traditional Christianity have finally begun to admit this truth. Much of that admission was prompted by the fact that Herbert Armstrong began as far back as the 1930s to publish and broadcast that truth. The publications and broadcasts he produced were so widely distributed that some concessions of truth had to be acknowledged by traditional Christianity. However, truth concerning major doctrines could not be conceded or it would completely undermine their faith.

Another account taught concerning Christmas is that there was a star shining down over the little village of Bethlehem that directed the way to where Christ was born. That too is a fable and contrary to astronomy. In truth, a star in scripture is often simply used when speaking of a spirit-created angelic being. It was indeed an angel that showed the way to where Christ was born.

Again, it is easy today to find such information by an easy search on the Internet.

The idea that Christ was born near the time of the winter solstice was assimilated into a religious observance by the Church of Rome in the 12th-century. At that time, a festival already existed that had been primarily established by another Roman emperor named Aurelian. Sol Invictus ("Unconquered Sun") was the official sun god of the later Roman Empire and a patron of soldiers.

On the 25th of December of AD 274, Aurelian made it an official deity alongside the other traditional Roman deities. The reason Christmas became recognized by the Roman Church is recorded in the annotation to a manuscript of a work by a 12th-century bishop Jacob Bar-Salibi. It is recorded:

> *"It was a custom of the Pagans to celebrate on the same 25 December the birthday of the Sun, at which they kindled lights in token of festivity. In these solemnities and revelries the Christians also took part. Accordingly when the doctors of the Church perceived that the Christians had a leaning to this festival, they took counsel and resolved that the true Nativity should be solemnized on that day."*

Christmas is the creation of that Roman Catholic Church. Christmas is the combination of two words. They are "Christ" and "mass" which is the central liturgical ritual of the Catholic Church. The overwhelming majority of those in traditional Christianity hold to this teaching and practice of the observance of Christmas, but this has never been recognized by God's Church and those calling themselves Christian who have their doctrine and lineage from that early Church of 31 AD.

Some will ask, what is the harm in observing such a thing if Santa Claus is a fable and Christmas really isn't the time of Christ's birth? It doesn't matter if you do not care that God instructs there is to be no intermingling of the practices and customs in the worship of other gods. But if you do care, then wouldn't you want to know what is true since God declares that we are to worship Him in spirit and in truth?

Major Differences in Doctrine
The expression of "the tip of the Iceberg" explains so very well what has been covered so far about the discrepancies and vast differences between the two groups, both calling themselves Christian. The meaning of this expression is that there is a small portion of something that can be seen, but there is a much larger part that is not yet seen. So it is with two opposing teachings about Christianity, and only a small part of some of these differences have been mentioned thus far.

WWIII and all that has been prophesied to occur in this end-time have everything to do with the questions being asked about the religions of this world and especially that of Christianity. The fact that people have not listened and heeded end-time prophecies that have been accurately foretelling events that are leading up to mankind's final war reveals the true attitude of mankind toward God.

There is a deeper reason that people have not chosen to listen to God's warnings about the end-time over the past 70 years. The real reason most choose not to listen is that they hate the truth that is taught by God's Church. Traditional Christianity does not want to change its practice of observing family-oriented holidays like Christmas and Easter or of Sunday morning worship together. It does not want to adhere to God's instruction for how we are to live our lives.

God reveals that, by nature, mankind does not like or want His laws to guide their lives, not even in traditional Christianity. It is actually revealed that many will resist and fight against Christ and his army when he returns. For 6,000 years, God's Son and those with whom God has worked to teach His truth have been hated, mocked, ridiculed, scorned, beaten, imprisoned, and killed. God's truth has been resisted and hated. We are now fast approaching the time that God is going to change all that.

What kind of world would it be if mankind kept just three of God's laws concerning human relationships? For example: not stealing, not committing adultery, and not killing others.

Within all the tens of thousands of denominations and nondenominational churches, most assume that what they are taught by religious scholars and ministers is true. However, that is not the case. Most major doctrines within traditional Christianity are vastly different from those taught by the apostles and God's Church. It is good to know what those differences are.

A simple list of differences between what traditional Christianity teaches and what God's Church teaches can quickly reveal what a person genuinely thinks about God's truth—whether they are drawn to it or whether they resist it because they so dislike it.

So which is true, and which is false? Only one can be true, and if neither is true, then they are both false.

The Christians of 31 AD are known by very specific doctrines. Others who call themselves Christians are following what became established after 325 AD, and they are also known by very specific doctrines.

The origin of "traditional Christianity" has its primary doctrines in what was established by the Church of Rome in 325 AD. Churches of traditional Christianity, though varying greatly in many ideas, teachings, and beliefs concerning God and Jesus Christ fundamentally share many of the same major doctrines.

The group calling themselves Christian from 31 AD forward all call themselves after whose Church it is, just as Christ said it should be—**the Church of God**. This group belongs to no other name or system.

Differences

Easily recognized differences between both groups calling themselves Christian will now be listed. This list will state first what was believed by the Church of 31 AD, then it will state what was **"NOT"** believed by it, but what most in traditional Christianity **do** believe. Following this list of differences, some will be addressed by clearly speaking of truth that has recorded proof (scriptural proof) of the doctrine of those original Christians beginning after 31AD.

• Observed the weekly seventh-day Sabbath (following Friday, the 6th day, and preceding Sunday, the 1st day of the week) as the day commanded for worship, **NOT** Sunday on the 1st day of the week.

• Observed Passover, **NOT** Easter.

• Believed Christ was in the grave (heart of the earth) for exactly three days and three nights, **NOT** for a day and a half (late Friday to Sunday morning).

• Believed Christ was resurrected to life again at the end of the weekly Sabbath, **NOT** on Sunday morning.

• Believed in taking of the symbols of Passover annually on that day, **NOT** a Communion that can be observed weekly.

• Observed the annual Holy Days of God, **NOT** annual holidays like Easter and Christmas.

• Taught the need for a resurrection to future life, **NOT** of an immortal soul where one instantly goes to heaven or hell upon death.

• Believed in a final eternal judgment, meaning one remains dead for all time as part of such judgment, **NOT** of being tormented or tortured in hell forever.

- Believed there is only One Eternal Almighty God (Yahweh Elohim) who has eternal self-existing life inherent in Himself, **NOT** that God is a Trinity which teaches there are three distinct gods in the godhead who also function as one god.

- Believed Christ was affixed to a pole, **NOT** on a cross.

- Taught that the name of Christ was commanded to be Joshua, **NOT** that the name of Christ is Jesus.

- Believed that Joshua the Christ has only existed since born of his physical mother Mary, **NOT** that he has eternally existed as God the Father has.

This has only been a partial list of some of the more important differences that begin to expose the greater part of the iceberg—the portion that is not seen by traditional Christianity. Many of these will now be addressed more fully in the remainder of this chapter, as there is much more that needs to be seen.

GOD THE FATHER NAMED HIS SON JOSHUA
In the newly organized official Church of the Roman Empire under Emperor Constantine, the body of believers had the custom of calling Christ by the name of Iesous in Greek or Iesus in Latin (both translated as Jesus in English). But that was not the name the disciples and others of the Church that began in 31 AD called Christ. They called him by the Hebrew name of Yehoshua (translated as Joshua in English).

The name "Jesus" (Iesous in Greek and translated to Latin as Iesus) was adopted by the Catholic Church after 325 AD, and then it was also accepted by the protestant churches once they formed and came into existence hundreds of years later.

God instructed that the name to be given to His Son once he was born of Mary was to be Joshua. That was the same name as the Joshua of the Old Testament who led the children of Israel into the promised land. The name means "the Eternal's (Yahweh's) salvation." In his physical life, the Messiah first came as the Passover lamb—indeed "the Eternal's salvation" offered to mankind.

Those who have spent more than an average amount of time studying the Bible know that names mean a lot to God. When God gives names, they carry important meaning. They are not just names that might have a nice sound to them.

Late in the 4th century the Catholic religion commissioned and adopted a Latin translation of the Bible—the Vulgate. In the Old Testament, they translated the name for Joshua as Iosue. This is actually closer in sound to the Hebrew name for Joshua (Yehoshua). However, in the Latin Vulgate of the New Testament, a different word is used—Iesus. They also did this to Joshua's name (the one who led the Israelites into the promised land) in Hebrews 4:8, where it was translated as Iesus. Perhaps they did not realize that this was not a reference to Christ.

In writing about Joshua leading the children of Israel into the promised land, the apostle Paul would clearly have used the correct name for Joshua. Then the question needs to be answered as to why the Vulgate didn't use the same Latin word Iosue as they did in the translation of the Old Testament.

Both the Greek and Latin translations in the New Testament altered the name for Joshua, but it could have been a clearer **transliteration** (a word that sounds the same in another language), just as it was done in the translation of that name in the Old Testament. Especially in the Latin Vulgate, the Catholic Church, whatever the motive, made a clear change between the name of Joshua in the Old Testament and the name that Christ should have been called in the New Testament.

In both languages, a name could have been **translated** that carried **the same meaning** as Joshua does in Hebrew, but they didn't. Yet this process of translating was done properly when the word for "Messiah" of the Old Testament was translated as "Christ" (Christos) in the New Testament. Both mean the same thing, which is "the anointed one."

That is the proper way to translate words—by their actual meaning in the language one is translating into.

However, the name given to Christ by the Catholic Church is not an actual translation of words that convey the same meaning, as it was done with the words for "Messiah" and "Christ." The name "Jesus" does not carry the actual meaning of the name "Joshua," yet it could have. It isn't even an accurate transliteration.

The books of Matthew, Mark, Luke, and John were written in Aramaic, which is a Semitic language that is of the same family as the Hebrew language. Today, most religious scholars want to discredit this and instead claim that the apostles only wrote in Greek.

Certainly, Paul wrote in Greek to the gentiles, as he had been highly educated and trained in Jerusalem when he was known as Saul. But the disciples of Christ spoke and knew Aramaic. They were even looked down upon and ridiculed by Jewish leaders in Jerusalem because the disciples didn't have the same high level of education of those Jewish leaders. Many Jews of that time in other regions of the Roman Empire did speak and write in Greek, but in this area where the disciples were from in the time of Christ, Aramaic was the language of the Jews.

The word "Jesus" in the English language did not even come into existence until the late 1600s. It was a transliteration of the Greek word "Iesous," and the same corresponding word from the Latin "Iesus." However, as it has already been stated, Iesous and Iesus are not even good transliterations of "Joshua." Indeed, if God's instruction had been followed, then the name translated would have been Joshua—the same as the Joshua who led the children of Israel into the promised land after Moses' death.

Here is that instruction given by God as the correct name is translated from Aramaic to English:

"Now the birth of Joshua the Christ was as follows: After his mother Mary was betrothed to Joseph, before they came together, she was found with child of the holy spirit. Then Joseph her husband, being a just man, and not wanting to make her a public example, was mindful to put her

away secretly. But while he thought about these things, behold, an angel of the Lord appeared to him in a dream, saying, 'Joseph, son of David, do not be afraid to take to you Mary your wife, for that which is conceived in her is of the holy spirit. She will bring forth a son, and you shall **call his name Joshua** [the Eternal's Salvation], *for he will save his people from their sins.' So all this was done that it might be fulfilled which was spoken by the Lord through the prophet, saying: 'Behold, the virgin shall be with child, and bear a son, and they shall call his name Immanuel,'* [Isaiah 7:14] *which is translated, 'God with us.' Then Joseph, being aroused from sleep, did as the angel of the Lord commanded him and took to him his wife, and did not know her until she had brought forth her firstborn son. And he* **called his name Joshua**" (Matthew 1:18-25).

Indeed, after nearly 2,000 years, God is about to send His Son as the Messiah—the Christ—to first save mankind from self-annihilation and then to establish the government of the Kingdom of God over all nations. The last great error to be removed from God's Church in order that it be made fully ready for Christ's coming is the correction of his very name. The name "Jesus" Christ represents all that began to be taught in error in a church calling itself Christian after AD 325. The name "Jesus" represents the teaching of that church in doctrines such as the Trinity, Easter, Sunday worship, Christmas, and much more that are in error and contrary to God's Word.

The one whose feet will soon be standing once again upon the Mt. of Olives, after nearly 2,000 years, is Joshua the Christ—the true Messiah sent from God to save mankind.

PASSOVER VS. EASTER

Perhaps one of the greatest deceptions and distortions of scripture by the world of traditional Christianity has been over this subject of Passover versus Easter.

Most people are fully unaware that there ever was a controversy over these two observances. As it was already covered, that controversy came to a head in 325 AD at the Council of Nicaea. This was the council that the Roman Emperor Constantine called and presided over. As previously explained, it was here that the Passover observance that was commanded by God in Old Testament scriptures became outlawed in the Roman Empire.

It was in this Council of Nicaea that the creation for the observance of Easter as the day of observance for Christ's resurrection began. It was here that Easter was newly adopted as the focal point of a new state religion. It was here that Easter officially became the replacement of Passover within the Roman Empire, and Passover became outlawed.

Nowhere in any scripture is the name Easter mentioned or given as a time to be observed by God's people, but Passover is. However, there are some translations where a Greek word, which clearly means Passover, has falsely been translated as Easter.

For hundreds of years, up to the time of Christ, the nation of Judah observed the annual commanded assembly of Passover in the springtime, which was on the 14th day of their <u>first month</u> [known as Abib, or Nissan] of a new year. Christ and his disciples kept this observance on the last day of his physical life on earth.

This observance first began when the children of Israel were enslaved in Egypt and God had chosen a very specific time in which to free them from that captivity. As the chapters that follow will show, God fulfills prophetic events in a very meticulous, exacting, and precise manner. It states on this occasion that God was fulfilling this event in just such a manner.

*"And it came to pass at the end of the four hundred and thirty years, **even the selfsame day** it came to pass, that all these hosts of the Eternal went out from the land of Egypt"* (Exodus 12:41).

Christ and his disciples kept the observance in the same manner as it was that first time in Egypt. A lamb was killed, roasted, and then eaten. The symbolism was about Christ himself who would come into the world to fulfill the first great phase of God's plan for the salvation of mankind. Christ came as the Lamb of God to fulfill the role of Passover—to have his blood spilled upon the earth as he was killed to fulfill his role as the true Passover of all mankind.

It would be good at this juncture to point out a very basic truth that traditional Christianity has twisted and used to deceive people into believing something different. What is stated is actually very clear and revealing. After the original disciples were chosen to be apostles and were sent to the Israelites, Christ later chose another apostle whose primary work would be to take God's truth to foreigners. Here is what this apostle, Paul, wrote:

"Thoroughly clean out the old leaven [yeast] *so that you may be a new lump of dough, even as you are already unleavened* [homes were unleavened—yeast and leavened bread products removed]. *For even Christ our Passover is killed for us. Therefore* **let us keep the Feast**, *not with old leaven, neither with the leaven of malice and wickedness, but with the unleavened bread of sincerity and **truth**"* (1 Corinthians 5:7-8).

Those in traditional Christianity have little grasp of what Paul is saying here because they have never been taught about it by their preachers and teachers. Instead, with verses like these, teachers use the false premise that God's law was done away with through Christ and the teaching of the New Testament, and that obedience to the observance of the 7th day Sabbath (that which follows the 6th day, Friday) was no longer required after the time of Christ's death and resurrection.

These verses and those preceding and following them were written over 20 years after the death of Christ. These clearly reveal that the Church still observed the commandment to observe the Passover and that which immediately followed it, which is called the Feast of Unleavened Bread that lasted for seven days after the Passover day.

Paul even emphasized the importance of keeping the commanded annual Holy Days that immediately follow the Passover day. At that time, he also spoke of not only the importance of its observance, but also told of its spiritual intent and meaning. Again, he stated, **"Therefore let us keep the Feast."**

These verses that were quoted are helping to show the meaning in the fulfillment of the observance of these days. God uses the symbolism of leaven (yeast used in bread) as a reflection of what sin does in a person's life. Leaven is likened to sin that puffs one up in pride. The Days (or Feast) of Unleavened Bread is a time where God commanded that all leaven (yeast) and leavened products are to be put out of people's homes and that everyone is to eat unleavened bread during this period. This reinforced the teaching that people are to get rid of the leaven (sin) in their lives, just as they also put leaven out of their homes and then eat only unleavened bread during those seven days.

Leavening is reflective of sin and pride, and being unleavened is symbolic of obedience (to be without sin). God's people are to live in obedience to His laws (ways) in "sincerity and truth" as Paul wrote.

It also clearly states here that Christ fulfilled the purpose for which he came the first time in human life—to fulfill the role of Passover in God's plan. He was the Lamb of God who did not resist his perverse prosecution or his death, but instead, submitted as a lamb to what was done to him. In doing so and dying in such a manner by having his blood spilled to the earth, resulting in his death, he became the Passover for all mankind.

Many believe that Christ died because of being nailed on the pole, but that isn't why he died. He died because a soldier had run a spear into his side while he was hanging there, therefore spilling his blood to the earth. This becomes very important later when another matter concerning this account is brought to light.

The following account that will be quoted is about Christ's death. But before this, it would be good to keep in mind the order of events. Throughout most of mankind's history, a day would begin at sundown, starting with the night, followed by the next daytime portion once the sun would rise again. Then at sundown on that particular daytime portion, a new day would begin. So Passover began at sundown on the 14th of the first month (Nisan) as it continued into and through the nighttime. The daylight portion of Passover followed once the sun rose. Then at sundown on that day, the first annual Holy Day for that new year began. It was the first day of the Feast of Unleavened Bread—which Paul wrote that we should keep.

Keeping this timing in mind, it is important to note that Christ observed the Passover with his disciples beginning with eating the roasted lamb during the nighttime portion of the Passover, which preceded the daytime portion of the Passover day when he was put to death.

Before reading these verses, it needs to be understood that the Jewish people spoke of a "preparation day" as a time to make ready for a weekly Sabbath or an annual Sabbath (Holy Day) observance. A preparation day for a weekly Sabbath was the last day of the week in which one might make any necessary preparations for the observance of the Sabbath to follow. So the Jewish people have always recognized Friday (the 6th day of the week) as one of those preparation days because it is the preparation day for the 7th day weekly Sabbath.

The day before any annual Sabbath (Holy Day) is also recognized as a "preparation day." Although the Passover, which is a commanded assembly, is not an annual Holy Day, it is a preparation day. The Passover is a preparation day because the following day is an annual Sabbath as recorded in Leviticus 23—the first Day of Unleavened Bread.

"Therefore, because it was the preparation [preparation day for an annual Sabbath] *and the Jews did not want the bodies to remain on the pole* [Gk. stauros] *on the Sabbath, for that Sabbath was an high day* [annual Sabbath]*, they asked Pilate that their legs might be broken* [to speed up their death] *so that their bodies could be carried away* [so that they do not remain there during the Sabbath]*. So the soldiers came and broke the legs of the first and then the other who had been nailed to poles with him. But when they came to Joshua they saw that he was already dead, so they did not break his legs. Because one of the soldiers had pierced* [had earlier pierced] *his side with a spear and immediately blood and water came out* [it was then that he had died]*"* (John 19:31-34).

Christ was pierced with a spear because he had to fulfill the symbolism of the Passover lamb's blood spilling out on the earth and then dying.

So Christ did not die in the late afternoon as the other two did. Instead, he died right after being pierced in the side with a spear, and that was in mid-afternoon.

"*Now from the sixth hour* [12 noon] *until the ninth hour* [3 pm] *there was darkness over all the land. At about the ninth hour* [3 pm] *Joshua cried out with a loud voice, saying, 'Eli, Eli, lama sabachthani?' That is, 'My God, My God, why have You forsaken me?' Some of those who stood there, when they heard* **that***, said, 'This man is calling for his God Yahweh* [mistranslated as the name Elijah]'" (Matthew 27:45-47).

It needs to be explained in this part of the story that translators have interpreted words used in this account to be the name of the prophet Elijah, but that is sheer nonsense! Christ was not calling out to some prophet who lived and died several hundred years before, but instead, he was calling out to his Father who was Yahweh Elohim—the Eternal God. The word Elijah means "my God is Yahweh," and those are the words that Christ used as he was calling out to "his God Yahweh."

"*Immediately one of them* [a soldier] *ran and took a sponge, filled* **it** *with sour wine and put it on a reed, and offered it to him to drink. The rest said, 'Leave him alone and let us see if his God Yahweh will come to save him.' Then Joshua cried out again with a loud voice and yielded up his spirit* [he died]" (Matthew 27:48-50).

Indeed, Christ died mid-afternoon during the Passover day. After having the spear run through his side by a soldier (Jn. 19:34) and his blood was spilling out on the earth, he cried out to God his Father and then yielded up his spirit in death. He fulfilled the role of the Passover Lamb who died for the sins of all mankind. The annual observance has very great meaning in God's plan of salvation.

So why did that newly established Roman Church during the Council of Nicaea in 325 AD outlaw the observance of Passover and establish a new observance called Easter? Easter is found nowhere in scripture, although a few have taken Hebrew and Greek words that clearly mean Passover and have falsely translated them as Easter. For hundreds of years, many teachers and preachers who call themselves Christian have been trying to altogether erase any truth and understanding about Passover and the Feast of Unleavened Bread.

DEATH ON A POLE OR ON A CROSS?

This question might seem absurd to many, but it needs to be asked because people have never been told the truth about how Christ died. The Passover of all mankind did not die on a cross. There are two plain truths regarding this.

The first and simplest of all concerns the actual word that is quoted and then translated as "cross." Although many so-called scholars like to argue and debate this since they have very much to protect, the truth is that they are not being honest with how the actual word that is mistranslated as cross is used throughout other historic literature and documents of that time.

As it was just shown in the previous quotation from John 19, the word that is translated as "cross" in scripture is not from a Greek or Aramaic word for "cross." It is a word that means "a pole, stake, or beam of wood." However, translators have taken the Greek word "stauros" and mistranslated it to mean a cross. But there is no such translation or usage of that word in ancient Greek literature that gives credibility to such a farcical interpretation.

There are words in ancient Greek that could have been used to identify or describe a cross, but this word "stauros" is most definitely not one of them! But once again, many will simply choose to believe what they want as being true.

The Purpose of Breaking Legs

There is **irrefutable proof** that goes far beyond any debate over the translation or mistranslation of words. The greatest proof as to whether Christ died on a cross or on a pole is in the very story just quoted about the account of the two who had been sentenced to death together with Christ.

One needs to understand this story for what is actually being told. Again, the teachers of Judaism of that time did not want the bodies of these three to remain on poles during the time of the High Day, their first annual Sabbath of the year—the 1st Day of Unleavened Bread. It was now coming toward the late afternoon of that Passover day (the preparation day), and they wanted the bodies taken down and carried away before sunset and the start of that Holy Day that was going to begin at sundown. They believed this was work that should not be done on their annual Sabbath.

However, when the soldiers went to break the legs of all three so that death would quickly follow, they found Christ was already dead because earlier a soldier had run a spear through his side. There is a question here that is begging to be asked. How would breaking the legs of anyone hanging there on a cross suddenly result in death?

It is quite simple and easy to understand. Grasping the truth of the clear answer to this reveals an undeniable truth.

There is one reason and one reason alone that soldiers were sent to break the legs of all three who were hanging there. If they had been on a cross, breaking their legs would not have resulted in the quick death that the Jewish leaders wanted. However, it does apply when nailed to a pole, and *that* is the truth of what actually happened.

When a person was sentenced to death and it was to be done on a pole, the practice was to nail both of the person's hands (or wrists) overlapping each other just like the feet. The feet were overlapped with one over the other and a single nail (spike) was driven through at the bottom part of a pole. The hands (or wrists) were also overlapped with one over the other and a single nail (spike) driven through them at the top, again, just as with the feet.

In such a position, as soon as the legs are broken, a person can no longer push themselves upward in order to breathe. The very reason for breaking legs is so that a person would then quickly suffocate, as they could no longer breathe.

Prophecy concerning the coming of the Messiah revealed that none of his bones would ever be broken. In addition, in order to fulfill the symbolism in the killing of a Passover lamb, his blood had to be spilled to the earth as the cause of his death. God was not going to allow His Son's legs to be broken, nor allow him to suffocate as the cause of his death because such symbolisms would not match that of how the Passover lambs were killed.

If these three had been on a cross, there would have been no purpose in having their legs broken because they would still have been able to breathe. Breathing would become more strained, but they could still breathe for many more hours, and the Jews wanted them to die right away.

When arms are stretched straight above the body, the weight of the rest of the body pulling downward from such a position will begin to choke off a person's ability to breathe. This is simply a physical reality.

Also, why would anyone go to far greater trouble to build a cross-type structure to stretch out the arms when it is so easy to simply overlap the hands in the same manner as the feet were when nailed at the bottom of the pole?

Many historical accounts of such death sentences on a pole show there have been various transformations of its use over the centuries. Even the practice itself took on various forms where the actual use of a cross-type of structure in executions was at times performed. In such executions using a cross, people lingered for longer periods before they died which was far crueler than being executed upon a pole since people were left to die after a longer period of suffering with the addition of greater hunger, thirst, and bare exposure to the elements. The very purpose for using a cross was to cause greater suffering, and this method often included various forms of torture that were used on the one affixed to a cross.

In the practice of using a pole and nailing a single spike through both wrists (or the palms) overlapping each other, the arms are stretched straight above the individual, and in such a position a person would have to push themselves up with their feet in order to keep breathing. Even without hastening death by breaking a person's legs, this practice would naturally lead to a quicker death than being nailed to a cross.

So again, a person affixed to a cross would live longer and suffer much longer. A person affixed to a pole would die more quickly. Because of the additional effort it took to continue pushing oneself upward in order to breathe, a person would become weak more quickly, unable to continue pushing themselves up, and then die. Being nailed to a cross rather than a pole was far more sadistic and cruel as it prolonged one's life because breathing was not encumbered in the same manner as being affixed on a pole. Regardless, both were cruel methods to be used in execution.

Yet even here, another question should be asked. If the technology had been around at the time and Christ had been killed with a rifle, would people be wearing the likeness of one around their neck in order to symbolize their Christian belief?

There are reasons the Church of Rome after 325 AD promoted the idea that their Christ had died on a cross rather than a pole. They are the ones who changed the narrative of the story. Much of their reason for doing so had to do with their customs connected with the belief in other deities and their use of crosses, and also because of a vision or dream that Constantine claimed he had.

Stories vary as to what exactly happened, whether Constantine had a vision or a dream or both, but the gist was that Constantine said he had a vision of a symbol or a sign in the sky. Then it is stated he had a dream the following night, before a great battle, where Christ told him he was to use the sign that he saw to conquer. The words he supposedly either heard or saw in the sky were, "In this sign, you will conquer" or in another translation, "By this, conquer!" Constantine then commanded his soldiers to use this symbol on their shields. The battle they fought the next day led to a great victory for his army, which led them to believe that God was on their side. These are matters of historical accounts that can be easily found in one's own search.

The story of Christ's death having taken place on a cross gained in popularity over time. Although the symbol from Constantine's vision was later depicted in different ways in stories and in paintings, a cross in the form of a "**t**" became the norm for what was used as the symbol for Christ's death. This shape eventually became the accepted narrative as the device on which Christ was nailed to and died upon.

However, what is recorded in history about what Constantine saw wasn't a cross like Christ was to have died upon; it was more like that which formed the shape of an X over a P. It was called the Chi-Rho symbol because it consisted of the two Greek letters X and P. This was further popularized because these two Greek letters are the first two letters in the Greek word for Christos (Christ).

If you want to see this symbol that was used by Constantine, you can find it under the name of the Labarum of Constantine.

Even in this, the truth is that among the commandments God gave to Israel, one of those commandments states that there is to be no use of idols or any kind of image as symbols for religious worship. But people like to use all kinds of images for the symbols of their belief and worship. The cross, images of Christ and Christ on a cross, images of a mother with a child, and so many others are symbols used in traditional Christianity today.

So, what is true in such matters and what is false? How is it possible that over centuries people have come to practice and believe things that are nearly opposite of what God clearly says in His word?

It is as though the clearest of statements made in scripture are just simply ignored or viewed as irrelevant to obedience concerning how we should live. It is like the simple example of what Christ said regarding teachers of religion. Christ clearly stated how they should never be addressed by others. The principle and instructions are not difficult to understand.

"But don't be called Rabbi, for one is your Teacher, the Christ, and you are all brethren. Do not call anyone on earth your Father, for one is your Father who is in heaven" (Matthew 23:8-9).

The principle should be clear. No one should use or be called by any religious title that belongs to Christ or God. Yet many religious leaders and teachers use the title of Rabbi, Reverend, Father, Holy Father, Pope, Pastor, Bishop, etc. The use of words like these and others as religious titles or greetings is clearly against the principle and instruction given by Christ.

However, it should also be understood that some words used in a religious context concerning a religious leader's job or duty should not be confused with religious titles. Such things should be simple and easy for anyone to understand, but so often they are not. Other scriptures show the balance and how it is perfectly acceptable to have job descriptions of a pastor, teacher, minister, elder, etc., but they are never to be used as a title.

CHRIST'S RESURRECTION NOT ON A SUNDAY MORNING

The clearest and most indisputable of all proof covered in this chapter concerning a falsehood about Christ is the truth that he was not resurrected on a Sunday morning.

One True Sign

Christ made some very dogmatic statements about his identity. He also stated that there would be **only one sign** given as proof as to who the Messiah truly was.

"Then certain of the scribes and of the Pharisees answered, saying, 'Master, we want to see a sign from you.' But he answered and said to them, 'An evil and adulterous generation seeks after a sign, and no sign shall be given to it, but the sign of the prophet Jonah. For as Jonah was three days and three nights in the belly of the great fish, so shall the Son of man be three days and three nights in the heart of the earth'" (Matthew 12:38-40).

Christ clearly stated that **only one sign** would be given to prove who he was—one sign that would identify the Messiah. That sign was that the Christ would be in the heart of the earth—the tomb—for exactly three days and three nights.

The manner in which this statement is made in Greek and even more so in Aramaic establishes there would be a total period in the heart of the earth of three full days and three full nights. The fact that it states this period of time would be the same as that of Jonah being in the belly of the great fish is even more specific. The Hebrew language in which this account was recorded makes it clear that the time for these three days and three nights is an exact measurement of time that is equivalent to 72 hours.

Traditional Christianity has a very hard time with this statement of Christ, and they try to excuse and support how they came up with their own timing. They work to change the very definitions of a day and a night, and even the actual year of Christ's death. They do all this for great reason. They have much to protect in their narrative of a late Friday afternoon burial and a sunrise resurrection on Sunday morning.

Indeed, the teaching of traditional Christianity is that the Passover that year was on a Friday (which it wasn't), and that "their" Jesus died in the late afternoon of that Friday. Then they go on to teach that he was resurrected on a Sunday morning. No one can squeeze three days and three nights out of this, although they do attempt to do just that. They actually claim this is what happened and that this is what fulfilled Christ's own words about three days and three nights.

Looking at this, it would mean he died late afternoon on Friday and was placed in the tomb just before the weekly Sabbath began at sundown. In order to have a Sunday morning resurrection, that would mean he was in the tomb for only Friday night and Saturday night—two nights.

Then traditional Christianity gets very creative when they say he was in the tomb for three days (daylight periods of time). They explain that since he was placed in the tomb while there was still a little daylight remaining on Friday that this constituted the first day. He then would have been in the tomb all during the weekly Sabbath—day two. Since they claim he was resurrected early Sunday morning at sunrise, then that very small daylight portion on that Sunday morning constitutes day three.

When added all together, however, this timing is hardly three days and three nights. Even if they were right about those three daylight portions being able to be counted as three days, they still miss out on one complete night. Thus, by Christ's own words, this would disprove that he was the actual Messiah. Yet it is this method of timing from late afternoon Friday to Sunday morning that traditional Christianity claims was fulfilled by "their" Jesus.

The truth about the actual timing of Christ's resurrection is not difficult to understand, but it does require true knowledge of what actually happened in the timing of events that led to Christ's death and then his resurrection. It is an incredible revelation and awesomely inspiring reality when one comes to see what actually happened.

The teaching about Jesus being the Christ is a story of him being in the heart of the earth for only half the time that Joshua the Christ is actually recorded as being there. When adding the actual time that scholars and teachers of traditional Christianity say that Jesus was in the heart of the earth, it is really only about half the time that is revealed in scripture as actually occurring.

Those who look to the one named Joshua as the Christ teach that after his death he was in the heart of the earth—in the tomb—for a complete period of time that was exactly three full days and three full nights.

In covering the actual timing of all this, remember that a new day always began at sundown. Each day was counted from sundown to sundown, not from midnight to midnight.

It is because of this method for telling time from one day to another that the Jews wanted all three who had been sentenced to die to have their legs broken. Then, after a quick death, the bodies could be removed and carried away before sundown on Passover. This is because at sundown on Passover their annual Sabbath observance (the first day of the Feast of Unleavened Bread) would begin, and no work was allowed during the time of the Sabbath.

But there is much more involved here and it takes a little time to have the exact timing explained and revealed in an orderly and clear manner.

The annual observance of Passover can fall on different days of the week from one year to another. In the year of Christ's death of 31 AD, Passover fell on the 4th day of the week. By our recognition of time today, that means Passover (a preparation day) began at sundown on a Tuesday and lasted through that nighttime portion of Tuesday and on through the daylight portion of Wednesday. That full period of time was recognized as being the 4th day of the week, and in 31 AD that was the time of the annual Passover observance.

It was on that Tuesday evening that Christ kept what many refer to as his "last supper." It was indeed a meal and it was his last one, but it was far more than simply a final supper. It was the Passover meal where a lamb had been killed, then roasted, and eaten by those who observed Passover at that time. This was the manner for observing the Passover that was first kept when the children of Israel were enslaved in Egypt.

After hundreds of years of observing it in this manner by killing, roasting, and then eating the Passover meal on the evening of Passover, Christ had come to now fulfill the greater meaning contained in that day. He came to die as the Passover Lamb for all mankind, through whom all sins could be forgiven.

This Passover observance with his disciples was the last to be observed in this manner. Christ and his disciples kept it as commanded, but after that Passover meal, he instituted the new manner in which it was to be observed. No longer was a lamb to be killed and eaten in that annual observance, but now God's people were to keep it in the new way that Christ revealed on that final night of his life.

It was an observance that contained meaning in the drinking of a small portion of wine and eating a small portion of unleavened bread. Traditional Christianity has misapplied this annual observance and has changed it to have a different meaning and timing of observance that they call Communion.

However, the taking of a small portion of wine and unleavened bread is about Christ's death in our stead. The wine is symbolic of the blood he spilled for us as the true sacrifice for sin. Such a sacrifice could only be made by one who lived a life free of sin—one worthy of being the sacrifice for the forgiveness of sin. Taking the small portion of unleavened bread in such a ceremony is symbolic of Christ "being without sin—being unleavened" in his life.

One can easily see for themselves how a couple of decades later that the apostle, Paul, reminded the Church of how to keep this annual

112   *Turmoil within Religion*

observance. He stated it was to be in the same manner Christ first revealed it should be observed.

*"For I have received of the Lord that which I have also delivered to you, that the Lord Joshua on the **same** night* [Passover night] *in which he was betrayed took bread* [unleavened bread], *and after he had given thanks he broke it and said, 'Take and eat of it* [a broken piece] *for this is my body which is broken for you. Do this for a remembrance of me* [a remembrance at every annual Passover].' *After the same manner he also took a cup* [of wine] *after dinner* [Luke 22:17-20] *and said, 'This cup is the new testament in my blood. Do this as often as you drink it* [on every Passover], *in remembrance of me. For as often as you eat this bread and drink this cup, you are proclaiming* [announcing] *the Lord's death until he comes. Therefore, whoever shall eat this bread and drink this cup of the Lord in an unworthy manner shall be guilty of the body and blood of the Lord'"* (1 Corinthians 11:23-27).

The Actual Timing of Christ's Death

All recognize that Christ died on the Passover day, but all are not in agreement with when the Passover actually occurred in the year of Christ's death. It takes a little while to go through all the scriptures that speak of this, but it is very worthwhile and awesomely revealing to go through a good part of that story flow.

Traditional Christianity teaches that Passover was on the 6th day of the week that year. The reason for this is that they failed to recognize that one of the Sabbath days being spoken of in the timing of Christ's death was not a weekly Sabbath. They have misunderstood this for centuries because they do not know or understand the timing of Passover in relation to the annual Holy Days that followed. They have not understood the observances of the Holy Days of the Jewish people over hundreds of years, ever since the time of Moses. These are all listed in order in the Book of Leviticus, chapter 23.

As it has already been mentioned, the day that follows the annual observance of Passover is an annual Sabbath—and annual Holy Day (High Day), the first day of the Feast of Unleavened Bread. In addition, they have not understood the Jewish tradition of recognizing days that precede a Sabbath as being a "preparation day" for getting ready for a Sabbath.

Those who began translating scripture from Greek and Aramaic into Latin in the 380s AD did not grasp these simple observances of the Jews, or they simply did not care. The Church of Rome determined to have scripture translated into a single work that would be for their use, so they commissioned that scripture be translated into Latin and this work became known as the Latin Vulgate.

Translations into other languages that followed many centuries later once the printing press was invented resulted in even greater confusion and mistranslation of scripture.

So when these early translators wrote about this story of Christ's death, burial, and resurrection they were confused and did not accurately interpret or understand what actually had occurred. They read about a preparation day and automatically believed that this was about the 6th day of the week—what we recognize as being Friday. But that was not the case. The complete story makes this very clear.

"Therefore, because it was the preparation [preparation day for a Sabbath] *and the Jews did not want the bodies to remain on the pole* (Gk. stauros) *on the Sabbath, for* **that Sabbath was an high day** [an annual Sabbath, an annual Holy Day], *they asked Pilate that their legs might be broken so that their bodies could be carried away* [so that they not remain there during the annual Sabbath]" (John 19:31).

Understanding this helps to reveal the **exact** day of the week that Passover fell upon and when Christ was actually resurrected. As it will come to be shown, this **annual High Day**, the annual observance of the 1st Day of Unleavened Bread, always follows the Passover day. On that year in 31 AD, this Holy Day was on the 5th day of the week—what we recognize as being Thursday.

So at sundown on the Passover day on the 4th day of the week (on Wednesday), the **annual Sabbath**—the annual High Day of the 1st Day of Unleavened Bread began. The Jews wanted all three to be taken down from the poles and carried away before that **annual Sabbath** was to begin. Then the story that follows is about how Christ's body was taken away and placed in a tomb.

"Then notice the man named Joseph who was a council member. He was a decent and upright man, and although a member of the council, he had not consented with their decision and deed [of the others of the council]. *He was of Arimathaea, a city of the Jews, who himself also waited for the Kingdom of God. This man went to Pilate and pleaded for the body of Joshua. He took it down and wrapped it in linen and laid it in a sepulcher* [tomb] *that had been cut in stone, wherein no one had ever been laid. That was the preparation day, and the Sabbath was drawing near* [about to begin]" (Luke 23:50-54).

Again, one needs to understand Old Testament law and the Jewish observance of a Sabbath. No work was to be done on any Sabbath day, so the day preceding every Sabbath was a preparation day in which to complete the normal work of the week and to make oneself ready for the proper observance of a Sabbath when no work was to be done. That is why the story that follows is so important to understand. The story continues.

"The women also, who came with him [Christ] *from Galilee* [to Jerusalem] *followed after* [after Joseph of Arimathaea to the tomb], *and they saw the sepulcher* [tomb] *and how the body was laid. Then they returned and prepared spices and ointments, and they rested on the Sabbath according to the commandment"* (Luke 23:55-56).

This juncture of the story becomes important because of what these women did. In the verses just quoted it says that they went to prepare spices and ointments. Afterward, they would take these spices and ointments and place them with Christ's body.

These women didn't have the foreknowledge that Christ was going to be put to death and die that afternoon on that Passover, so they obviously wouldn't have these spices and ointments prepared in advance. Therefore, they had to wait until there was time to buy and prepare them.

By the time Christ died and was taken to the tomb, the Passover day was at an end, and they certainly had no time then to buy any spices, let alone prepare them. They couldn't buy them after Passover because that next day was an annual Holy Day, and no spices could be purchased or prepared on a Sabbath.

It states that they rested on the Sabbath, and that should be easy to understand. They could not do that work on the Sabbath that followed the Passover. The body of Christ had been placed in the tomb just before sunset on that Passover day. Christ was barely in the tomb once that annual Sabbath began. So the women could not work on that annual Sabbath, and therefore, they rested as commanded.

When did they prepare the spices? It wasn't on the annual Holy Day that followed the Passover, but they were able to prepare them on the following day. That following day was the 6th day of the week (Friday). They worked on that day, which was the weekly preparation day for the weekly Sabbath. Yet they also had to do something else first before they could begin to prepare those spices and ointments in the customary fashion for a burial. A single and simple scripture is recorded in Mark's account that makes this clear.

"*When the Sabbath was past, Mary Magdalene, and Mary* **the mother** *of James, and Salome, went to purchase spices so that they might come and anoint him* [Christ's body]" (Mark 16:1).

What is being shown here is that the women had to first purchase the spices before they could prepare them. So they purchased and prepared them on the following day—the 6th day of the week, Friday. They could not buy or prepare these on a Sabbath day.

If traditional Christianity interpreted this account directly as it is stated, due to their not understanding the timing of the Jewish holy days, they would have looked upon this as being about the weekly Sabbath. However, in doing this they missed the obvious because if this were the case then the women would not have been able to buy the spices until Sunday. But that doesn't fit, or make any sense, as it is clear they had these purchased and prepared by the time they came to the tomb on Sunday morning.

It took them all day to both buy these spices and ointments and then do the work of preparing them. The account that follows reveals that they did not have time to do all this (on Friday) and to also take it to the tomb that same day in order to complete the work of placing Christ's body in a proper burial, as his body had been hastily placed in the tomb at the close of Passover. The next verse simply goes on to tell the rest of the sequence of events.

"And very early in the morning, on the first day of the week (Sunday), *they came to the tomb when the sun had risen"* (Mark 16:2).

These two verses in Mark simply tell a story of how the women had to wait until after the annual Sabbath to purchase and prepare spices for Christ's burial. They did the work on the 6th day of the week (Friday). Then once the work on that preparation day ended, they rested again—this time on the weekly Sabbath. Since the weekly Sabbath isn't over until sundown on that 7th day of the week, they did not take the spices to the tomb because darkness was now setting in. So then on the morning of the first day of the week, on that Sunday morning, they came to the tomb to anoint Christ's body.

If one has a good understanding of the observance of the Sabbath and the preparation days, then this story fits together quite clearly and simply. The women could not buy or prepare spices on a Sabbath, so they did so on the first day possible. That was on the 6th day of the week (Friday).

It took them a long time to do that work, but once the weekly Sabbath (Saturday) was drawing near they had run out of the time required to go to the tomb to finish the work of properly preparing Christ's body in his burial. If they could have purchased and prepared the necessary spices and ointments, and then taken them to the tomb on that preparation day (Friday), they would have done so. Instead, they had to wait and rest through the time of the weekly Sabbath.

The weekly Sabbath would end after the daylight portion of the 7th day and then the 1st day of the week would begin at sundown, but nightfall would also quickly follow. So they had to wait until morning to take the spices and ointments to the tomb.

As a person reads all these stories that are written from the different vantage points of all four who recorded the account of these events, this entire story becomes even clearer. It is so important to include and compare the witness of disciples and others who knew and saw these events, which are recorded in Matthew, Mark, Luke, and John.

The Sunday After Christ's Resurrection
Another area of misunderstanding and misinterpretation regarding the annual Sabbath and weekly Sabbath that followed this Passover is in Matthew's account.

"In the end of [or **"After"**] *the Sabbath* [**Gk. plural—"Sabbaths"**]*, as it began to dawn toward* [**into**] *the first of the week, Mary Magdalene and the other Mary came to see the sepulcher"* (Matthew 28:1).

This account of Matthew states that there were "Sabbaths" that had come to an end before Mary Magdalene and Mary the mother of James came to the tomb on Sunday morning. Most have mistranslated this with the Sabbath being made singular, but in Greek it is plural. There had been two Sabbaths directly following the Passover of Christ's death and burial. It is simply stating here that there had been two Sabbaths that had passed before the two Marys came to the tomb at the dawning of the daytime portion of that first day of the week.

It is clear then that there were two Sabbaths contained in this period of time and we have also seen the period of time spoken of where they had purchased and prepared these spices. Clearly, traditional Christianity does not account for these two Sabbaths or even the preparation day between them.

The truth of such a matter can be exceedingly exciting, inspiring, and illuminating to finally come to see. But such a truth, when having believed for a lifetime in a Friday crucifixion and Sunday morning resurrection, is not so easy to face and then address in one's life. That is not the fault nor condemnation of any who have been deceived by others. However, it is the fault of those who mistranslated scripture and of those who since then have come to know the truth but have refused to teach it.

This matter in the timing of Christ's resurrection is also clouded in confusion and darkened by the teaching and tradition surrounding the observance of Easter. The idea of a sunrise service because Christ was purported to have risen at that moment in time is not at all factual.

"The first day of the week Mary Magdalene came early, **when it was yet dark***, unto the sepulcher, and saw the stone taken away from the sepulcher"* (John 20:1).

There were others following right behind them and it states the sun was just beginning to rise, but Mary Magdalene and Mary (the mother of James) arrived while it was still dark and the sun had not yet risen. Although much of this has been translated in very awkward ways, the story is consistent and clear: both Marys arrived first, while it was yet dark, and the rest then began arriving with the spices just as the sun was beginning to rise. The message is the same; Christ had risen. He had already been resurrected before they ever arrived. He wasn't resurrected at that moment when the sun was about to rise, nor at the moment when it did rise. He already had been resurrected earlier!

"Now after the Sabbath, as the first of the week began to dawn, Mary Magdalene and the other Mary came to see the tomb" (Matthew 28:1).

After the Sabbath, the first day of the week begins at sundown on the 7th day of the week. It then becomes dark, so the dawning of the first day of the week is in the morning when the rays of the sun begin to lighten the sky.

Next is the account of how the great stone had been rolled away from the opening of the sepulcher by an angel. It records that the women had concern about how they were going to get that stone moved so that they could properly anoint the body with their spices, but when they arrived it had already been removed and Christ was not there—he had already been resurrected earlier.

"Very early in the morning the first of the week, they came to the sepulcher at the rising of the sun. And they said among themselves [had earlier stated their concerns], *'Who will roll away the stone from the opening of the sepulcher?' But when they looked, they saw that the stone*

was [was already] *rolled away, for it was very great"* (Mark 16:2-5).

The way the stone had been rolled away before they had arrived is described in that same account of Matthew 28. Starting with verse one again:

"Now after the Sabbath, as the first of the week began to dawn, Mary Magdalene and the other Mary came to see the tomb. And behold, there was [had earlier been] *a great earthquake, for an angel of the Lord* [had] *descended from heaven, and came and rolled back the stone from the opening, and sat on it. His countenance was like lightning, and his clothing as white as snow. And the guards shook for fear of him, and became as dead. Now the angel answering said to the women, 'Do not be afraid, for I know that you seek Joshua who was nailed to the pole. He is not here, for he rose, as he said. Come, see the place where the Lord was lying'"* (Matthew 28:1-6).

This account of those who were first exposed to the truth that Christ had already been resurrected is stated in translations many different ways. No matter how it is written, the fact is that when they came to the tomb, he was not there, for indeed he had already been resurrected. No scripture says that he rose or had risen at the moment of sunrise or anywhere around that timing. But that is the narrative of Easter and its teaching.

There is no need to cover all the scriptures that surround this story, as they all speak of the same thing. Christ was no longer in the tomb. He had been resurrected earlier. But is there any way to know how much earlier? Yes!

It is good to be reminded of what Luke had to say about this account.

"Now upon the first of the week, very early in the morning, they came to the sepulcher, bringing the spices which they had prepared, and certain <u>others</u> [came] *with them. Then they found the stone had been rolled away from the sepulcher, and they entered in, and did not find the body of the Lord Joshua. It came to pass, as they were very perplexed about all this, behold, two men stood by them in shining garments* [two angels]. *As they were afraid, and bowed <u>their</u> faces down to the earth,*

they [the angels] *said to them, 'Why do you seek the living among the dead? He is not here, but has risen. Remember how he spoke to you when he was yet in Galilee, saying, "The Son of man must be delivered into the hands of sinful men, and be hung on a pole, and the third day rise again."' And they remembered his words"* (Luke 24:1-8).

Once again, we are brought back to this issue of what Christ had to say about **the only sign** that would be given of who the true Messiah was. He would be in the heart of the earth—in the tomb—for three days and three nights. Then on the third day, he would be resurrected—at the exact end of that third day.

The timing is that just before sundown on Passover day, just before the annual Holy Day was to begin, Joseph of Arimathaea placed Christ in the tomb. That was right before sunset on that 4th day of the week, which was at the end of the Passover day. Then the annual Holy Day of the 1st Day of Unleavened Bread began—an annual Sabbath. This day was the 5th day of the week.

This means that the time from just before sunset on the 4th day of the week and up to sunset of the 5th day of the week (of which the vast majority of that day was that annual Sabbath) would constitute the first day of Christ being in the tomb.

Then just before that first day in the tomb was coming to an end, at the end of that **annual Sabbath** just before sunset, day two would begin and then end just before sunset of that 6th day of the week, which is known as the **preparation day** for the weekly Sabbath (a Friday as we would see it).

Then the third day of Christ being in the tomb was from just before sunset on that preparation day and the beginning of the weekly Sabbath. That third day in the tomb ran through that night of the weekly Sabbath and into its daytime portion of the Sabbath all the way up to just before sundown when that third day and that weekly Sabbath would come to an end.

To fulfill what Christ stated about the Messiah being in the heart of the earth for three days and three nights, he had to be resurrected toward the very end of that weekly Sabbath. It would have been just a little while before sunset on that Sabbath when a new day was about to begin. That new day after sunset on the weekly Sabbath was the first day of the week—Sunday. The first day of the week (Sunday) always began after sunset on the weekly seventh-day Sabbath.

To fulfill the sign of who the Christ truly was, he had to be resurrected exactly three days and three nights later—three full days after being placed in the tomb. That period ended toward the end of the weekly Sabbath. The Christ—the true Messiah—had to be resurrected at the end of the weekly Sabbath day in order to prove who he was. He was not resurrected during any moment of the first day of the week. He was not resurrected on Sunday.

TWO CHRISTIANITIES

Indeed, there is a vast difference between two strongly opposing groups that call themselves Christian. Since 31 AD, one group has been called the Church of God. A vastly different organization began to form in 325 AD and it has grown very large into what can be best described as "traditional Christianity," which is now made up of tens of thousands of denominations and nondenominational churches.

One group of Christianity believes Joshua is the Christ and is the one who was dead and in the tomb for exactly three days and three nights until he was resurrected to everlasting spirit life at the end of a weekly Sabbath day, just before the first day of the week (Sunday) began.

The other group of Christianity believes Jesus is the Christ and is the one who was resurrected on a Sunday morning at sunrise—on Easter, after being in the tomb for a day and a half.

The world is soon going to be introduced to Christ when he returns with an army of 144,000 who will at that time establish the Kingdom of God to reign over the nations of the earth, and who will then establish one true Church for all mankind.

Chapter 5

END-TIME DESTRUCTION IN TWO CHRISTIANITIES

THE BOOK OF REVELATION IS first and foremost about prophesied events that will be fulfilled in the end-time. But even as this book has been showing, many of these events have already been fulfilled over the past 70 years, yet the world has been fully unaware of them.

Of all those prophesied events, most have occurred over the past 30 years and the fulfillment of these events are speeding up and becoming far more intense. Remember that the fulfillment of these prophesies is following the pattern of a woman in labor pain. Yet as explained, the magnification of these events and their greater fulfillment will finally begin to be recognized by this world once the United States is attacked and conquered during the first five Trumpet events of Revelation.

In addition to physical destruction, the Book of Revelation also foretells of cataclysmic end-time events that would occur within the two vastly different groups of Christianity that were described in the previous chapter.

Events of disastrous proportions have already occurred in the group of Christianity that began in 31 AD, the one named as God's Church. The fulfillment of the first five Seals of Revelation is about those **apocalyptic events**, and they will be covered in the latter part of this chapter.

END-TIME DESTRUCTION OF THE CHRISTIANITY OF 325 AD

The group within traditional Christianity which had its organized beginning in 325 AD is prophesied to yet experience catastrophic destruction. To better grasp what is prophesied in Revelation about these events that will be fulfilled during WWIII, it is needful to know some related history.

These events are directly tied into what was covered in Chapter 2 concerning the seven prophesied revivals of the old Roman Empire, and the last revival that consists of ten nations of Europe.

The Origin of Europe

There is a term that one can look up for themselves that has much to do with the formation of Europe and its modern-day religious beliefs. It is **Europa**. The name comes from Greek mythology. This was the name of a Phoenician princess that was abducted by Zeus who had taken the form of a white bull and who then carried her (Europa) to Crete. It is from this name that the continent of Europe received its name. This has much to do with the eventual establishment of religious ideas in that region of the world, which later spread throughout all the world.

As an aside, it is interesting to note that when the euro was established as the new currency of the European Union, each country had symbols placed on the two-euro coin. The symbol that was printed on the coin for Greece was a woman riding a bull—the symbol for Europa, and much more. The representation is very symbolic in the Book of Revelation.

"Then one of the seven angels who had the seven bowls came and talked with me, saying to me, 'Come and I will show you the judgment of the great harlot who sits on many waters, with whom the kings of the earth committed fornication, and the inhabitants of the earth were made drunk with the wine of her fornication.' So he carried me away in the spirit into the wilderness. There I saw a woman sitting on a scarlet beast, full of names of blasphemy, and having seven heads and ten horns" (Revelation 17:1-3).

These verses are prophetic concerning the seven revivals of Europe that lead up to the final one that has ten horns. These "ten horns" represent the ten nations that will come together in military might and use nuclear weapons during the period of the fulfillment of the Fifth Trumpet.

God has used this depiction of a woman on a beast to describe the connection between rulership and false religious beliefs within the prophesied European empire and its revivals through time. The influence of many deities runs deep in the beginning formation of the rise of the Roman Empire—the beginning of a prophetic empire—a European empire that would continue up to the very end-time and the last war on earth.

A heading in Wikipedia entitled "List of Roman Deities" actually captures in the very first paragraph what a person needs to grasp concerning the foundational formation of the Roman Empire from the beginning.

"The Roman deities most familiar today are those the Romans identified with Greek counterparts, integrating Greek myths, iconography, and sometimes religious practices into Roman culture, including Latin literature, Roman art, and religious life as it was experienced throughout the Empire."

As partially explained in the previous chapter, the practice of the early Romans was to adopt the deities and religious practices within the different regions of the Empire and mix them. The resulting religious practices and beliefs went through many transformations and gradually changed over hundreds of years and eventually morphed into what became known as "Christianity in the Roman Empire."

That is why today a person can come to recognize and identify the actual beginning for the kinds of mysterious teachings and beliefs that have no connection and no origin to any scriptural truth, doctrine, or teaching from the Bible. Instead, the ideas, origins, and teachings of Easter, Christmas, trinitarian symbolisms, symbolisms contained in crosses, sun and Sunday sunrise worship, mother with child worship, rabbit and egg fertility symbolism, and much, much more, have morphed into the current teaching and practices of over 2 billion people on earth. Simply put, the origin of these ideas used in the creation of this new Roman religion came from religious ideas and practices from those who believed in the ancient deities.

God has much to say about mixing false teachings and practices from the belief in other deities with what He has revealed as the true ways of worshipping Him. Since mankind has ignored God and has further polluted His truth with fables and false religious practices, He is now bringing the world into judgment for doing so. It is during this time of judgment that He will bring an end to mankind's self-rule and religions as He establishes His Kingdom to rule over all nations on earth.

Full of the Names of Blasphemy

Going through history from the time the Roman Empire began and seeing the transformation of religious ideas can help a person better face the actual truth of what has morphed into what we see today in "traditional Christianity." The birth of traditional Christianity has its roots in the very custom of mixing widely varying beliefs.

Indeed, the Romans incorporated the custom of blending religious beliefs and mingling other peoples' gods with their own. After conquering a nation, they were accepting of others' beliefs because it made it easier for them to merge different groups of people together to unite their expanding empire. This practice not only mixed beliefs from the Greeks, Celts, and Germanic people but also beliefs from Judaism and those who held to true Christian beliefs and teachings in the empire.

These widely varying beliefs also included the belief in many deities. It is for this reason that God described this beast in Revelation 17 the way he did. His description of this beast is reflective of the mythical god Zeus who disguised himself as a white bull carrying the princess Europa on his back to Crete. Crete is the largest and most populated island of Greece, and it has a deep history of being the center of Europe's first advanced civilization, the Minoans, from 2700 to 1420 BC.

Although this mythological bull was white in color, God describes it as a scarlet-colored beast with seven heads and ten horns. Scarlet is used here to prophetically reflect the system of government and religion of the Roman Empire. The color scarlet was a symbol of the wealth and power of that empire.

This color is also used prophetically to depict prostitution and adultery, which is how God prophetically describes what took place in the religious practice of the Roman Empire that produced a false Christianity. In those verses quoted from Revelation 17, it spoke of judgment that was coming to "the great harlot who sits on many waters, with whom the kings of the earth have committed fornication, and the inhabitants of the earth were made drunk on the wine of her fornications."

So when it states, "I saw a woman sitting on a scarlet beast, full of names of blasphemy," then one needs to understand the purpose for such a statement. The name for Europe coming from this mythological story epitomizes the very process that created a "false Christianity." The custom within the Roman Empire of blending mythology, religious beliefs and practices, and concepts relating to many different gods was used in much of what formed a false Christianity.

Since this practice was so deeply incorporated into the creation of traditional Christianity, it is prophetically described as being full of names of blasphemy. Blasphemy is a matter of assuming the right to change or act against what God has given as true and right regarding how one is to properly worship Him.

That which is described as "a woman sitting on a scarlet beast, full of names of blasphemy" is exactly what was described in Revelation 13.

*"Then I stood on the sand of the sea, and saw a beast rising up out of the sea, having seven heads and ten horns, and on his horns ten crowns, and on his **heads a blasphemous name**"* (Revelation 13:1).

"So they worshiped the dragon [referring to Satan] *who gave authority to the beast, and they worshiped the beast, saying, 'Who is like the beast? Who is able to make war with him?' And he was given a mouth speaking great things and **blasphemies**, and he was given authority to*

*continue for **forty-two months**. And he opened his mouth in **blasphemy against God, to blaspheme His name**, His tabernacle, and those who dwell in heaven"* (Revelation 13:4-6).

As shown through these verses, the formation of false Christianity is filled with blasphemy. Some of that has been addressed already as in the example of how God began to be called a Trinity. It has also been covered how the very name of Joshua was corrupted by using the name Jesus instead. Although it is difficult to fully prove after so many hundreds of years, there are some who give a pretty good argument to the belief that the name Jesus actually has its roots in the name of Zeus.

Although this description of "names of blasphemy" is given, it is about more than just literal names. It also includes those things that were described in mythology as being used in various practices of worship. Even art and sculpture used in worship in mythology have been mixed into worship in false Christianity. These too fit the description of carrying the "names of blasphemy."

Indeed, there are a very large number of things that fit this description that have become incorporated into false Christianity. Although much of this has been mentioned, some bear repeating.

God's Sabbath day on the seventh day of the week was changed to a weekly worship on the first day of the week, which is a day named after the sun—Sunday. The formal ceremony of baptism where an adult chooses to repent of their sins and is then immersed in water has been blasphemed. It has been changed to a ceremony of christening by sprinkling water on the head of a child and calling it "baptism," even though the very word translated as baptism comes from the Greek word meaning "to immerse."

There is a considerable amount of artwork with symbols and objects that has originated from the practice and teaching about false gods and false doctrines from these false deities. Much of this has been adopted and used in the exact same representations in false Christianity. The artwork involving these false gods often depicts scenes from heaven and hell. The symbols of crosses and other religious objects like a mother and child statue were used to worship false gods centuries before Christ was born of his mother Mary. All these things have been mingled into a false Christianity.

It is also good to be reminded of all the blasphemous things done by Constantine, who called together and presided over the Council of Nicaea in 325 AD and helped create a new state religion that called itself "Christianity."

God commanded that Passover was to be observed **yearly** by His people for all time. Yet in that **annual** observance of partaking of the symbolism contained in eating a small portion of unleavened bread and drinking a small portion of wine, they changed the partaking of these symbols to a ceremony called Communion that can be observed **weekly**.

Part of the very definition of blasphemous is about "that which is sacrilegious against God or sacred things, and is simply a lack of showing respect to God."

Calling the name of God's Son by some other name than what He instructed it should be is blasphemous. Calling God a Trinity is blasphemous. God clearly reveals that He alone has had eternal existence inherent in Himself and that no other God has eternally existed. Even before His own Son was born from a physical woman, God made this clear.

*"I am the LORD [***Heb.- Yahweh, meaning the Eternal***], and there is no other; There is no God [***Heb. – Elohim***] besides Me. I will gird you, though you have not known Me, that they may know from the rising of the sun to its setting that* **there is** *none besides Me. I am the LORD [***Yahweh, the Eternal***], and there is no other"* (Isaiah 45:5-6).

*"For this is the word of the LORD [***Yahweh, the Eternal***], who created the heavens, who is God [***Elohim***], who formed the earth and made it, who has established it, who did not create it in vain, who formed it to be inhabited: 'I am the LORD [***Yahweh, the Eternal***], and* ***there is*** *no other'"* (Vs. 18).

God explains here and in many other areas of scripture that He alone has eternal existence. But a church rose up in the Roman Empire that stated God is a Trinity. That is the definition of blasphemy.

The Council of Nicaea established the observance of Easter after outlawing the observance of Passover. The Roman Empire accepted a religious observance called Easter, which has its origin in the goddess of many ancient cultures.

The Christianity of the Roman Empire taught a false timing for Christ's death, a false timing of his resurrection, Sunday morning worship, Christ's supposed death on a cross, the distortion of his name, the use of his name in an observance of his birthday—a birthday that did not occur in winter, and so much more. Do such things fit the definition of being blasphemous?

As it has also been covered, the religious titles pertaining to God that Christ commanded should never be used by religious teachers have been attached to the names of thousands of people who have called themselves ministers of God.

The leaders of this church and those who have come out of her have blasphemed God's name by usurping the title of Father, Reverend, Pope, Cardinal (wearing scarlet), and more. Her religious leaders have taken to themselves the right to absolve people of their sins, of which only God Almighty can do. It is through the sacrifice of His Son as the Passover who spilled his blood to the earth for that very purpose—so mankind, through Christ, can become forgiven of sins.

The question in all this should actually be, "What is true and what is false?" Only that which is false can blaspheme God and His name. It is the misuse of His name and of His true words that are given throughout scripture. By definition, to twist, distort, and mistranslate what God has spoken is a matter of blasphemy.

The Woman on the Beast

So who is this woman who rides on the beast in Revelation 17? Each reader has covered enough already to give a truthful answer to this. It is good to read the verses again and then continue in order to learn much more about this seventh and last revival that is right now being fulfilled.

"Then one of the seven angels who had the seven bowls came and talked with me, saying to me, 'Come and I will show you the judgment

*of the great harlot who sits on many waters, with whom the kings of the earth committed fornication, and the inhabitants of the earth were made drunk with the wine of her fornication.' So he carried me away in the spirit into the wilderness. There I saw a woman sitting on a scarlet beast, full of **names of blasphemy**, and having seven heads and ten horns"* (Revelation 17:1-3).

The woman who is likened to Europa symbolizes the religion that became established in the Roman Empire. Prophetically, a woman pictures a church. God's own Church is referred to as a woman—and is even described as "the mother of us all." God has intended that His people be nourished and fed by the Church. However, the description of this woman is not about God's Church but about one that is responsible for feeding (nourishing) in a blasphemous manner—making others drunk on what she gives them.

*"The woman was clothed in purple and scarlet, and adorned with gold, precious stones, and pearls, and having in her hand a golden cup full of **abominations** and the filthiness of her fornication. On her forehead a name was written: Mystery, Babylon the Great, the Mother of Harlots and of the Abominations of the Earth. I saw the woman, drunk with the blood of the saints and with the blood of the martyrs of Joshua. When I saw her, I marveled in great astonishment. But the angel said to me, 'Why did you marvel? I will tell you the mystery of the woman and of the beast that carries her, which has the seven heads and the ten horns'"* (Rev. 17:4-7).

When the meaning of the representation of a "woman" is understood here, it is quite easy to see what God is describing by such prophetic symbolism. The woman as a church is described as being clothed in bright and costly colors and pictured as having great wealth and making a display of it. She is a church and she stands out to all who see her. In Europe, she stands out as the center of cities in order to be seen by all, as much sacrifice and wealth went into such constructions.

The woman is depicted as having a golden cup, another symbol, but which also is actually used in one of its religious practices that reflects its teachings and use of the word of God—to blaspheme. God's people are commanded to drink a small portion of wine once a year on the night of Passover. As this was covered earlier, this is symbolic of the blood of Christ that was spilled for us in order for our sins to be forgiven and to reflect that he fulfilled the meaning of Passover and died as our Passover Lamb. Those taking of this small portion of wine on the annual observance of Passover **do not do so** from a golden cup or chalice.

But the teaching of that great church of the Roman Empire is that it can be done weekly in what is called Communion during the second most important part of its worship service. That service is referred to as mass and specifically during this second portion of mass is the Liturgy of the Eucharist. In the eucharistic prayer, this church "commemorates Jesus Christ and his redeeming work, especially his sacrifice for the sake of all humankind through his crucifixion."

So what is true and what is false? Is it the observance of a Communion service in a ceremony referred to as the Liturgy of the Eucharist or is it Passover that is observed only once a year? Do such things matter to God? The truth is that such an altered observance from what God and Joshua the Christ commanded is **an abomination** to God. God refers to changing what He has commanded, especially in the practice of customs from the worship of manmade deities, as a form of adultery and **spiritual fornication** because it reflects **unfaithfulness to God** and His true word.

So this woman is referred to as a harlot—one who practices adultery—or who is simply **casual** in her approach to sexual relationships with others (the mixing of religions with God's word). When looking at this on a spiritual plane in what a relationship with God should be, one faithful in spirit and in truth, then this has a much deeper meaning.

This woman is described as "the harlot" who rides the beast and also the mother of harlots. In other words, many other harlots came out of her. The truth of that should be obvious as well for anyone who is willing to face the truth of it. Many churches did come out of that great church that became established in 325 AD as the state religion of the Roman Empire. Her daughters took with them most of her false doctrines.

She is referred to as "Mystery Babylon" because her teachings (words) are like a mystery because they claim their validity comes from God, yet they do not agree with God's words. Babylon is a good description because the word is derived from the word "babel" meaning "confusion," and is defined as something that is unclear or confusing due to the result of mixing many voices together. This church actually states that their most important teaching, which is about the Trinity, is not from scripture, but it is a "mystery given to the church, as something that cannot be truly comprehended."

This reference to Babylon is given for two reasons. The first concerns what began to happen shortly after the flood in Noah's day when false religion once again began to spring up in different cities, one of which was Babel. Those living in that city had determined to build a tower that would reach up into the heavens. This pursuit was mingled with false religious ideas. Corruption and pride were accelerating at such a fast pace in the minds of those living there that God had to intervene to slow down the process of further corruption once again.

At this point in time after the flood, all people spoke the same language. The means by which God was going to slow mankind in their evil pursuit was to confound the people with different languages. This is the origin for the basis of differing languages today. God changed a portion of the spirit in their mind in an instant so they had understanding and ability to speak another language. When God did this, different groups could no longer understand each other, and they were only able to understand those who were given the ability to speak the same language as themselves.

It would be like everyone speaking English one day, and then all of a sudden, certain groups could only speak French, others Japanese, while yet others spoke only Russian, and so they would divide into groups. It may be hard to imagine such a thing happening, but that is exactly what occurred. For a person who spoke a single language on one day and a completely different one on another, it was as if they had always known the new language they were now speaking and had no memory or understanding of their previous one.

The name of the city became known as Babel. The term Babylon, which became one of the first prophetic world-ruling empires, carries that same meaning. It was that first prophetic kingdom depicted by the head of gold in Nebuchadnezzar's statue.

Babel and Babylon both mean "confusion." That term has become synonymous with the way of religion and governments of this world. They are man-made systems that only create confusion, turmoil, division, and wars. These are all opposite to the way of God that produces unity, soundness of mind, and true peace.

An even deeper understanding can be derived from the use of the expression "Mystery Babylon" since that is where the formation of false religion actually began. After the flood, it was in the city of Babel that false religious ideas and practices began to form. These evolved into the worship of different false deities that stemmed from the same ideas when there was still one language spoken by all in Babylon.

After people became divided and then separated into different regions with those of the same language, the names of these deities varied because of those different languages. Each culture then began to develop a little differently in religious beliefs and practices. That is true with the worship of the sun gods, and the moon and planets, as well as gods of fertility.

The histories of the worship of Tammuz, Ishtar, Astarte, Diana, Zeus, Artemis, Ra, Aton, Apollo, and so many others all have their roots in Babylon. It is from what began in the city of Babel that the evolution of false religion began and then finally worked many of its practices and ideas into what later became organized in 325 AD and called itself Christianity. That was the birth of false Christianity, and that is why it is indeed referred to as "Mystery Babylon."

These verses also state that it is this woman, this church, that has been drunk on the blood of the saints. The word "saints" is simply a term used by the apostles to describe members of God's Church who were faithful to living God's way of life. Saints are not what that church has pictured them to be.

That church has been responsible for persecuting, imprisoning, and killing many of God's people through time. After all, it was the Roman government that created this church and it was that government that convicted the Son of God, Joshua the Christ, to death by nailing him to a pole. It was also that same government that beheaded John the Baptist.

It is even believed through writings and traditions passed down that all of the early apostles were imprisoned, some several times, and that all but one was eventually killed at the behest of the Roman government. It states that Herod killed James, the brother of John, with the sword. Records reveal that John, who was imprisoned on the Isle of Patmos, was likely the only one not killed by the Roman government.

Paul, the apostle to the gentile world, was beaten, stoned, imprisoned, and then kept under house arrest in Rome for an extended period of time before he was eventually killed. Candidly, ever since that time, people have continued in great hatred of the message that God's apostles and teachers have brought, and as a result, many other leaders of God's Church have been imprisoned and/or killed.

Satan and the Bottomless Pit

After John described the woman riding on the beast, the angel went on to explain that he would tell him the mystery of the woman and the beast that has seven heads and ten horns.

"The beast that you saw was, and is not, and will ascend out of the bottomless pit and go into perdition. And those who dwell on the earth will marvel, whose names are not written in the book of life from the foundation of the world, when they see the beast that was, and is not, and yet is" (Revelation 17:8).

As we continue through the story, it will become evident that the beast symbolizes Satan. He is the one being described as being responsible for supporting and carrying the woman—of giving strength and power to this church. He is behind all the consecutive revivals of the prophesied European empire. Indeed, Satan is described as a beast—one like a great dragon and the other being a scarlet-colored beast that has seven heads—the seven revivals of the European empire that would occur over a span of time just over 1,450 years from the time of the first revival which happened under Justinian.

That which is written about the beast that will ascend out of the bottomless pit is partially in the form of a riddle. It has already been mentioned that this beast carries the woman—this Roman church. It is the beast that gives the woman even greater power and prominence. This beast is Satan, and the term "beast" also describes much of the role of the nations with whom he specifically works to carry and lift up that church to greater power and prominence during each revival.

These revivals are for the purpose of war. That church was always involved in one way or another in those revivals that covered that first 1260 years up to the time of the fall of Napoleon, which was also the time that marked the beginning in the progressive decline of the power and influence of the Catholic Church over the European empire. That decline in power and influence has been ongoing ever since, just as it is today, and it is leading to the end-time destruction of that form of Christianity that began in 325 AD.

Most of the involvement of that church in those revivals and wars during that period took place behind the scenes and in secret. Nevertheless, this has much to do with this description of the beast that supports that church because he is the actual power behind it—Satan and the demonic spirit world.

Satan is the one in scripture who is referred to as being restrained in a "bottomless pit" and who then ascends out of it for a short period of time. The timing of these references that use the form of a riddle is very specific.

This "bottomless pit" is first referred to in events that result from the blowing of the Fifth Trumpet. In that specific account, smoke symbolically begins to ascend out of the pit at a time when a spiritual phase of the Fifth Trumpet was being fulfilled (Rev. 9:1-3). That phase was fulfilled and more will be covered in the second portion of this chapter, which is about end-time destruction that came upon the original Christianity—God's Church. This destruction occurred in December 1994. It is about massive persecution that Satan was allowed to exert upon God's Church, and now that period has passed.

However, the physical phase of Satan being released from the bottomless pit is yet to be fulfilled. When Satan is fully released again he is pictured as **ascending** out of the pit, which simply means he will be without restraints so that he can influence and move ten nations of Europe into one last great war—an all-out thermonuclear war—WWIII.

God has allowed Satan to influence the different revivals of the European empire. When one revival has come to an end, then that is when God has restrained Satan once again from exerting such power and influence for war until it is God's time to allow him to do so again. The time when Satan will be allowed to fully ascend out of that pit, which is to be released from his restraint this next and final time, is when it is God's time to allow those ten nations of Europe to be brought together for the purpose of war. When those nations are able to fully unite as a single power without the drag of the rest of the current European Union it will be the time that leads into a full-scale world war—WWIII.

It is so very important to try to grasp the significance of what is being said in the next paragraph.

If God did not control the timing of all this and release Satan when He does, these nations would still come to war. This is especially true in this end-time. The nations of the world are headed toward WWIII no matter what, for the simple fact that people and nations have become so corrupt in their thinking. If God did not intervene in exactly the way He does (and will), that war would last much longer and bring far greater agony and suffering from the long-lasting, hideous upheaval in the world. So not only is God going to intervene to stop mankind from destroying itself, but He is also shortening the time that would otherwise multiply the intensity and length of mankind's suffering.

The **"bottomless pit"** is simply a physical description derived from two words. One has the meaning of an "abyss" (translated as "bottomless") and the other word "pit" is often used to describe a cistern (literally, "a place prepared for holding water").

It is rather difficult to describe things that exist in a spirit realm using physical explanations or examples. This place is simply a specially prepared spirit state that restrains Satan's ability to exert his full spirit power. It is a condition or state that holds back and contains much of his power, primarily the power to lead people into war. It is something that God does not allow him to do until a specific moment in time. Again, such things can be difficult to understand, but they are all timed to serve God's greater purpose in how to most effectively help deliver mankind.

While in the abyss, Satan is not able to use his full power. However, he is still able to broadcast a strong spirit attitude that influences mankind. There is a time coming at the very end of this age just before the Kingdom of God is established in the Millennium that Satan will be **sealed** in complete restraint so that he will have **NO** ability to use **any powers** upon mankind throughout those 1,000 years.

The timing of Satan **ascending** out of the bottomless pit from this condition of spirit restraint is toward the very end of this last and seventh revival that began to form back in the 1950s. It is this last revival that is represented by the ten horns. This will be spoken of again a few verses later. It will be over these ten horns (ten nations) that Satan is able to exercise his greatest power to influence and move those leaders to agree to go to war. However, even though Satan can work to try and influence and lead these rulers to do his bidding, the decision to heed such influence is still in their own hands.

The Beast that Was and Is Not
This verse in Revelation 17 about the beast, Satan, "that was, and is not" reads like a riddle. The only way to comprehend this is to understand that for all these revivals, God does not restrain the full powers of Satan.

The beast "that was" can refer to any time Satan **was** active during one of the revivals in Europe when he was not being restrained by the spirit abyss. However, this section of scripture is referring to a very specific period— the last time he **was unrestrained**. It was when he **was** stirring up Germany and Italy through the power of influence, which he used directly upon Hitler and Mussolini.

Once WWII was brought to an end, Satan was restrained again, and it is in that current restraint that he "**is not**" exercising his full power because he is restrained by the spirit abyss, as has been the case for close to 75 years now.

Even when in spirit restraint, Satan has always been able to exercise his influence and powers to broadcast his spirit attitude in order to manipulate and deceive people, but he has not been allowed to always use his greater powers of influence to destroy as "the Destroyer" in war. Satan has many names that describe his evil actions and another one of those mentioned in scripture is Apollyon, which means "the Destroyer." This verse goes on to foretell what will follow after this period ends: *"The beast that you saw was, and is not, and* ***shall ascend out of the bottomless pit****, and go into perdition"* (Rev. 17:8).

Satan is now described as ascending out of the spirit abyss, his place of restraint. This is the time that he is able to use all his power to speed up the inevitability of an all-out WWIII. After that is over it states that he then continues until he finally comes to his time of "perdition."

This word "perdition" is one that has a wide variety of uses and can mean "waste, destruction, and death." This has a dual purpose as it is used here because once Satan is released, he will quickly move people and nations into a full-scale nuclear WWIII. His actions lead to great destruction, waste, and death of hundreds of millions. However, this is also the **last time** Satan will be allowed to stir up a war that causes massive destruction, although he will still try one more time.

Europe will respond to Satan in the way he wants them to, and they will become engaged in a great nuclear war with others, but to the degree they do so is a matter of their own choosing.

WWIII truly is the war that will end all war. God will never allow another war once He brings an end to mankind's self-rule on earth. Once God intervenes and brings WWIII to a close, He will establish a peace that will reign on earth for the next 1,000 years of mankind. God will not allow war ever again. This is actually part of the true "good news" (gospel) of the Kingdom of God because it is about the very establishment of peace and God's rule on earth.

As Satan stirs up one last great war that causes massive destruction and death, he will also be pressing forward toward his own destruction and death. Once he has engaged in one last war, he himself will be headed straight toward his own perdition, although that will come much later.

Now, "the Beast that Was, and Is Not, and Yet Is"
The last part of this same verse is still written as a riddle, but it is different from what was stated in the first part of the verse. Notice:

"The beast that you saw was, and is not, and will ascend out of the bottomless pit and go into perdition. And those who dwell on the earth will marvel, whose names are not written in the book of life from the foundation of the world, when they see the beast that was, and is not, and yet is" (Revelation 17:8).

One must first understand who those people are whose names **have already** been written in the book of life. This is not a matter of predestination like some doctrines teach. As it was mentioned earlier, those who are written in this book of life are those whom God has worked with at different times throughout the past 6,000 years who will come with Christ to rule on earth. They are those who have been called to that purpose since the foundation of the world when mankind was first placed on earth.

They are the ones who will be resurrected to spirit life at Christ's coming, who are composed of spirit essence but able to manifest themselves in physical form just as Christ did after his resurrection. God's plan from the beginning, **"before the foundation of the world,"** was that there would be 144,000 that will return with Christ at his coming.

They are those whom God has "chosen" over a period of 6,000 years to be part of the first resurrection to spirit life at Christ's coming—the ones written in the book of life to this point in time. Many of these are named in scripture, but many more are not.

The others spoke of here, "whose names have **not yet been written** in the book of life," are those who live during that millennial period under the rule of God's Kingdom. They live during the time when they will know (see) what Satan has done for 6,000 years against God and mankind. They will marvel and they will know that this being and the demonic world are no longer able to be in the presence of mankind to deceive and hurt.

All who live during the Millennium will know that Satan was the beast that "was," and now "is not," because he is no longer around mankind. They will also understand (see) that he still exists—he "yet is." The people living during that 1,000 years know and believe the truth that is already recorded in scripture that this being will be completely removed from mankind and released only for a short time once the Millennium is over.

So indeed, this verse is very prophetic about the beast—about Satan. It is about the 7th and last revival. Then it focuses on the time that follows it when Satan is finally placed in the bottomless pit (spirit abyss) and a seal placed completely over it for 1,000 years, beginning right after Christ returns.

The End of Mystery Babylon
This chapter is entitled, "End-Time Destruction in Two Christianities." One Christianity that became fully organized in 325 AD has been described as the "woman sitting on a beast," and on her forehead a name that was written: "Mystery, Babylon the Great, the Mother of Harlots and of the Abominations of the Earth."

It is at the time of Christ's coming with his spirit army of 144,000 that God brings a complete end to this false Christianity. It is recorded in Revelation as being a time when seven angels pour "the wrath of

God" out of their bowls, meaning "the judgment of God against it," which brings final destruction upon that system to completely destroy it. This is about what began to be quoted at the beginning of this chapter concerning the destruction of this false system.

"Then one of the seven angels who had the seven bowls came and talked with me, saying to me, 'Come and I will show you the judgment of the great harlot who sits on many waters, with whom the kings of the earth committed fornication, and the inhabitants of the earth were made drunk with the wine of her fornication.' So he carried me away in the spirit into the wilderness. There I saw a woman sitting on a scarlet beast, full of names of blasphemy, and having seven heads and ten horns" (Revelation 17:1-3).

The end-time judgment upon this great harlot results in destruction that is mighty upon it.

"Then he [the angel] *said to me, 'The waters which you saw, where the harlot sits, are of peoples, multitudes, nations, and languages. The ten horns which you saw on the beast, these will hate the harlot, make her desolate and naked, eat her flesh and burn her with fire. For God has put it into their hearts to fulfill His purpose, to be of one mind, and to give their kingdom to the beast, until these words of God are to be fulfilled. Even the woman whom you saw is that great city* [Babylon] *which has reigned over the kings of the earth'"* (Rev. 17:15-18).

This false religious system that has held great sway over rulers and people's lives for centuries will be brought to an end toward the end of WWIII. God will allow Satan, the beast, to sway ten nations to enter into nuclear war, but God will also put it into the minds of these leaders to turn against this woman—this false church—because of its evil influence, approval in counsel for war, and the catastrophic results for having listened. They will, in turn, as it says, strip her naked and make her desolate as being thoroughly burnt up with fire—devoured and destroyed.

The next chapter of Revelation continues by describing the complete destruction of Babylon. All that will remain are the foul spirit beings consisting of Satan and the demonic realm as they are placed in total restraint for a period just beyond the Millennium when they will once again be released.

"After these things I saw another angel coming down from heaven, having great authority, and the earth was illuminated with his glory. He cried out mightily with a loud voice, saying, 'Babylon the great has fallen, has fallen, and has become a dwelling place of demons: a prison for every foul spirit, a cage for every unclean and hated flying creature [speaking of Satan and the demons being placed in spirit restraint—all that is left of Babylon]. *For all the nations have drunk of the wine of the wrath of her fornication, the kings of the earth have committed fornication with her, and the merchants of the earth have become rich through the abundance of her sensuality'"* (Rev. 18:1-3)

It is made clear through these latter chapters of Revelation that the religious system of the harlot who rides the beast and carries the name of Mystery Babylon is destroyed.

"Then a mighty angel took up a stone like a great millstone, and threw it into the sea, saying, 'Thus with violence shall that great city Babylon be thrown down, and shall be found no more at all'" (Rev. 18:21).

Just before the 1,000-year reign of Christ and the 144,000 begins, God will destroy the counterfeit Christianity that emerged in 325 AD. Then indeed, Christ will begin his reign as King of kings as he begins to establish God's rule—the Kingdom of God—on earth. This also means that he will establish God's Church as the only religious organization on earth. All other systems of religion will be destroyed and only the truth of God will remain.

END-TIME DESTRUCTION ON THE CHRISTIANITY OF 31 AD
It was stated in the beginning of this chapter: "Events of disastrous proportions have already occurred in the one group of Christianity that began in 31 AD, the one named as God's Church." This destruction began on the 17th of December 1994. Yet the world was oblivious to those major prophetic events becoming fulfilled because it was unaware of the existence of God's Church.

The fulfillment of the first five Seals of Revelation is about those **apocalyptic events** upon God's own Church. These events and the timing that has followed reveal a timeline that is leading up to Christ's second coming—his return as the Messiah—the Christ of all mankind.

Not only has the world been unaware of the existence of God's Church, but traditional Christianity has led people astray from what is true about the end-time. Although most do not even address it, those who do have the wrong interpretations of what God has to say about the subject.

The major misinterpretation about end-time events concerns what Revelation has to say about the first four Seals of Revelation that describe catastrophic end-time events through the depiction of four horsemen who are riding different colored horses, with each one representing different end-time destruction that follows. Since none of those major events that they misinterpret are happening in the world, they believe that WWIII must yet be far off. However, the truth is that this war is about to begin at any time, and they are not prepared.

Four Horsemen of the Apocalypse
Some have come to view the end-time through misguided stories about the Four Horsemen of the Apocalypse. Knowing why people believe as they do will help give a better understanding of what is actually true concerning the timing and actual fulfillment of these prophetic events that have already happened.

Some organizations in traditional Christianity do teach about the four horsemen. However, they believe that these horsemen are about **great physical tribulation**. They also believe that this massive worldwide tribulation is what will later lead into a full-blown WWIII. But again, that is not true!

The meaning of the word "apocalypse" has changed over the centuries. That is primarily due to confusion that was created by traditional Christianity over their many interpretations of what is written in John's Book of Revelation. The word "apocalypse" first appeared in both Greek and Latin. The Greek word "apokalyptein" was used by John in his writing of the book, as that word carried the definition "to uncover, disclose, and reveal."

It was nearly 300 years later when the Catholic Church commissioned the Bible to be translated into Latin that the word "apocalypsis," then meaning "revelation," began to be used.

Much later, during the period of Middle English, this word carried the meaning of "insight or vision" and even of "hallucination."

Then, in the mid-1800s, writings about the meaning of things written in the Book of Revelation began to give credibility to this word "apocalypse" as bearing prophetic meaning of cataclysmic events and belief of an imminent end of the present world.

Over the past few decades, traditional Christianity has gone way off base and highly exaggerated how it uses such terminology. They have created interpretations or ideas that now carry a definition of a complete final destruction of the world, the end of the world, of great catastrophic tribulation on earth before WWIII begins, of theories about a final Armageddon (the last and completely destructive battle of mankind) and other nonsensical interpretations.

It is because of such flawed interpretations as these that the first four Seals of Revelation have taken on some of these distorted definitions when speaking of the four different horsemen that are described in these Seals.

The first four Seals of Revelation that are depicted by four different horsemen are not at all about a modern-day apocalypse that brings about great physical destruction on earth. These apocalyptic ideas about an end to this world are false. The very expression and teachings associated with the "Four Horsemen of the Apocalypse" are sheer nonsense!

The truth is that the first four Seals are about events that have already happened to God's Church—prophetic events that would be the very sign that signaled the beginning of a specific countdown in this current end-time. While many are waiting for the events of the Four Horsemen of the Apocalypse to be revealed, they do not know that those events have already taken place.

In order to grasp what these first four Seals are really about, it is necessary to know a little bit about God's Church that exists today—a Church the world does not know. It is important to know what God has been doing through His Church in these end times.

God's End-time Church

For nearly 70 years now, God's Church has been striving to warn people that we are in the end-time that is prophesied throughout the Bible. That warning is about one more world war—a nuclear war. It is about the prophecy that Europe will once again play a major role in great war. As it has already been covered, those warnings from God's Church, through Herbert Armstrong, began right after WWII had come to an end.

For over a decade now, God's Church has heightened end-time warnings, and people still will not listen. It is simply the nature of mankind to ridicule and dismiss what God's Church has been proclaiming ever since it began in 31 AD. As a result, end-time events have remained hidden.

It is difficult for the human mind to believe that there is any authoritative source that can know what God's will and purpose actually is for mankind. It is difficult for anyone to believe that God's true Church has remained small throughout the centuries while other organizations claiming to be Christian have grown large. Human nature tends to believe that the larger a church organization is, the more likely God is working through them.

It is even far more difficult for the human mind to believe how it could be possible that over two billion people have been deceived about traditional Christianity. Yet that is what has happened over the centuries. This is true about traditional Christianity just as it is true of other religions of different deities, wherein billions today are deceived.

This book has laid out proof to show what is true and what is false concerning many teachings and doctrines about God and Christ. It is by the truth that is taught that you can identify God's Church. There is no other organized group on earth that teaches what this book has already covered as being true.

However, it also needs to be stated that God's Church does not yet have all truth. That is because God has progressively been revealing what is true over the past 6,000 years. Only after Christ returns will God's Church then be given all that is true.

Over the centuries, God's Church has struggled to survive and through time it grew weaker and smaller until it nearly died out. It was at this point in the 1930s that God raised up an apostle, Herbert Armstrong, through whom He began to restore truth to His Church.

God gave prophecy to John, in the early 90s AD, about seven eras that would exist in His Church up to the end-time. The fifth era was known as Sardis and it had nearly died out by the late 1920s, just as God said would happen. As God was bringing the era of Sardis to a close, he raised up Herbert Armstrong to restore truth to His Church in an era known as Philadelphia.

God's apostle was not only to begin restoring truth to His Church, but he was to begin fulfilling a commission that God gave to him concerning this end-time. Herbert Armstrong often spoke of that commission since God had revealed to him that this is what he was to fulfill.

"And this gospel [good news] *of the kingdom will be preached* [proclaimed] *in all the world as a witness to all the nations, and then the end will come"* (Matthew 24:14).

This book has already covered the incredible extent to which Herbert Armstrong proclaimed the good news of the coming Kingdom of God that will rule over this world once Christ has returned as the King of kings. The massive worldwide circulation of *The Plain Truth* magazine, the worldwide broadcasts of radio and weekly television program of *The World Tomorrow*, as well as his meetings with numerous world leaders, were all part of fulfilling that commission.

This was indeed a "witness" to the nations of the world that the end-time was upon mankind and that God's Kingdom would soon be established. But the people and nations of the world rejected what was proclaimed to them, and this too is a witness against mankind of their refusal to listen to God. Then after that commission was completed by the time of his death in January 1986, end-time events did begin to emerge as the seventh and final era of God's Church came on the scene—the era of Laodicea.

It is toward the end of this era known as Laodicea that major end-time events occurred in God's Church that fulfilled the first four Seals of Revelation that are commonly referred to as the Four Horsemen of the Apocalypse. These were prophetic concerning God's Church and not about physical end-time events that would happen to this world.

Prophetic Timing for Christ's Second Coming
During the Church era of Philadelphia, God gave to his apostle, Herbert Armstrong, a very specific prophetic key concerning the first four Seals of Revelation. He understood that the Olivet prophecies of Matthew 24 were the key to understanding these four Seals, but he did not see that these were not about physical end-time events.

Christ gave the Olivet prophecies to his disciples when on the Mount of Olives on the last night of his life on the Passover of 31 AD.

Although this key was given to Herbert Armstrong, God did not reveal the full meaning of those prophecies to him, and neither was he given the ability to use that "key" because it was not yet time for the Seals to be opened. He was not given to see that it was a prophetic matter concerning the very Church of God, so instead, he mistakenly believed the First Seal was about the physical "religious" world of traditional Christianity.

Matthew 24 and the other accounts of the Olivet prophecy parallel this account of the Seals found in Revelation 6. Even within the Church, it wasn't until after the First Seal was opened that these first four Seals were starting to be seen in a different light, as something other than being physically fulfilled. So it is no wonder that even within the world these things have been viewed as having a physical fulfillment about great physical tribulation on the earth.

As mentioned, these first four Seals are often referred to as the time of the Four Horsemen of the Apocalypse because they have been viewed as being "apocalyptic" in their physical, destructive power over the earth. Apocalyptic destruction **will** come on this world once the events of the first four Trumpets of the Seventh Seal begin to lead to the destruction of the United States. However, these earlier Seals are about the powerful destruction that occurred in God's own Church. They were of an apocalyptic nature spiritually.

The following verses describe the disciples walking with Joshua around the temple as he prophesied about God's Church at the end-time. Then the conversation moved to questions and answers concerning that time.

"Then Joshua went out and departed from the temple and his disciples went with him to view the buildings of the temple. Then Joshua said to them, 'Do you not see all these things? Truly I say to you that there shall not be left here one stone upon another that shall not be thrown down'" (Matthew 24:1-2).

Those things that Joshua was telling his disciples were perceived by them as being something physical in nature. That is the natural human response to the teachings of Joshua the Christ. Mankind, by nature, deals with the "physical world" that surrounds it. That is because mankind cannot see or measure that which is spiritual.

The Book of John is filled with such examples. In chapter 3, Joshua was speaking to Nicodemus, a great leader of the Jews. Nicodemus could not understand what Joshua was talking about when he spoke of the need to be "born again" of spirit. He asked how one could be born again once he is old. He knew he could not enter again into his mother's womb and be born a second time.

Even traditional Christianity embraces a wrong interpretation of this. They believe that being born again is some kind of "spiritual experience" while still in this physical body. But Joshua was explaining a literal change that has to take place in human life. That change is part of God's purpose for mankind. Mankind has the opportunity to be born of spirit essence into the Family of God as an eternal living, spirit being.

John 4 records the account of a Samaritan woman who met Joshua at a well. He explained to her that she could drink from the water in that well, but she would become thirsty again. He then said he had living water to give, and if a person drank of it, they would never again thirst. She asked for that water so she would never have to return to the well daily to draw water for drinking. She didn't understand that he wasn't speaking of physical water, but of being able to "drink in" of the "spiritual water" of the Word of God.

Then, in John 6, Joshua spoke of some of the future symbolism for the observance of Passover, which Paul later explained in 1 Corinthians 11:23. Joshua told his disciples they would have to eat of his flesh and drink of his blood. In John 6:66 it is recorded that many of his disciples (not the twelve) quit following him after that because they abhorred what he had said. The Jewish people have always accepted the laws of clean and unclean foods. They knew that eating human flesh and drinking blood was a flagrant and obvious breaking of God's law.

But Joshua was not speaking of a literal physical interpretation. He was beginning to lead his disciples to understanding what would later be given about the future observance of the Passover. In that future ceremony, drinking a small amount of wine would serve as a reminder of his spilled blood, and the eating of a piece of unleavened bread would symbolize his flesh—his physical life, sacrificed for the sins of mankind, as the Passover.

The Book of John continues with more stories that were interpreted on a physical plane but were intended to be interpreted spiritually. This is the same case as with the story of Joshua the Christ talking to his disciples concerning the stones of the temple being cast down. This was not intended for a physical interpretation, but a spiritual one. Although the physical temple was later destroyed by the Romans during the first Church era of Ephesus in 70 AD, Christ was not referring to that event. This prophecy was about the Church at a future time—the end-time.

The stones of the temple are spiritual. They are about God's own Church.

*"Now therefore you are no more strangers and foreigners, but fellow citizens with the saints, and of the <u>household of God</u> [a spiritual temple], and you are being built upon the foundation of the apostles and prophets, with Joshua the Christ himself being the chief corner stone, in whom the whole building is being fitly framed together and **growing into a holy temple** in the Lord, in whom you also are being built together for an habitation of God through the spirit"* (Ephesians 2:19-22).

Paul explained here that those whom God has called into His Church are described as being part of a spiritual temple—a holy temple in the Lord. The apostle Peter explained this in a similar fashion.

*"To whom coming, as unto a living stone, rejected indeed of men, but chosen of God, and precious, you also as **lively stones** are being built up as a spiritual house, a holy priesthood, to offer up spiritual sacrifices, acceptable to God through Joshua the Christ"* (1 Peter 2:4-5).

Members of the Church of God are being described as being like "living stones" (spiritual) that are being built into a spiritual house. That spiritual house is the temple of God.

In this Olivet prophecy, as Christ explained that the stones of the temple would be cast down, he was speaking of a future time for the Church. He was speaking similarly when he told the Jews, "Destroy this temple and in three days I will raise it up." On that occasion, he was speaking of himself, and he was foretelling his death and resurrection that would follow after being dead and in the tomb for three days and three nights.

After Christ told the disciples that there would not be one stone left upon the other in the temple, they then wanted to know more about what he was telling them.

"As he sat on the Mount of Olives, the disciples came unto him privately, saying, 'Tell us, when shall these things be and what shall

THE FALL OF THE UNITED STATES 151

*the **sign** of your coming be, and of the end of the world* [Gk.—age]?'" (Matthew 24:3).

Do you see the context of this prophecy? It not only involves the Church but here it makes clear the timing for when these things would occur. The disciples asked Joshua about the timing of events surrounding the stones of the temple being cast down. By their very question, it is clear that they knew he was speaking of the time for his coming (in his Kingdom) and the end of the age. This prophecy is about those things that would happen to the Church at the end-time, just prior to the return of Joshua the Christ to establish the Kingdom of God on earth.

As future accounts reveal, the disciples wanted to know when the Kingdom of God would become established, but they had no idea it would not be in their lifetime. Instead, they believed it would be soon. At this point, they still did not understand some of the things he had been telling them about the fact that he was going to be killed. This same account is worded a little differently in the Book of Mark.

"*Tell us, when shall these things be and what shall be the **sign** when all these things shall be fulfilled?*" (Mark 13:4).

Joshua was telling his disciples about the timing for when he would actually come as King of kings in the Kingdom of God, and the very sign that would lead up to that time. The sign He would give would involve the Church—events and **signs that would occur in the Church of God**—not signs that would occur in the world, even as the following verse should clearly show.

"*This gospel* [good news] *of the kingdom shall be preached in all the world as a witness to all the nations, **and then the end will come***" (Matthew 24:14).

In these accounts, Christ began to reveal more to them that would become fulfilled in God's Church over time. Then he began to narrow in on the events that would lead directly into the end-time. It is here that he revealed a specific event. The fulfillment of this event was when the commission that God had given to His apostle, Herbert Armstrong, was completed. It was accomplished by the massive work he did in spreading the gospel through publications, radio, and television worldwide, and directly to world leaders. Indeed, the gospel of the kingdom was preached in all the world, and after that was completed, Christ said that "then the end would come."

It was after Herbert Armstrong's death that the last Church era called Laodicea then came on the scene. More is stated in the Olivet prophecy of the very sign of Christ's coming and it came to pass just as he said it would. The disciples had asked what that sign of his coming would be, and he answered exactly what that was—when the end-time countdown would begin. After Christ stated that "then the end would come," he went on to show what would reveal the beginning of those end-time events that would lead up to his second coming.

*"Therefore, **when you shall see** the abomination of desolation, spoken of by Daniel the prophet, stand in the holy place (whoso reads, let him understand), then let those who are in Judea flee into the mountains"* (Matthew 24:15-16).

Christ was revealing what would come to pass on a spiritual plane by giving the analogy of what had occurred before in the physical temple concerning an abomination with which they were all familiar. There was the event that was known as the "abomination of desolation" that occurred in 168 BC when Antiochus IV Epiphanes desecrated the temple by erecting a statue of Zeus in the temple and having a pig offered before it upon the altar.

The account in Daniel had a dual prophetic fulfillment. The first fulfillment was a physical one in 168 BC, but Christ was explaining that there would be a spiritual fulfillment as well. That spiritual fulfillment would come about when an abomination of desolation would occur in God's Church—in the spiritual temple.

This event would be so devastating to God's own people (referred to here as Judea—about spiritual Judah—the Church) that they were warned to flee into the mountains. This will be explained more fully, but it is about a time in which the Church would be scattered. In prophecy, "mountains" are used to symbolize governments. It is about a time of scattering of God's own Church when even the organized government of the Church (within the ministry) would itself become scattered.

There are many groups who look at these prophecies concerning the sign of Christ's coming and they believe that this abomination of desolation will involve something that happens in Jerusalem in the temple mount area. Some believe that these verses can begin to become fulfilled if construction of a new temple becomes desecrated soon after, even if it is only with a few stones being delivered and erected in that location. Some believe that this could even become fulfilled if only an altar were to be placed in that location so that a pig could once again be offered upon it. Such ideas are ludicrous and too far-fetched to be considered realistic.

The Olivet prophecy is indeed the key to understanding that the first four Seals of Revelation are about God's own Church and what would happen once a "spiritual" abomination of desolation would occur within the Church—the true spiritual temple of God. The fulfillment of these Seals is not about physical tribulation that would come upon the world, but of spiritual tribulation that would come upon God's Church.

Indeed, God's word reveals that great destruction would come upon two different Christianities in the end-time. As has been addressed, once it is time for WWIII to be brought to an end, the institutions of traditional Christianity that first became organized in 325 AD will begin to become completely destroyed.

In addition, God's word reveals that His own Church would undergo massive destruction, which Christ foretold in the Olivet prophecies that would come to pass in the end-time, leading up to his coming to establish God's Kingdom. Understanding the true meaning of what has become known as the Four Horsemen of the Apocalypse, which is about the events of the first four Seals of Revelation, reveals an actual timeline that is leading up to WWIII and Christ's second coming.

Chapter 6
GOD'S CHURCH IN THE END-TIME

THE JOURNEY FOR THOSE of God's Church since 31 AD has been an arduous one that has been fraught with persecution and danger. Its members have generally experienced much ridicule, mocking, and hatred. Throughout its history, there have been those who were stoned, beaten, tortured, imprisoned, and killed because of their belief.

Yet in this end-time, the Church has experienced a level of destruction that has been far beyond anything that happened since it began in 31 AD. It was a destruction that was spiritual in nature—far worse than anything physical.

This destruction was prophesied by Christ on the last night of his physical life before he was killed the following afternoon in order to become the Passover for all mankind. A few decades after Christ's death, Paul was given additional information about that destruction that would come to pass as a result of an end-time apostasy.

Then even later, God gave much more for John to record about this in the Book of Revelation. That destruction, which would begin to come to pass upon God's Church, would serve to reveal a countdown to Christ's second coming and the events that would lead up to WWIII.

God allowed this destruction to come upon His own Church in this end-time. It serves as part of His plan of salvation for all mankind. That which the Church experienced through the destruction in the first four Seals will eventually work to help produce some of the greatest results ever in the salvation of mankind.

The Apostasy and Abomination of Desolation
For many years after the Church first began in 31 AD, God's people, including His apostles, were looking for when Christ would return to establish the Kingdom of God on earth. They did not know that Christ would not return until over 1900 years later.

The prophecy that Christ gave Paul concerned signs that would come to pass in God's own Church that could only be recognized by His people. These signs, which could not be seen by the world, reveal when a countdown would begin to WWIII and Christ's return.

"Now we ask you brethren concerning the coming of our Lord Joshua the Christ, and by our gathering together unto him, that you not be soon shaken in understanding or be troubled, neither by spirit, nor by word, nor by letter as coming from us, as though the day of Christ is at hand. Let no one deceive you in any way, for **that day will not come** *unless the falling away* (Gk.— apostasy) *come first, and that man of sin be revealed, the son of perdition"* (2 Thessalonians 2:1-3).

The context of Paul's prophecy is very clear since he specifically referred to the timing of its fulfillment four distinct times. Notice the phrases: 1) *"the coming of our Lord Joshua the Christ"* 2) *"our gathering together unto him"* [the gathering of the Church—the 144,000—at the coming of Christ] 3) *"as though the day of Christ is at hand"* and 4) *"for* **that day will not come** *unless."* This prophecy given through Paul makes it clear that what he is going to tell them concerns what all of them want to know. When is Christ returning?

Paul is explaining to the Church that very specific events must first occur within the Church before the return of Joshua the Christ—before the Kingdom of God will be established (the time for "our gathering together unto him").

This warning to the Church parallels the one that Joshua the Christ gave in the Olivet Prophecy concerning the time for his coming and the fulfillment of end-time events.

"Then Joshua answered and said to them, 'Take heed that no one deceive you. For many shall come in my name, saying, I am the Christ, and shall deceive many'" (Matthew 24:4-5).

Again, this is about the Church and not about the world. The world has always been deceived from what is true about God because it has not yet been His purpose to reveal His will and purpose to it. God only revealed His purpose to a few up to the time of Christ, and then after that, only to the Church.

The only ones who can become deceived are those to whom God has given His truth. This warning was given to God's Church so that they not lose that truth by becoming deceived.

Christ was giving a clear warning that part of the sign of his coming would entail many who would come along and try to deceive the Church. Who can come to the Church in the name of Joshua the Christ? Only the ministry of the Church! Joshua said **many** would come **in his name** and try to deceive many in the Church.

Before Joshua was killed upon a pole, many of those following him already believed that he was the Messiah (the Christ) sent from God to take over the reins of government from the Romans. Before he died, they wanted to know when he was going to do this. Even after his death and resurrection, they still wanted to know. They did not understand that he was there at that time to fulfill the role of becoming the Passover of all mankind and that God's Kingdom would not be established until nearly 2,000 years later at the end of this age.

Paul gave this prophecy about an apostasy to the Church. Then questions followed. How could an apostasy or a falling away from the truth happen in God's Church? How could any of God's people become so deceived that it would be possible for an event of such magnitude like that of an "apostasy" to occur within God's own Church? Paul continues in this prophecy by giving an outline of the kind of events that would occur in order to fulfill this.

Paul stated that the **first** thing that would take place before Christ would return was that Apostasy. This word from the Greek, apostasia, is translated in several different ways. Some examples of that include: a falling away, a Great Apostasy, a rebellion, a revolt. All of these are accurate definitions for the meaning of that Greek word.

Secondly, he stated that the "man of sin," the "son of perdition," must be revealed. There is only one other person who has ever been referred to previously in scripture as "the son of perdition." It was Judas Iscariot. He was one of the original twelve disciples and the one who **betrayed** Joshua the Christ for thirty pieces of silver.

Long before the creation of mankind, the first apostasy ever recorded was that which concerned the angelic realm when the archangel Lucifer betrayed God and led a third of the angels in rebellion against Him. That archangel then became known as Satan. He was indeed the first son of perdition, as angels are referred to as the sons of God in the angelic realm, for He created them. Satan was also the first son of sin—the very first in all God's creation to sin—the author and originator of sin.

So what Paul's prophecy records is an incredibly heinous thing that a single person would be guilty of doing within God's own Church. Paul states more about what this man of sin would do.

"Let no one deceive you in any way, for that day will not come unless the <u>falling away</u> (Gk.— apostasy) come first, and that man of sin be revealed, the son of perdition, **who opposes and exalts himself** *above all that is called God, or that is worshiped, so that he as God* **sits** *in the temple of God, showing* ['showing' in the Greek means 'to show forth, expose, reveal'] *himself that he is God"* (2 Thes. 2:3-4).

Knowing that this prophecy is about God's Church, it becomes apparent that there would arise an individual who would have such prominence that he would be able to exercise much sway over others in the Church. The warning given was to be on guard against any such person who might try to deceive the Church—to lead them away from the truth God had revealed to them.

It states in those verses that this man of sin would exalt himself above God. This is exactly what Satan did within the angelic realm. It is about the power and influence he wanted to have over the angels. He believed his ideas and ways were better than God's, so he opposed God and went about to work against His ways and establish his own.

Satan's very name means "adversary" which means he was against God and worked against God's plan and purpose. In a similar manner, the man of sin, the son of perdition, would rise up in God's Church and he would betray God and Christ. He would become an adversary—he would oppose and act against God and against Christ.

Part of this prophecy given by Paul became well known in the early Church and they believed that someone would rise up within their midst and seek to deceive many. They believed that there would be a falling away in the Church before Christ would return.

Nearly 1900 years later when Herbert Armstrong became an apostle, once again the Church came to believe that there would be a falling away in the Church before Christ would return. However, no one had any concept that what would happen would be as massive and destructive as it was.

In addition, they also did not understand or see at all the fact that this man of sin would come from a leader within the Church itself. It was only believed that a great falling away had to occur before Christ would actually return, and as time progressed, many came to believe that this grand deception would come from outside the Church—from the world of traditional Christianity.

The apostle John made mention of this man of sin in later writings and referred to him as the Antichrist. But John also taught that there were in fact already many antichrists active in the environs of God's Church. However, they understood that **the** Antichrist was yet to come.

By the time John wrote these things, several decades after Paul's warning of the Antichrist, there had already been individuals and ministers within the Church who had risen up and turned against Christ (became anti-Christ), but they were not **the** Antichrist spoken of by Paul.

With the description of the "man of sin" and the "son of perdition," this individual would clearly be one who would betray God and His Son Joshua. His sin and betrayal would be so heinous that it is described as him "showing" or "setting forth" himself to be as God. Such an expression means he was one who had the ability to have powerful influence to raise up (as in idolatry) his own ways and teachings above what God had given to the Church.

This event is exactly what eventually came to pass during the last Church era—Laodicea. The fulfillment of this prophecy about an apostasy in the Church would be the event that would signal the countdown to the coming of Christ—that his return was now imminent.

In that final era of the Church, the betrayal by the son of perdition who turned against God and Christ was the cause of "the Apostasy" that did occur in God's Church. His actions became the spiritual fulfillment of the "Abomination of Desolation" spoken of by Christ in the Olivet prophecy. The original abomination was about massive destruction and desecration of the physical temple of God by Antiochus IV Epiphanes in 168 BC. The second abomination was about massive destruction and desecration of the spiritual temple—the Church of God—once the Apostasy occurred.

The Emergence of the Man of Sin
God raised up Herbert Armstrong as His apostle during the sixth Church era of Philadelphia. His commission was to fulfill what Christ said would occur just before the end-time would come. That commission was to proclaim the good news of God's coming Kingdom to all the world, which he did.

As Herbert Armstrong entered his 80s, his health was waning, and carnal human nature was beginning to work its way into some of the ministry at the headquarters of the Church. Some ministers were being lifted up with self-importance while experiencing the power and authority of being over various operations and congregations of the Church. They started seeing Herbert Armstrong as frail and began to look at who might replace him. This included several evangelists, who were the highest ranking in the ministry, and even his own son, Garner Ted Armstrong.

In the mid to late '70s a wrong spirit began to work its way into the lives of far too many ministers who were beginning to maneuver and work for position, power, recognition, and doctrinal change within the Church. This marked the beginning of the rise in what Christ gave strong prophetic warning concerning the ministry in the end-times. He said that "many will come in my name and deceive many." This could only be something that could happen in God's Church and it had to come from the ministry, as they are the only ones who can come in the authority of Christ's name. This was not about deception that would happen in the world to those who were already deceived.

Some of these ministers, including evangelists, had to be removed from their positions and separated from the Church because they were already turning against truths that God and Christ had delivered to Herbert Armstrong. This was the emergence of many antichrists, but not yet of **the** Antichrist. It was during this period that there were a few thousand people who followed some of these ministers out of God's Church during these times of trouble and turmoil.

Over the last decade of his life, Herbert Armstrong had to deal with many battles that were beginning to emerge within the Church, which were mostly originating within the ministry. Not only were these battles coming from within the ministry, but the worst were from those directly under him in authority. They were the ones who over the years had become ordained as evangelists, most of whom were students of his in classes he personally taught when Ambassador College (a college of the Church) was first established.

An undercurrent struggle for power began within the Church as it was becoming more apparent that Herbert Armstrong was likely to die before Christ's return and that someone would be moved into his place as the one who would then lead God's Church. It is almost unimaginable that such a thing could happen within God's very own Church. This reveals the spiritual condition that many were beginning to drift into within the Church—a Laodicean spirit, defined as a spirit that was "lukewarm," and neither hot nor cold for God's way of life.

It had come to the point that Herbert Armstrong did not feel he could fully entrust the Church to any of these long-ordained evangelists, let alone to entrust them with some of the most important positions within the organization of the Church. At one point, he even reached out and brought in a pastor to the Church in Pasadena, California, where the organization of the Worldwide Church of God was headquartered. This man, Leroy Neff, was the pastor of the Church in Houston, Texas. He had proven himself to be a man who was a faithful minister and could be trusted, and so Herbert Armstrong made him the Treasurer of the Church, as he felt he could not give this job to any of the evangelists.

Even when Herbert Armstrong came to the point of believing he was nearing death, he did not believe he could pass along his responsibilities to any of the evangelists, who were of the highest rank within the administration of the Church under him. So he began giving greater responsibilities to a man who had been serving for a long time as an elder in the local congregation.

In the late '70s, Herbert Armstrong took notice of this man's service, who was then later ordained to an evangelist and was brought into the administration of the Church. That evangelist was Joseph Tkach, Sr., and Herbert Armstrong placed him over all the ministry of the Church worldwide, as again, he did not believe he could entrust it to any of the other longtime evangelists.

Within the headquarters itself, God was allowing Satan to stir up distrust, suspicion, jealousy, lust for power, and even doctrinal division. God did not intervene to stop it but allowed individuals to continue choosing the way that they would go, even if that way was wrong. The Church was becoming weaker spiritually and heading into what would become the Laodicean Era, as people were becoming lifted up in pride, and trusting in self more than trusting in God. The Church was becoming ripe for an apostasy. Nothing like this had happened in its nearly 1,950-year history.

Joseph Tkach, Sr. was the primary person conversing with Herbert Armstrong toward the end of his life when he was confined in his home because of ill health. As his health deteriorated, more of the administration of the Church was being taken over by Joseph Tkach. It was told to the Church that when Herbert Armstrong believed his death was imminent, he transferred all responsibility of leadership to Joseph Tkach, Sr.

Finally, the time for a complete transition from one Church era to another came in January 1986 when Herbert Armstrong died. At the time of his death, the Philadelphia Era ended and the Laodicea Era began—the seventh and last prophetic era that would exist before Christ's coming.

Joseph Tkach, Sr. was now in the role of leadership over God's Church. In the beginning, he seemed supportive of Herbert Armstrong's past leadership and teaching. It seemed as though he was doing things in faithfulness in upholding the truths God had delivered to the Church through Herbert Armstrong.

By the end of the 1980s and into the first couple of years of the 1990s, that began to change. Administrative changes began to be made that seemed somewhat innocent in the beginning, but they were not.

Over the early years of his leadership, slowly but surely, Joseph Tkach, Sr. was elevating himself and his importance within the organization of the Church by surrounding himself with many of those younger in the ministry, and at the same time, trying to diminish the role of others who had carried greater responsibilities during Herbert Armstrong's ministry as God's apostle.

The Church began to take on a new air and attitude because of those Joseph Tkach, Sr. had placed in positions of leadership, including his own son. It was an air of self-importance, of spiritual arrogance and pride, of being spiritually "rich and increased with goods." This was coupled with an already weakened condition within the Church of spiritual lukewarmness and complacency. Christ had forewarned that this would come to pass in the last era of the Church. The mixture of all these components was disastrous for the Church.

Paul's prophecy of an apostasy stated that the man of sin, the son of perdition, would "**sit** in the temple of God, showing himself that he is God." This portion of Paul's prophecy is very telling. This temple of God being spoken of is not the old physical temple in Jerusalem that was destroyed. Many who try to explain these verses do so in great error as they try to connect this event with that physical temple. But in other writings, Paul is very clear when he speaks of the temple because he does so in the context of it being the spiritual temple of God—the Church.

The word "sits" reveals even more about an individual who would be in the temple—the Church. This is not a physical matter of someone sitting around in a building, but it is a spiritual matter involving the spiritual temple—God's Church.

No one could be in this temple of God unless they are part of the Church of God. Yet there is **much more** to this description. This is in the context of someone in authority who is **set** in the Church, bearing authority. This word in such a context in Greek actually means "to cause to set" as in "to set, appoint, or to confer a kingdom unto one."

A couple of examples from scripture are quoted below:

"To him who overcomes will I grant to **sit** *with me on my throne, even as I also overcame, and am* **set down** *with my Father on His throne"* (Rev. 3:21).

"Joshua said to them, 'Truly I say to you, that you who have followed me, in the regeneration when the Son of man shall **sit** *on the throne of His glory, you also shall* **sit** *on twelve thrones, judging the twelve tribes of Israel'"* (Mat. 19:28).

Toward the end of his life, Herbert Armstrong stated that it had never been made clear to him who should lead the Church if he should die, but as stated before, it was reported that he had transferred all responsibility of leadership within the Church to Joseph Tkach, Sr. just before his death. Only one man in the end-time **became appointed—set**—to have great authority in the Church of God, yet he was never an apostle of God. Whether he was **set** there by Herbert Armstrong or whether he **set** himself there, it is not truly known, but one day it will be.

The manifestation of the betrayal by the son of perdition became the cause of **the Apostasy** in God's Church. His actions became the spiritual fulfillment of the Abomination of Desolation spoken of by Christ in the Olivet prophecy.

The Actual Event: The Apostasy
Joseph Tkach Sr. began to place young, inexperienced men into important positions of administration within the operations of the Church. These were not long-time ministers, but mostly newer ones. This large, new group of ministers who were being merged together had a unity with one another of a mindset that was opposed to the past.

This group became a secretive kind of brotherhood that was determined to see the Church become more "mainstream" like the churches of traditional Christianity. These men disliked Herbert Armstrong and his teachings and began to work on turning the entire Church in a different direction. Much of their "behind the scenes" activities did not become fully known until 1995.

However, beginning in 1992, there were many in the older leadership of the Church who were becoming aware of massive doctrine changes that were being planned and were going to be introduced to the Church. However, these individuals **did nothing to warn the Church or ministry** of this conspiracy in the headquarters of the Church. They did not take a stand against what was happening. They did not stand up for God, Joshua the Christ, or God's Church—God's people.

Within this group of younger ministers, some individuals had been conspiring as to how they could lead the Church away from the truth God had given it through Herbert Armstrong. They had tried to diminish the memory of Herbert Armstrong and at one time there was even a movement to destroy his books and literature that were still in large supply at the headquarters of the Church. These ministers had begun to make plans to change literature that would reflect major doctrinal changes that would bring the Church into closer agreement doctrinally with the churches of mainstream traditional Christianity.

Joseph Tkach, Sr. and his son, Joseph Tkach, Jr. were heading this conspiracy to change the doctrines of God's true Church and to lead the Church into a false Christianity.

Although this secretive group of ministers who were plotting to overthrow God's Church had planned to prepare literature to launch these changes, they were caught off-guard when their plans were exposed too early by Joseph Tkach, Sr. when he made a sudden change to a sermon he was going to give in Atlanta, Georgia. In this visit to the Atlanta area congregations of the Church, Joseph Tkach, Sr. was confronted with problems and rumors that were emerging over these changes. He had to make a choice and he felt he needed to address it during that visit.

It did not become known until later, but he had prepared to deliver a different sermon from the actual one he ended up giving in Atlanta. Some things were coming to a head quicker than this conspiring group had planned and Joseph Tkach felt forced into giving a completely different sermon on that day of December 17, 1994.

In that sermon, which was later sent out to all the churches worldwide, Joseph Tkach, Sr. began to inform **God's Church** that every major doctrine was being changed. In addition to Atlanta, he also gave two more sermons on this same subject in two additional locations on the consecutive weekly Sabbaths that followed. All three sermons contained much of the same overall message of these major changes in doctrine.

That sermon in Atlanta declared that the 7th day Sabbath was a matter of personal choice as to when it could be observed. It could be observed on the seventh day of the week (Saturday) as all were accustomed to, or on the following day, the first day of the week (Sunday), like traditional Christianity does. It was no longer to be seen as a commandment required by God.

In addition, God's annual Holy Days were being treated in the same manner, as the Church was being told that they were not really commanded to keep them, and although much of the Church would continue doing so, it was more as a matter of tradition and not of commandment. Also, Christmas and Easter were not forbidden as in the past. There were numerous other changes being mentioned, even down to saying that the laws of God concerning what was unclean for mankind to eat were not valid.

Needless to say, that sermon was the beginning of a **great apostasy!** Here was a man who was seen as sitting in authority over God's Church on earth who had now put himself **in the place of God**, as he set out to change the very laws of God.

That which Paul stated about the man of sin, the son of perdition, had then come to pass: *"Who **opposes** and **exalts himself above** all that is called God, or that is worshipped, so that **he as God** sits in the temple of God, showing* [revealing] *himself that **he is God**"* (2 Thes. 2:4). God does not change His way and truth, but Joseph Tkach, Sr. believed he could.

In our modern history, when has there been a religious institution that has experienced someone rising up within its own ranks who at a single moment in time went about changing every major teaching and doctrine of that organization? Yet, God's own Church did experience exactly that, just as God foretold would come to pass in the end-time.

The Seals Began to be Opened

There are some in the world who are waiting for the time of the opening of the First Seal of Revelation so that they will then be able to know that Christ is coming. There are those who believe that when the First Seal is opened that Christ's coming will then be three and a half years after that tribulation begins. However, such people will be fully caught off-guard, because the first four Seals are not about physical tribulation in the world, but about spiritual tribulation and destruction that has already occurred in God's Church.

The First Seal was opened on the 17th of December 1994, when Joseph Tkach, Sr. gave that sermon in Atlanta, Georgia. This was the beginning of the Apostasy. It was the beginning of great tribulation within God's own Church. It was the beginning of a prophetic countdown to the actual second coming of Joshua the Christ.

"I saw when the Lamb opened one of the seals, and then I heard as it were the noise of thunder as one of the four living creatures said, 'Come and see.' Then behold, I saw a white horse and he who sat on it had a

bow, and a crown was given unto him, and he went forth conquering, and to conquer" (Revelation 6:1-2).

This is about the one who was set in authority (given a crown to rule) in the temple of God. This prophetic picture is about one who used his power to wage war to conquer and overthrow God's Church—to desecrate and destroy God's Church—to commit the "abomination of desolation" in the temple of God.

Then, the next three seals that were opened were simply the result—the effect—of the first.

"Then another horse went out that was red, and it was given to him who sat on it to take peace from the earth, and that they should kill one another, as a great sword was given to him" (Revelation 6:4).

Once Joseph Tkach, Sr. gave his desecrating sermon in Atlanta, the floodgates were opened to free-flowing doctrinal perversion and widespread private interpretation of God's Word through human reasoning and demonic influence. Peace was taken from the earth in every area where God's Church was.

The growing unrest that was building over the previous years with the doctrinal battles and fighting amongst brethren and ministers who were increasingly yielding to distortion of doctrine was now unleashed upon the Church in a massive onslaught, almost overnight. Ministers and brethren began to choose different sides and fight over doctrinal differences.

The opening of this Second Seal followed instantly behind the first. Nearly three-quarters of the ministry yielded to this new doctrinal format. They turned towards this newly embraced false way; they turned away from the truth. Many ministers fully adopted the new teachings of Joseph Tkach, while others adopted only portions of them. Nevertheless, a broad movement toward false doctrine in a false Christianity was thrust upon the Church.

This emergence of so many false ministers led to quicker dissemination of false doctrine and teaching. Those ministers were no longer wielding the sword of God's word, in spirit and in truth, but a false sword that served to take truth from brethren and destroy spiritual lives.

As the peace of God was taken from their midst through this process, brethren entered into the greatest time of spiritual warfare the Church had ever experienced since it began on Pentecost in 31 A.D. Multiple thousands of brethren began to lose their spiritual lives as people began to kill one another spiritually. The sword of false ministers was false doctrine, and with that came great devastation and spiritual murder.

"When he opened the third seal, I heard the third living creature say, 'Come and see.' I looked, and behold there was a black horse, and he who sat on it had a pair of balances in his hand. Then I heard a voice in the midst of the four living creatures saying, 'A measure of wheat for a penny, and three measures of barley for a penny, and see that you do not hurt the oil and the wine'" (Revelation 6:5-6).

These two verses are well understood by most who read them as pertaining to famine. The Church has always understood that this was about a time of famine that would come upon the world at the end-time, but it was only seen as a time of physical famine. Such a time will indeed come upon all the world physically, but these verses are about the Church and spiritual famine that followed this Apostasy.

These actually fulfilled an Old Testament prophecy that was to occur in the end-time. *"Behold the days come, says the Lord Eternal, when I will send a famine in the land—not a famine of bread, nor a thirst for water, but of hearing the words of the Eternal"* (Amos 8:11).

As false ministers and false doctrine grew in power, brethren became weak and fell victim to a growing spiritual famine. The truth of God—the Word of God that brethren needed to eat and digest in order to be fed spiritually was becoming very scarce. A time of great spiritual famine did indeed come upon God's people.

The result of the Apostasy created widespread destruction and desecration in God's Temple. The destruction that followed parallels a prophecy in Ezekiel 5 about this very thing, as it describes how the effects of the devastation were divided into three specific segments.

As soon as the Apostasy occurred, right at one-third of the Church turned away from all the truth they had been given. They went back to embracing the false Christianity that God had delivered them from when He first opened their minds to see and understand His truth.

Over the next few months, another third of the Church simply gave up in despair and had a complete loss of faith. They abandoned everything. They had no understanding of how or why these events could possibly have happened to a Church that was God's. They had no answers and no hope—nothing left for which to fight.

Then there was a final third that tried to hold onto some form of what they had believed when God had first opened their minds to understand the truth. By the time of the Apostasy, the Church had grown very weak spiritually just as it had been forewarned concerning the last era of Laodicea. It was prophesied to become a church that was spiritually lukewarm and that would begin to drift into a spiritual sleep rather than being spiritually alert and watchful as Christ said it should be.

God declared that since the Church would become so sluggish spiritually due to its own neglect and lack of zeal that He would spew it out of his mouth, meaning that it would be fully separated from Him—from receiving His favor and holy spirit. That is exactly what happened to a very weakened spiritual body. God additionally stated that in the very end-time He would only deliver a small remnant of His people from the third of the Church He was going to allow to become scattered, who still wanted to hold onto some form of their past beliefs.

That final third of the Church became scattered because great confusion had struck them due to the Apostasy. Many of these wanted to hold onto doctrines and truths they had received from God when they were first called. Different splinter organizations began rising up as they began trying to rebuild what had existed in the past. Confusion was multiplied as weakened scattered members had to decide with what organizations they might affiliate. There were vast disagreements between the various groups concerning matters of church structure, leadership, and doctrine.

There was no single group that stood out clearly as being a definitive continuation of God's Church—of where God was working.

Within only months, over 600 separate organizations formed and each one carried the underlying belief that they were the rightful ones through whom the true Church of God would continue.

This last era of the Church was prophesied to be an era that was lukewarm in spirit, while at the same time being lifted up with pride, self-reliance, and self-righteousness of belief in "being right" above that of others. That attitude carried on into most of these many organizations—each believing that they were right.

However, God makes it clear that His Church is **one body—one Church**—that is **united** in truth, belief, and spirit. Only God can reveal what is true. Through that truth, He reveals where His Church has continued on as the small remnant of that very large, scattered body of the former physical organization of the Worldwide Church of God.

Satan Was First to Declare Who the Man of Sin Was
This massively destructive event of the Apostasy within God's own Church began to occur in December 1994 when Joseph Tkach gave his sermon in Atlanta. However, the Church did not grasp that this event was the beginning of the Apostasy. It did not know that God would soon reveal the man of sin to His people—those who were truly willing to repent of letting down spiritually and of becoming lukewarm—of becoming Laodicean.

However, five years before this prophetic event occurred, there was a minister in the Worldwide Church of God organization who had been removed as a minister and disfellowshipped from God's Church in December 1989. This individual, Gerald Flurry, then formed his own church organization. He was opposed to minor changes that Joe Tkach, Sr. was making in the Worldwide Church of God, which was the reason for his dismissal.

A couple of years before the Apostasy, some few were becoming more vocal about their desire to change toward Protestantism, but it had not yet been officially announced by the administration of God's Church. However, well before all this, Gerald Flurry set himself against Joe Tkach, Sr. since he did not like the kinds of changes being made within the Church. He became vocal against the government that was still working within God's Church.

Doctrinal truths were not yet being changed. Those changes did not begin until Joe Tkach, Sr. officially announced them in Atlanta several years later. It was that announcement of a complete overhaul of doctrines that set off the events that produced the Apostasy, which in turn would begin to be what would later reveal who the man of sin was.

Indeed, what Gerald Flurry did was grounds for removal from the ministry. He was stirring up divisiveness within the Church, which is against the instruction of God regarding the spirit of unity, support, and cooperation that is to exist within the government of the ministry of His Church.

After being removed from the ministry, Flurry set out to begin a new church that was supposedly established for the purpose of carrying on the work of Herbert Armstrong and his teachings. Yet this man did not know that the work of carrying out the commission God had given to Herbert Armstrong was already completed—it was finished once he died.

Flurry's church began to promote the idea that the era known as Philadelphia was continuing through him and that all others who would not join him were now Laodicean. As he set out to establish his church, he advanced the notion that he was the true torchbearer of the commission previously given to Herbert Armstrong, and that he would now carry on that same work.

As he set out to build his church, he aggressively used the name of Herbert Armstrong. That tended to give the impression to some, who themselves were becoming disgruntled with the administration of Joe Tkach, Sr., that he indeed might be the one through whom God was now working. Although he used Herbert Armstrong's name to such an extent, his church did not truly reflect Herbert Armstrong or the spirit of his teachings.

Mystifyingly so, toward the beginning of his new ministry, Gerald Flurry actually made the claim that Joe Tkach, Sr. was the prophetic man of sin well before the Apostasy had even occurred. However, he later changed this teaching about who the man of sin was when Joe Tkach, Sr. died because his death did not fit into Gerald Flurry's scenario and belief of what the man of sin would later fulfill.

The reason for mentioning these things is because this individual, although initially correct in what he stated about Joe Tkach, Sr., was also exceedingly presumptuous and wrong for having made such a declaration about him. Instead, it was God's purpose that He would later reveal who the man of sin was by an unmistakable judgment He would pass on him once he caused the Apostasy.

Nevertheless, there is a being who did know who would become the man of sin before it ever happened. That being was Satan and he was already working through Joe Tkach, Sr. to eventually bring about the Apostasy that God was going to allow to happen in His timing. It clearly states how the man of sin, the son of perdition, was able to exercise the kind of power that he did in order to influence others in the Church in such an adverse manner. It was because of Satan's own power that was working through him.

The revelation that Paul gave about the Apostasy that is recorded in II Thessalonians 2 states this about the man of sin: *"whose coming is after the working of Satan with all power and signs and lying wonders"* (Vs. 9).

Well before the Apostasy ever occurred, Satan was working through Joe Tkach, Sr. to give him the kind of power and influence he desired that would in turn come to fulfill his role as the man of sin. Since Satan already knew who this man was, it was an easy thing for Satan to lead another man, Gerald Flurry, to believe that Joe Tkach, Sr. was the man of sin long before he would actually bring about the Apostasy.

Gerald Flurry was easily led by Satan to believe this about Joe Tkach, Sr. because he had already been in strong disagreement and dislike of him anyway. After all, it is that vocal disagreement that led to him to being put out of the ministry and the Church by Joe Tkach, Sr. himself.

The fact that Gerald Flurry made such a proclamation about Joe Tkach, Sr. being the man of sin, before God actually revealed it, was in itself a spiritually deceptive and perverted act. It should come as no wonder since that revelation actually came from Satan himself who is exceedingly deceptive and perverted.

The Man of Sin Revealed by God
For several months after the Apostasy, the third of the Church that was becoming scattered was in shock and could not grasp what or why this was happening to God's people.

In this story flow, there is more that needs to be seen concerning Paul's prophetic writing about the Apostasy, which now becomes relevant.

"*Now you know what <u>withholds</u>* [Gk.– "**holds back**, restrains, detains"] *so that <u>he</u>* [the man of sin] *might be <u>revealed</u>* [Gk.– "to be made known, to disclose what before was unknown"] *in his time. The mystery of iniquity is already at work, but for now it is only <u>withheld</u>* [same Gk. word – "**holds back**, restrains, detains"] *until <u>he</u>* [the man of sin] *<u>is taken out of the way</u>.* **Then** *shall that wicked be <u>revealed</u>* [Gk.– "made known, **illuminated**"], *whom the Lord shall consume with the spirit of his mouth, and shall destroy with the brightness of his coming*" (2 Thes. 2:6-8).

This prophecy is about the man of sin—that wicked one—who **would be revealed** "whom the Lord would consume with the spirit of His mouth (by what God commands), and shall destroy with the brightness of his coming (illuminating Christ's coming)." Most who were scattered after the Apostasy have not been able to understand this verse because they only see this as being fulfilled in a literal, physical way. They believe this prophecy can only be fulfilled at the time of the actual coming of Joshua the Christ on the very day the end-time comes to a close.

But it is this very verse that shows how God alone would <u>reveal</u> (**illuminate, make known**) the identity of the man of sin and what this was to mean for the Church. The timing of Christ's coming and the events that would precede his coming were being "held back" (**from being known—seen**) until the Apostasy and the revealing of the man of sin would take place.

Although most had neither "ears to hear nor eyes to see," God did make it abundantly clear that He was the one who would reveal the man of sin. After Joseph Tkach, Sr. betrayed God and Christ by giving that defiant sermon, the spiritual Temple of God—the Church—became defiled. An abomination of unprecedented proportion had taken place.

Exactly **40 Sabbaths** (to the day and hour, in his time zone) after Joseph Tkach, Sr. gave his infamous sermon in Atlanta, he died. This was God's own declaration. God revealed His judgment against the man of sin by taking his life. God revealed that Joseph Tkach, Sr. was indeed the "son of perdition"— "the man of sin." By this, God also revealed that the world had entered a countdown for the end-time. This was finally the time, after nearly 6,000 years, for end-time prophecies to begin being fulfilled, starting with the fulfillment of the First Seal of Revelation. That process began on the same day Joseph Tkach, Sr. gave his apostatizing sermon, but it was God who had to later reveal it.

This prophetic fulfillment of God destroying the man of sin is the very event that declared—**illuminated**—the coming of Joshua the Christ to God's own people. The time for his return had now come and was **no longer being held back** from view to the Church. The time had come; the countdown to Christ's coming had arrived!

In scripture, the **number 40** is used as a declaration from God of His **judgment**. Because of mankind's rebellion in the days of Noah, God's judgment was carried out through a flood that lasted for 40 days and nights. Another example is in the account of what happened to Israel after God had delivered them out of Egypt. Because of their rebellion right after being delivered from slavery in Egypt, God extended their time and let them wander in the wilderness for 40 years before He allowed them into the promised land.

Joseph Tkach, Sr., who was seen as having been set in authority in God's Church, directly under Christ, declared that the seventh-day Sabbath was no longer a commandment for God's people. Is it any wonder then that because of his rebellion, God gave a judgment upon him that would be accomplished in exactly **40 Sabbaths**—to the hour—from the very Sabbath when he declared the Sabbath day itself was no longer relevant?

So the first thing God revealed to His Church concerning a countdown was the matter of the importance of the period of the 280 days (**40 x 7**) that revealed His judgment, where **40** is used prophetically for **"judgment"** and **7** is used to show God's purpose being **"complete."**

When Joseph Tkach, Sr. gave his sermon that polluted and desecrated God's Temple—the Church of God— the prophesied "Abomination of Desolation" of the spiritual Temple of God became fulfilled. This prophecy of Paul concerning the Apostasy had begun. God revealed a very specific judgment that He had personally executed upon the man of sin, this son of perdition. Exactly 280 days later, **God took his life.**

God Revealed His Remnant Church

By God revealing the identity of the man of sin to His people and that an apostasy had occurred in the Church, He was also beginning to reveal to His people the identity of His remnant Church. This would be the organization through whom He would continue to work until Christ returned. It would be the organization that would be the continuation of His Church—the Church of God.

As it was explained, once the Apostasy came upon God's Church, it scattered and soon had splintered into over 600 organizations. For the first 3 ½ years after the Apostasy, there was much confusion that had gripped God's people who had become so dispersed. It was unclear where or through whom God was working, if indeed He even was.

During the era of Philadelphia, God revealed much truth through Herbert Armstrong. These truths in themselves revealed the truth that it was Herbert Armstrong who was chosen to be God's apostle to His Church. God always establishes truth given to His people through His prophets and apostles.

Truth can only come from God and has to be given by Him. Mankind cannot come to the truth of God on its own. God makes it clear that He is building a spiritual temple and has been doing so on the foundation of what He has established through His prophets and apostles, with Joshua the Christ being the chief cornerstone. It is the fact that much truth was given through Herbert Armstrong, in a final age of mankind, when God's truth on earth had become nearly nonexistent, that proves who God's apostle was during the Philadelphian Era.

After the Apostasy, God once again began revealing more truth to His Church. It was truth that was not known until God gave it. It is through the giving of so much new truth that God began to reveal where His Church was continuing in the midst of all that had become scattered, and through whom He was working. It is through the many truths that God has revealed since the Apostasy that He has revealed who the apostle is through whom He is working until Christ's coming.

When Herbert Armstrong was fulfilling the commission God had given him to carry the good news of the soon-coming Kingdom of God into all the world, the Church of God took on a unique name as an organization. It carried the name of the Worldwide Church of God, an organization that no longer served as God's Church once the Apostasy came to pass.

Of the hundreds of organizations scattered after the Apostasy, God raised up one that would continue to serve His Church until Christ returns. This Church became established by God on the day of Pentecost in 1998, exactly 3 ½ years (1260 prophetic days) after the Apostasy. The organization's name is the Church of God – Preparing for the Kingdom of God (PKG). The name reflects the commission that God has given to it.

Once again, as with Herbert Armstrong during the era of Philadelphia, God began revealing new truth to His Church. No other group that was scattered after the Apostasy knows or teaches these truths.

These groups have not even accepted a truth that should be obvious to them all—that the Church experienced the prophesied Apostasy recorded by Paul in II Thessalonians 2. They have not believed that

Joe Tkach, Sr. was the man of sin, the son of perdition. They do not believe that God rejected the era of Laodicea because all had become spiritually lukewarm just as Christ gave to John to prophesy. These do not believe that the Apostasy reveals the truth about what Christ said would happen to the Church in that all the stones of the temple—the Church of God—would be cast down before his coming.

God said that in the end-time He would raise up a remnant of His scattered Church that would continue on to Christ's second coming as the King of kings. To raise up this group He began revealing many new truths to it. In the beginning, those truths were about the revelation of who the man of sin was and that the Church had experienced an apostasy and at that time was spewed from God's mouth—rejected by Him. God further revealed that what Christ had declared about an abomination of desolation that would defile the temple of God—His Church—did indeed happen just as he said it would.

As a result of these truths being revealed, God built upon the understanding of those events to reveal even more. It was shown how the first four Seals of Revelation paralleled the end-time prophecies of Matthew 24 that were about great destruction that took place in God's Church due to the Apostasy.

Many other new truths then followed as God worked to restore and spiritually revitalize His Church once more – a Church that would be fully prepared for Christ's coming. It was revealed that exactly 144,000 who had been chosen over the past 6,000 years would return with Christ and that no others would return with him, as some believe that an innumerable multitude will also return with Christ.

There are many ideas in various groups of traditional Christianity about what and who the Antichrist spoken of by John is all about. It is not about a world leader or some well-known religious leader in this world. God revealed to His remnant Church that this was prophetic about the man of sin—the son of perdition.

Furthermore, God revealed that He alone is Yahweh Elohim, and He alone has eternally existed, and that Christ has not eternally existed, but that his life began when he was born of Mary into physical life. Only God's remnant Church knows this truth concerning both God the Father and Joshua the Christ.

There are many other truths that God has continued to give to His remnant Church and these truths are witness—testimony—from God of who His one true Church is in this end-time. There is a list of those additional truths given since the Apostasy which are listed on the Church website (cog-pkg.org) in the Publications section in an article entitled "57 Truths."

The first three of those truths were all that remained toward the end of the Sardis Era when God began to raise up Herbert Armstrong to be His apostle to His Church. God then began to reveal and eventually restore 18 truths to His Church during that new era of Philadelphia.

Truths given through Herbert Armstrong were testimony, evidence, and proof that he was God's apostle. In like manner, the additional truths given since are evidence that the Church of God—PKG is indeed God's Church and that He is now working through an apostle to prepare His people for the return of His Son, Joshua the Christ, to become King over the nations of this world.

Chapter 7

THE SEVEN THUNDERS A PRELUDE TO WWIII

THE FALL OF THE UNITED STATES is the beginning of the end of mankind's time to govern itself. It needs to be repeated that in this final period of the end-time, God is going to allow mankind to come to the brink of self-annihilation.

Finally, after 6,000 years of self-rule, God is revealing to mankind that it cannot successfully rule itself. Mankind's way has only led to power struggles, divisiveness, domination, corruption, excessive taxation, economic hegemony, prejudicial governance, biased judiciaries, and horrifying wars. That is the true history of mankind!

It is toward the very end of this period of time, just before mankind would annihilate itself, that God is going to intervene and stop that self-destruction. Through the fast advancement of modern technology, mankind now has the ability to end all life on earth. Yet God will not allow it.

It is at this point that God will intervene to change the world from its own rule to that of His rule. Before that kind of change can happen, a change in **the attitude and spirit** of mankind must first take place. That is why the prophetic events of this end-time are designed to **humble** mankind so that people can begin to be taught the only way to real peace.

The title of this book, *The Fall of the United States,* emphasizes the moment when the world will be awakened to the start of another world war. This will be when the events of the first five Trumpets of Revelation are coming to pass. It is about the complete collapse of the wealthiest and most powerful nation the world has ever known.

Although the nations of the world bring about the cataclysmic events of a world war, for which they are fully responsible, there are yet other prophetic events that precede this obliterating war. Those events have already been happening for several years now and they will continue escalating right up to when this final war begins. After it begins, then these will intensify far more, right up to the end.

As with the Seven Seals and Seven Trumpets of Revelation, these events were also spoken of by John in the Book of Revelation, but he was told not to record what those events were. The reason for this is because it was to be given later in the end-time. These events are known as the Seven Thunders.

Seven Thunders

It has already been described how the Sixth Seal of Revelation was opened on 9/11. Additionally, that same day also marked the beginning of prophetic "thunder." It was the very first rumbling of the First Thunder of Revelation.

There are Seven Thunders, and each Thunder will itself have multiple thunders—rumblings—that will occur throughout this entire period of time.

Thunder is the perfect analogy for describing the events of this prophetic period of a worldwide storm that has been brewing since 9/11 with ever-growing thunderous sounds and shakings. Often, as a great storm is approaching, thunder accompanies it and becomes louder the closer it gets.

Prophetic Thunders have been sounding for many years now, gaining in frequency and intensity. However, once this book has been published, those Thunders will become even more dramatic in power.

The prophet John heard the sound of Seven Thunders but was not allowed to write what he heard, therefore these were not recorded in the book of Revelation.

*"Now when the **seven thunders** sounded, I was about to write, but then I heard a voice from heaven saying to me, '**Seal up** the things which the seven thunders sounded, and **do not write them**.' The angel whom I saw standing on the sea and on the land then raised up his hand toward heaven and gave oath in Him who lives forever and ever, who created heaven and the things that are in it, the earth and the things that are in it, and the sea and the things that are in it, that there should be time <u>no longer</u>* [Gk.- "any further"]. *But in the days of the sounding of the seventh angel,* **when he shall begin to sound,** *the* **mystery of God <u>should be finished</u>** [Gk.- "shall or should be completed, fulfilled, accomplished"], *as He declared to His servants the prophets"* (Revelation 10:4-7).

So as John was about to write what he heard, God told him that it was to be sealed up. That was accomplished by John simply not writing about it. This is exactly like what God told the prophet Daniel when he wanted to know what the prophecies that he had been given were all about. God told him that the words of the prophecy were to be closed up and sealed until the end-time.

The reason God spoke to John in this manner is that He had pre-determined that John would have a counterpart whom He would give to proclaim these Thunders at the end-time—at the time when these would begin to become fulfilled. The specifics of the Seven Thunders were left for this end-time in order to be declared and revealed by God's end-time prophet and apostle who would be John's counterpart.

There are only two people whom God has used to fulfill the role of both a prophet and an apostle. Their role as prophets would be to declare explicit and chronological prophecies for the end-time. John was given to record those prophecies, but he did not know what they meant. God is using John's counterpart to reveal fully what those prophecies mean. Both individuals were also given the role of apostles, as God revealed truth through them that was to become established in His Church.

These Thunders, that John had not been allowed to write about, first began to be declared in this end-time, back in 2006, in a book entitled *2008 – God's Final Witness*. Those Thunders had never been announced before that book. Everything else that John concerning the Seven Seals, Seven Trumpets, and the Seven Last Plagues had been declared by an angel, but the Seven Thunders were not.

Indeed, a worldwide storm has been brewing, and the warning of that approaching storm has been contained in seven distinctive types of prophetic Thunder. However, the world has not known what to listen to in order to identify those Thunders. Nevertheless, these have still been sounding even though the world has been deaf to them.

For the very few who have been able to hear the thunder, it has served to help them become better prepared and alert to what is coming. These Thunders have been a prelude to the actual storm that is now almost here—a prelude to WWIII. Once that war begins, these Thunders will be magnified many times over, just like thunder continues once the storm arrives. Remember, the purpose of these Thunders is to amplify the ability to humble mankind.

Those Thunders that were first revealed in the book, *2008 – God's Final Witness*, will be repeated and updated here.

This thundering is like the analogy given of a pregnant woman with labor pain. All Seven Thunders will increase in intensity as this great end-time storm approaches, but one type of thunder will be more pronounced than another—from one great labor pain to another. Each type of Thunder will continue to rumble, but at certain times one will be much louder than all the others.

The First Thunder

September 11, 2001, was a day that thundered so loudly that the very mention of it is recognized all over this world. Mention that day anywhere on earth and people know what happened. However, people do not yet recognize the real meaning behind why this day is so vastly important.

What happened in New York, Washington D.C., and a field in Pennsylvania is not what is most important about this day. What happened on a Biblical plane is of far greater significance!

This date became etched in the minds of people throughout the world, and so did another word. The association to that date began to put the thought of **terrorism** into the minds of all who had 9/11 etched into their memory.

The greater reality for that day is its Biblical significance because it is prophetic in nature. The prophetic symbolism of these events is the very thing that will lead to the beginning fulfillment of the Seven Trumpets of Revelation and a full-blown World War III.

Terrorism and war are not new to mankind. This has been the way of man for thousands of years, but this terrorism is part of end-time prophecy, and this is what makes it different from all other acts of war.

#1: The **First Thunder** is the beginning **terror of war** for the end-time. This is war that is prophetic for the end-time.

Most of these Thunders contain things that have occurred on the earth in one way or another ever since man's beginning. Terrorism is not new. Wars are not new. But what is happening now, in these Seven Thunders, is new because it is part of end-time prophecy. All these things will lead directly into the final period of great physical tribulation on all the earth with ever-increasing intensity.

The success of al-Qaeda's terrorist attack on 9/11 was the beginning of the First Thunder. This was the very day the Sixth Seal of the Book of Revelation was opened. So the events of this day have very great Biblical and prophetic significance!

Terrorism is war, and war is terror. An American Civil War General, William T. Sherman, is recognized for a famous quote, in which he said, "War is hell." Any way you address it, war reigns terror wherever it strikes.

Since 9/11, we have seen more rumblings from the "terror of war." These rumblings have been continuous and striking with far greater power than that of 9/11. That is especially the case when simply looking at the kind of destruction and loss of life alone that has occurred since then that is in direct response to the events of that day. Look at what has happened since the description of these Thunders was first published.

The United States began bombing Afghanistan on October 7, 2001, in what was called Operation Enduring Freedom. However, in much of the world, this stirred up greater resentment and hatred toward Americans more than it produced any promotion of freedom.

The U.S. called an end to that war on August 30, 2021. The manner in which this was done caused even greater bitterness in the world toward the U.S. This even caused her allies to feel betrayed, which has, in turn, created far deeper distrust than ever.

So rather than freedom, this terror of war produced far greater death than 9/11. The Watson Institute of Brown University in its publication, *Costs of War*, states that U.S. troops killed in the fighting in Iraq and Afghanistan by the end of 2019 had reached over 7,000. Several hundred allied soldiers were also killed. Even more shockingly, the paper also concluded that as a result of psychological wounds, over 30,177 service members and veterans of the post-9/11 wars have committed suicide.

The total number of U.S. soldiers who died as a direct result of terrorism since 9/11 is more than 12 times as many who died on that day.

The paper further stated that approximately 177,000 national military and police allies from Afghanistan, Pakistan, Iraq, and Syria had died.

Under their "Summary of Findings," this publication states that, in total, "At least 929,000 people have died due to direct war violence, including armed forces on all sides of the conflicts, contractors, civilians, journalists, and humanitarian workers. Many times more have died indirectly in these wars, due to ripple effects like malnutrition, damaged infrastructure, and environmental degradation." In addition, "38 million people have been displaced by the post-9/11 wars in Afghanistan, Pakistan, Iraq, Syria, Libya, Yemen, Somalia, and the Philippines." These are the direct effects of the terror of war in this end time!

THE FALL OF THE UNITED STATES 185

These are only a few of all the conflicts in the world that have contributed to the terrors of war that have occurred since the First Thunder sounded on 9/11. The reality of this should have brought about a noticeable lessening of pride and haughtiness that exists in people and nations, but it has only humbled a very few so far.

The Second Thunder
There is another rumbling that has been increasing in intensity over the past couple of years. It is the direct result of a marked increase in destructive power being unleashed by the earth itself.

#2: The **Second Thunder** is the increasing destruction generated by **earthquakes**.

There have always been earthquakes and very destructive ones throughout the world, but this Thunder will become far more prominent before this end-time is over. A part of the destruction that comes from earthquakes also produces volcanic and tsunami activity.

One of the more pronounced events to follow 9/11 was the 2004 Indian Ocean earthquake, known by the scientific community as the Sumatra-Andaman earthquake. According to the United States Geological Survey, the earthquake and its tsunami killed more than 283,100 people, making it one of the deadliest disasters in modern history.

The Third Thunder
In terms of an economic impact on property, and even loss of life, one of the most destructive forces that is taking a dramatic turn for the worse is being caused by an escalating change in our weather.

Some will argue that the current weather conditions reflect normal cycles of change over time. It is true that the weather follows cycles. Yes, there have always been times of intensity when destructive powers have been unleashed. However, now is different because the destructiveness and change in weather patterns is going to continue to increase dynamically, not following normal patterns.

Some regions will experience abnormally large amounts of rainfall, while others, that normally receive large amounts, will receive little to none. The consequences of this will be a marked increase in flooding and mudslides in some areas, while other areas will experience growing problems with drought, which as we have seen in recent years, results in widespread fires and extensive damage to property, homes, livestock, and crops.

Further, some regions will experience normal amounts of rain, but it will come at the wrong time to benefit agriculture. Too much cold and too much heat at the wrong time will also add to this destructive power. Those who have their livelihood in agriculture have always had to contend with such things, but these conditions will become worse.

#3: The **Third Thunder** is the growing **destructiveness from weather**.

The destruction from hurricanes, cyclones, tornadoes, excessive heat, cold, drought, flooding, and wind will only continue to escalate in magnitude of power and frequency.

Just in hurricanes alone, it is reported that twelve of the sixteen most devastating and costly storms to ever hit the United States have occurred since 2001.

From the publication *Business Insider*, dated September 10, 2018, there is an article entitled, "The 16 most destructive hurricanes in U.S. history," with the top three most notable and costliest ones: 3rd—Hurricane Sandy 2012 at $71.4 billion, 2nd—Hurricane Katrina 2005 at $108 billion, and 1st—Hurricane Harvey 2017 at $125 billion.

Since 2001, there has been a large number of fatalities in this thundering, and the economic loss since then has been over $420 billion just from hurricanes alone, which also adds to the next Thunder.

The Fourth Thunder
Each one of the previous prophetic Thunders will have an impact on the Fourth Thunder. The result of nations fighting terrorism and engaging in war, along with the devastation caused by earthquakes

and the increasing impact from destructive weather, will place a greater burden on a crushing global economy.

#4: The **Fourth Thunder** is **global economic upheaval.**

The world is entering into a time of final upheaval for the global economy. The stock market cannot continue its masquerade of being healthy and robust while being falsely propped up by a "positive spin" that is filled with false confidence, pseudo-exuberance, and creative forecasting. The day of reckoning is now on the world's doorstep. Many deeply-felt pangs of panic will reverberate throughout the world as we draw nearer to a huge global crash.

Some nations are already indicating a shift from the dollar to the euro as a better assurance for future stability. Although many in the United States scoff at such a possibility, that is precisely what the trend will continue to be as confidence in the dollar continues to wane.

With corporate scandals and corruption on an alarming rise, along with a loss in confidence in a sick economy, the United States is drawing nearer to an economic implosion. Strong warning about this was given when these Thunders were first published in 2006 in a book entitled, *2008 – God's Final Witness.*

Later, in 2008, the world was confronted with the real state of the economy. However, God did not allow it to fully collapse at that time because other important prophetic events were not yet fully set in place for Him to allow such a global event to occur at that time.

Quantitative easing and other sleight of hand maneuvering have extended the inevitable. Yet unsound government interference and manipulation along with continued corporate and other financial market gimmickry has only worsened since 2008. The reality, in the long run, is that there will be no bouncing back from the cancerous greed that has nearly choked all life out of free-market capitalism.

Add to all these economic woes the problem of trade deficits, money manipulation, volatile oil markets, disastrous results of a worldwide pandemic, rampant inflation, a list of other global ailments; and you have a sure formula for global economic upheaval, the likes of which this world has never seen.

The world has experienced times of great economic upheaval, but it has always bounced back in one way or another. This time, there will be no bouncing back because the world will experience a complete economic meltdown to a level that not even the hoarding of gold and silver will solve. Indeed, the stability of the global economy is on very shaky ground.

The Fifth Thunder
The next three Thunders have a duality that includes both the Church of God and the world.

#5: The **Fifth Thunder** is **death**.

Death has always been part of mankind's experience with temporary mortal life, and the first three Thunders obviously include a marked increase in death from an escalation in worldwide devastation. However, this Thunder is in addition to these and will occur in a specific manner.

In small part, the Fifth Thunder has already begun within the Church of God that was scattered after the Apostasy. The world will be fully unaware of the first phase of this Thunder because they do not know God's Church. However, the Church that was scattered will become fully aware of its reality!

This Fifth Thunder is divided into three specific phases of death. **(1) The first phase** is death within the Church of God that was scattered. It will be specifically about a marked increase in the death of its leadership (the ministry). **(2) The second phase** will be a sudden escalation in the death of notable people in the world. **(3) The third phase** will be a sudden escalation of death in the world from plagues. Remember, these Thunders were first published in 2006.

(1) This first phase of this Fifth Thunder has already begun in a small way upon the Church of God that was scattered, after the prophesied apostasy. This phase of the Fifth Thunder is given as a strong chastening to those who have been scattered so that they might potentially be shaken from the deep spiritual sleep where they so proudly rest.

Sadly, spiritual arrogance and pride are so deeply entrenched in the hearts and minds of those who have been refusing to hear God's warnings, that many will not be able to humble themselves enough to accept what God's end-time prophet and apostle has been telling them. They will not acknowledge his words, which are from God to them, because they do not like the way they are being addressed or who it is that God is using. Instead, these individuals will stubbornly cling to their own ideas of how they believe God should teach them through their own organizations.

This specific phase of the Fifth Thunder is given in order to spiritually awaken those who will listen, who became scattered after the Apostasy. All who fail to accept what God is revealing will die in the final tribulation and be awakened to judgment at the end of the 1,000 years of God's reign on earth. After God had delivered the Israelites out of Egypt, He prevented tens of thousands who had rebelled from entering the promised land. God can easily prevent a few thousand from the scattered Church from entering a new age that they have longed to see.

This Thunder has already been ongoing in these scattered groups for several years now, but they seem oblivious to it. In the book, *2008 – God's Final Witness*, when this Thunder was first revealed, there is more that is stated about this that is directed to the Church that became scattered. However, no one listened then, and perhaps no one will listen now, even though they have been given the opportunity to do so many times.

The sound of this Thunder soon will be intensified by the deaths in the leadership of the Philadelphia, Restored, Living, and the United church organizations, as well as several other prominent church organizations that became scattered.

(2) The second phase of death will be upon notable people in the world. It will begin small and increase in intensity as all the Thunders do. These notable people will include political leaders and well-known entertainment and sports figures, and it will include notable religious figures within the various religions of the world.

(3) The third phase of death will come from epidemics and pandemics in the world.

The worldwide death toll from COVID-19 has already surpassed 5.5 million people and such things will only increase.

Again, this same message was published in 2006.

These three phases are not about an order in which these will occur, but that there are three distinct phases of thunder that comprise this Fifth Thunder.

The Sixth Thunder
This Thunder also concerns both the Church and the world. The rumbling started with the publication of my first book, *The Prophesied End-Time*. Then, in 2006, with the second book, *2008 – God's Final Witness*, that Thunder became louder as it made known that I am John's counterpart.

The larger portion of God's Church that has remained scattered since the Apostasy has ridiculed such a possibility. They especially take delight in the fact that Christ did not return in 2012 as I began proclaiming in 2008. None of them have listened to why God did not allow Christ to return at that time and why his return was moved forward.

This alteration in the sequence of end-time events is used by many in the Church that had been scattered and by some in the world to be their evidence that I am a false prophet and not an apostle of God. Their greater "proof" that I am not who I say is in how I was convicted of income tax evasion and sentenced to three years in a federal prison camp.

People can be very quick to believe what they want. And so it is that very few have ever believed that I may be innocent. However, as events move closer to the start of WWIII, many of those same people are going to see more clearly how poorly mankind governs itself and that includes its judicial systems.

Many choose to believe in their judicial systems. They believe that judges are just, unbiased, and not political, but that is not true. Even prosecution is far more about winning than it is about justice. Thankfully, God is going to change every system of mankind's government.

The growing manifestation of proof of God's end-time prophet and apostle being the spokesman of His two end-time witnesses is a Thunder that will become powerfully stronger all the way up until the very return of Joshua the Christ.

#6: The **Sixth Thunder** is the growing **revelation of God's two end-time witnesses**. It reveals that God's current prophet and apostle to His Church is the spokesman of God's two end-time prophets—the spokesman of His two end-time witnesses.

Indeed, the gradual revelation of who God's two witnesses are before Christ's return is what this Thunder is about. Part of that has already begun, but there is much more that is yet to be revealed that not even God's own Church knows at this time. All that these two will fulfill and how they do so will become manifest by God's own hand and in His timing.

It is right after John wrote about the Thunders that God spoke to him about these two witnesses.

"*I* [**speaking of God**] *will give to my two witnesses that they shall prophesy a thousand two hundred and sixty days, clothed in sackcloth. These are the two olive trees, and the two candlesticks standing on earth in the presence of God so that if anyone chooses to hurt them, fire proceeds out of their mouth and devours their enemies. So if anyone chooses to do them wrong, for doing so they will die. These have power to shut heaven, that it not rain in the days of their prophecy, and have power over waters to turn them to blood, and to strike the earth with any blow, as often as they choose*" (Revelation 11:3-6).

The matter of what was to be accomplished in the period of 1,260 days is believed to have already been fulfilled. The matter of being clothed in sackcloth is about a time of humility they were to endure. The fire that proceeds out of the mouth is symbolic of what is spoken and the consequences that follow. That which is stated in these verses will not become known to most until it is explained to them after Christ has returned.

This Sixth Thunder will grow louder as the events described in the previous Thunders continue to unfold with ever-increasing intensity, proving the validity of what has been written, and therefore, that such revelation could have only come from God.

The Seventh Thunder
This last Thunder, as with the previous two Thunders, concerns the Church and the world.

#7: The **Seventh Thunder** is **the accelerated revelation of God** to mankind.

This book has explained how mankind has never really known God and that there is great confusion and contradiction in religious beliefs concerning Him. It has also been shown that through the entire time of mankind on earth only a little more than 144,000 people have truly and deeply known God.

God has only revealed Himself to a very few throughout the past six millennia. Those few who did come to know God were rejected by the rest of mankind. The prophets and apostles were rejected, and because of that, mankind was not able to know God. God taught His ways to only one nation beginning in Moses' time, but even most of that nation rejected His words.

The history of mankind (the true witness of mankind) is that it does not want God's ways. People have not wanted God to govern their lives. So, in the past 6,000 years, God has called a very few into a special relationship with Him in order to be taught and trained for a future world-ruling government—the Kingdom of God.

Much of this has already been explained, but it needs to be understood that God is getting ready to do what He has never done before. God is getting ready to reveal Himself to the entirety of mankind. This revelation too is similar to thunder.

This Thunder has already begun to sound within God's Church. It is about to sound powerfully throughout the world as the other Thunders grow louder. Then once the events of the Trumpets begin and all the remaining end-time events that God has prophesied unfold, this Thunder will become deafening.

God's revelation to mankind will continue to accelerate as we draw closer to the end of man's rule on earth and the coming of Joshua the Christ when God's rule begins. Mankind has not known God, but all this is beginning to change.

Mankind Must Change
The world is about to begin experiencing the worst times of suffering and destruction it has ever known! God has warned mankind of this period known as the "end-time." Actually, the vast majority of prophecy throughout the Bible is about the end-time. Because of mankind's physically created existence and the human nature that this produces, God has always known what mankind would do through the ages. But that is exactly part of His plan.

In that plan, God allotted 6,000 years for mankind to choose its own ways to live life. Except for a very few whom God selected and worked with over the millennia, mankind, as a whole, has been blindly chasing after its own wants and desires. This has led to endless wars and destruction that have plagued our history.

Mankind's horrible history is all part of a learning experience. We can learn from our mistakes, but mankind has not yet learned that it cannot govern itself. We have 6,000 years of proof that shows exactly what our own self-rule has been able to produce. God's plan has always been to allow mankind to fail because there is no other way it can learn this greatest lesson in life.

Yes, God has allowed for failure, but not because He wants to see us fail. It is because, sadly, that is the **only way** we will finally begin to listen to Him—to begin to see that His way is vastly superior to that of our own and the only way that truly works.

God has a purpose—a plan—wherein He desires to give mankind life that extends beyond temporary mortal life to that of everlasting life. But with our track record, why would He? And what would the purpose be? So that there could be everlasting wars and suffering? Everlasting destruction? God's way is about peace. Destruction, drama, and divisiveness are the way of selfishness—the way of Satan, and that has been the way of mankind.

Mankind's way is that of selfishness and that is why our self-rule has never worked.

So in order for God to fulfill His plan for mankind, He has to have willing participants. The problem is that mankind, at this point in time, is still in denial of its destructive ways. On the contrary, mankind is filled with pride.

Today this prideful attitude is worse than ever before. That is in large part due to advances in science, physics, and mathematics that the world has seen develop over the past century. Never before in the history of mankind have we seen so much progress that has in so many ways benefited mankind.

Consider the evidence that can easily be seen in world population figures. It is estimated that from 1500 to 1800, the world population grew from nearly 600 million to just under 1 billion. However, today there are now approximately 8 billion people living on earth! It took 5,800 years to reach 1 billion people and only 200 years to reach 8 billion.

Although mankind has benefited from such advancements, it has also misused these to a point that now reveals the potential for such destruction on earth, which could lead to extinction.

God is the one who has allowed the population to grow by such leaps and bounds. He is the one who gave mankind the knowledge to be able to make such advances. Yet mankind has taken full credit to itself which reflects the depth of its distorted pride.

It should be clear by now that mankind, when left to its own self-rule, will always cause destruction. It is inevitable.

So God is going to allow mankind to come face to face with its own self-annihilation. The truth is that the **only way** to stop this self-destructiveness is for God to intervene and stop mankind from governing itself by instead establishing His own government—His own Kingdom to reign.

That is why mankind must first be **humbled** in order to achieve a genuine willingness to begin to truly listen to God, exactly in the manner that God directs. Indeed, a change must begin to take place within mankind, and there is only one way for that change to begin to take effect.

Mankind is so deeply entrenched in its own ways, so deeply filled with human pride, that it will not accept what is actually from God. People who see themselves as being religious or Christian do not see themselves in this manner. Yet it would be good to consider what God says about our very nature.

God states that "there is a way that seems right to a person, but the ends thereof are the ways of death" (Proverbs 14:12). This states well the attitude and spirit of mankind. It is just natural within the mind to believe that one's own ideas, thoughts, and judgments are right. We tend to simply think that we are right and that others who think differently are wrong. This is a basic result of human pride, for only God can tell us what is truly right and what is wrong.

As a simple example, consider all the thousands of divisions in different denominations, and non-denominational churches in traditional Christianity. Those who support and belong to a specific one have a belief that they are right, and they generally believe others are wrong (or less knowledgeable and less truthful) in matters concerning doctrine and teaching about God and Christ.

Yet God declares that there is only **one faith, one truth, one church,** and **one way** of life to be lived. The problem is that mankind is filled with pride—with belief that it is right, justified, and/or more insightful than others.

God further states that "the carnal mind is enmity [opposed to, an enemy] against God, for it is not subject to the law of God and neither indeed can be" (Romans 8:7). Mankind resists laws that are contrary to what it actually wants. This includes resisting the laws and ways of God.

It is because of such thinking that mankind has not listened to the prophets and apostles of God throughout the past 6,000 years. We now live in a time where God is going to address this. God is not going to allow this to continue any longer!

That is why this was alluded to at the beginning of this chapter. A paragraph needs to be repeated here that was addressing the moment in time when God will intervene to establish His government over mankind.

"It is at this point that God will intervene to change the world from its own rule to that of His rule. Before that kind of change can happen, a change in **the attitude and spirit** *of mankind must first take place. That is why the prophetic events of this end-time are designed to* **humble** *mankind so that people can begin to be taught the only way to real peace."*

There is absolutely no other meaningful and lasting way to begin to bring about a complete change in **the attitude and spirit** of mankind except for God to allow for end-time events to happen in the exact manner they are said to be fulfilled.

The prophetic events revealed in the Seven Seals, the Seven Trumpets, the Seven Thunders, and Seven Last Plagues are all designed to help people make this change—a change from pride, with reliance upon self, to that of humility and looking to God to lead them. All this is necessary so that mankind can begin to learn the only true ways that produce real peace and lead to everlasting life—life that will be filled with real and lasting happiness, fulfillment, love, and true peace forever.

Chapter 8

GOD'S HOLY DAYS REVEAL HIS PLAN

THIS BOOK HAS FOCUSED UPON those things that are leading up to a third world war. Mankind's history has been riddled with wars over the past 6,000 years. But now, we are at the threshold of entering a new age where there will be no more wars—ever!

Although scholars and educators debate how long mankind has been on earth, God reveals that we are now at the end of 6,000 years of self-rule. He then reveals that we are about to enter a new and exciting age in the next 1,000 years where His Kingdom is going to reign on earth over all nations.

During this age that is about to be ushered in, there will not be any form of manmade government that will rule. God is going to remove all forms of human socialism, totalitarianism, communism, oligarchies, aristocracies, dictatorships, democracies, and any other type of human devised government.

Through the millennia, the world has not known why God created mankind or what His plan is for having done so. Yet the very thing that mankind has refused to do, not observing God's weekly and annual Holy Days, is the very thing that reveals His plan and purpose for creating us. Mankind's insistence upon keeping its own holiday observances is the very thing that has kept it in darkness.

God's Holy Days reveal why mankind was given an initial temporary human life to live, and from the beginning, He has purposed that most all of mankind will actually live a physical life twice. He set aside 7,000 years for all humans to be born, and during this same period of time all will die. Yet He has set aside another 100 years that follow in which the vast majority of all who have ever lived will be resurrected to physical life once again.

God's Holy Days are exciting once a person comes to understand His purpose for such an incredible plan that spans 7,100 years. This time span of human existence is fully revealed through these Holy Days. Then what lies beyond is even more incredible and awesome beyond human imagination.

It was on Passover night of the day Christ would be put to death that he said to his Father in one of his prayers, "Your word is truth." God is the source of all that is true and absolute. This book has set out to illuminate truths that He has revealed through His Church.

The Reason for Religious Confusion

As this book has shown, there are many conflicting ideas about God and what His purpose is for the creation of human life. People are confused and often conflicted as to what really happens at death and what happens afterward. If there is life after death, then what kind of life is it?

Long ago, God gave mankind specific days that they were to observe and set aside for holy use and purpose. These days were given to reveal what His purpose and plan is for giving life to us and of what lies beyond death. Learning what these days are about leads to great understanding of God Himself and why He created physical, temporarily existing human life.

The reason most of humanity does not know or understand God and His plan and purpose for its existence is because it does not know about the observance of these days, and therefore, it cannot learn what these days reveal. That is the very reason God commanded mankind to keep and observe these days in the way He has shown so that it can come to truly know Him and His love for His creation.

Instead, mankind's nature is one of resisting God, and one of changing the truth about God to be something that is more palatable to a basic selfish nature that seeks to please self in whatever way it chooses to live life. Mankind does not want someone telling it how life should be lived, so it has worked to make religion and ideas about God easier for such a pride-filled nature to accept.

It seems so contrary to sound thinking that mankind would resist and reject God's instruction about how life should be lived. After all, He created us and He knows what will produce healthy relationships and peace, as well as happy and productive lives. Even a parent can see how one's own child can resist them as they work to teach them what they believe is best for them. God's wisdom and love are infinitely far beyond any human parent, and He **knows absolutely** what is best for us, yet He is resisted by His children.

The place to begin developing a true and meaningful relationship with God is in a person's obedience to the observance of His Sabbaths. The overview of God's plan is contained in the **weekly Sabbath**. Then, even more detail and specifics about that plan are contained in the **annual Sabbaths** that God also commanded to be observed in the manner He has shown.

Calendars Have Created Confusion
Before looking more closely at the command to keep the 7th day weekly Sabbath that follows Friday, the 6th day of the week, it is first needful to understand how calendars around the world vary concerning the placement of the days of the week. This has caused much confusion when it comes to someone trying to understand when to observe God's Sabbath.

Most people today don't know that calendars in most nations have been altered to be different than what God has shown concerning how to keep a yearly record of time. There has been great effort throughout history to change the cycle of the Biblical 7th day Sabbath. The motive behind this is what has been the catalyst for many in changing dates and times, although most people are unaware of this.

In recent history, nations have tried to standardize measurement systems throughout the world. Certainly, in this modern age of technology, manufacturing, and invention, it is good when standardization can be implemented, especially when focusing on worldwide commerce. Vast numbers of measuring systems have now been standardized. As an example, many nations have accepted the metric system, and yet some few still stubbornly refuse.

However, when it has come to the standardization for marking time, there has always been much confusion and disagreement. The United Nations in recent history has played a great part in all this. The International Organization for Standardization (ISO) set out to standardize the calendar in a publication called *ISO 8601:1988*, and as stated in the title, it was published in 1988. In this system, the weekly cycle established that Sunday is the seventh day of the week and Monday is the first day of the week.

Even before this change was made in 1988, several countries in Europe had already done so. What many have failed to understand in partaking of such standardization is that there has actually been a conspiratorial purpose that was involved in making these changes. This change by many has been masqueraded as an effort to establish a workweek where the first five days of the weekly cycle begin on Monday and end on Friday. Thus, the last two days of the weekly cycle are Saturday on the 6th day of the week, which would make Sunday the 7th day of the week.

Uniquely so, such a change gives all new generations the false assurance that when they read about God's Sabbath being on the seventh day of the week, then Sunday seems perfectly appropriate. Nevertheless, that would be a wrong assumption.

The timing for the weekly Sabbath of God has never been lost in Judaism. Christ concurred with the Jews concerning the fact that the day they were observing as the seventh day of the week was indeed the weekly Sabbath God had commanded. Before, and ever since that time, the Jews have always known the correct day for the observance of the seventh-day Sabbath.

Only a handful of nations today have a calendar that shows what is true, which corresponds to the true weekly cycle. On those calendars, Sunday is correctly listed as the first day of the week and Saturday is the seventh, which is the true time for the observance of God's Sabbath.

However, calendars that begin the weekly cycle with Monday are incorrect as they list Sunday as the seventh day, and yet this is the calendar that most nations use. Sunday is not the Biblical seventh day of the week. It is not God's 7th day Sabbath.

Changing the cycle of the week is nothing new. Throughout the world, it has been shuffled around many times over the centuries. However, whenever mankind engages in such practices, they work against what God established long ago. From the beginning of the counting of time on earth, God gave a basic weekly cycle of seven days within the months of each yearly cycle.

WEEKLY SABBATH
Our Creator

A true and right relationship with the One Eternal Self-Existing Almighty God can only begin as a person comes to the point that they will humble themselves before Him and observe the true weekly Sabbath that He commanded. No one can have a true relationship with God unless they observe and worship Him at the times that He has revealed they should. Anything else is disobedience and blasphemy against God.

This book has clearly shown times that are false and times that are true. God desires that His creation listen to Him and worship Him truthfully just as Christ said.

"But the hour is coming, and now is, when true worshipers will worship the Father in spirit and truth, for the Father seeks such to worship Him. God is spirit, and those who worship Him **must worship** *in spirit and* **in truth**" (John 4:23-24).

There is no other way to worship God. He requires it be done **in** truth. So as these verses show, there is a time coming when the world will begin to practice worshipping God in the truth. That will begin worldwide in the Millennium once Christ returns. Some few did begin such worship in Christ's time and continued doing so within God's Church once it became established in 31 AD.

God reveals the importance of the weekly Sabbath day and how it became established. It has everything to do with the very purpose for why He created mankind. The weekly Sabbath is to remind everyone of the very creation week in which mankind was created and that He is our Creator!

"Thus the heavens and the earth were finished, and all the multitude in them. On the seventh day God ended His work which He had done, and He rested on the seventh day from all His work which He had done. Then God blessed the seventh day, and <u>sanctified it</u> [**set apart for holy use and purpose**]*, because that on it He rested from all His work which **He created** and had done"* (Genesis 2:1-3).

Although it is explained in much greater detail in the literature from God's Church, many people think that this account of creation being spoken of in Genesis 1 and 2 is about the time when God created the earth and universe itself. That is simply not true. The earth was created at least hundreds of thousands of years, and perhaps even millions of years earlier. That should be easy to understand by scientific evidence itself.

Living creatures and plant life existed on the earth after it was first created, and there is an exceedingly vast amount of fossil evidence to this truth that exists all over this earth. However, people have not known that Satan at one time destroyed all life on earth after he had rebelled against God. The devastation he brought happened in an instant as he tried to destroy the earth itself.

Satan possessed the power to rip apart vast regions of the earth, shaking it off its normal orbit and rotation, as well as completely darkening the atmosphere itself. As a result of what happened so quickly within the atmosphere of the earth, temperatures dropped so low that plant life and animal life froze completely within an instant.

So when one begins to read about what God did during those first six days, it isn't describing the earth being created at that time. It had not been completely destroyed, so it was already there. It had remained uninhabitable for tens of thousands of years, and perhaps hundreds of thousands.

The context of Genesis 1 and 2 is one of the earth already being here and of God remolding and refashioning it so that life could be created upon it once again. Then, on that sixth and last day of creating, God created temporarily existing human life comprised of physical matter. As God reveals throughout scripture, this is the beginning stage in the pinnacle of His creation.

"For in six days the Lord made [**to do, accomplish, perform—His work**] *the heaven and the earth, the sea, and all that is in them, and rested the seventh day. Therefore the Lord blessed the Sabbath day, and sanctified it"* (Exodus 20:11).

The word here most often translated as "made" does not mean "create," but is a word that simply means "to do, to perform, to accomplish" work that one has set out to complete. God did, or accomplished, work that He set out to do within those six days, and then He rested on the seventh. He accomplished what He desired to do in the heaven (the atmosphere), the earth, and the waters of the earth. That is exactly what is being stated in this verse.

The verses that precede this are God's command that the weekly seventh day is to be observed as a Sabbath and kept holy—as the true holy day of the week. The first lesson that the weekly Sabbath day should teach us is what this verse states about God: He is the one who created life once again on the earth—**He is our Creator**. If one cannot grasp or believe that God created us, then why listen to anything He says; but if He is our Creator, then indeed we had better listen closely.

God Established Time

The weekly Sabbath is on the seventh day of the week, and it has been since the days of Adam and Eve. Just as the week was established in the creation week to be seven days, so was God's plan for mankind set to encompass a period of 7,000 years.

The first six days were set aside for mankind to do his own work, but the seventh day was God's time—the Sabbath. Mankind has also been allotted 6,000 years to live its own way, but like the seventh-day Sabbath, the last 1,000 years belong to God, and it is to be lived God's way! It is God's time!

Few believe the story about God delivering Noah into a new world. We live at a time when people find it even harder to believe that God is about to deliver mankind into a new world again, but this time where the Kingdom of God will rule all nations. Yet that time is exactly what is rapidly approaching! It will be the establishment of the Millennium—1,000 years of the Kingdom of God ruling over mankind.

It should be clear that God set apart the seventh day by personally sanctifying it. God didn't do that for any other day of the week. The Biblical definition for being sanctified means to be **set apart for holy use and purpose**. God didn't set apart the sixth day (Friday) or the first day (Sunday) for holy use and purpose. God's purpose from the beginning was to set apart the seventh day for all time, as a weekly Sabbath for mankind. God established the cycles for time, and He told mankind how to observe those cycles.

"Then God said, 'Let there be lights in the firmament [**Heb.—expanse**] *of the heaven* [**atmosphere, sky**] *to divide the day from the night, and let them be for signs* [**for the "marking" of time**], *and seasons* [**Heb.— appointed times**], *and for days, and years'"* (Genesis 1:14).

The Hebrew word for "seasons" means "appointed times," much like we speak today of appointments. Time is exact. God made the keeping of time a calculable factor of life. We can establish and set specific moments in time for any purpose we choose. From the very beginning of creation week, God established specific times that He personally set for mankind, which are to be appointments that we should keep with Him. The weekly Sabbath is one such appointment that never changes. Every seventh day mankind should keep this appointment with God! God even magnifies that point.

"The Eternal spoke to Moses, saying, 'Speak to the children of Israel, and say to them, The feasts [**Heb.— "appointed times" and not the Hebrew word for "feasts"**] *of the Eternal, which you shall proclaim to be holy convocations* [**Heb.—commanded assemblies**], *even these are*

My feasts [**Heb.—appointed times**]. *Six days work shall be done, but the seventh day is the Sabbath of rest, a holy* convocation [**Heb.—commanded assembly**]. *You shall do no work because it is the Sabbath of the Eternal in all your dwelling places. These are the feasts* [appointed times] *of the Eternal, even holy* convocations [**commanded assemblies**], *which you shall proclaim in their* seasons [**Heb.— appointed times**]. *In the fourteenth day of the first month at* even [**after sundown**] *is the Eternal's Passover. On the fifteenth day* [**an annual Holy Day—annual Sabbath**] *of the same month is the* Feast [**this word in Hebrew does mean "feast"**] *of Unleavened Bread unto the Eternal. Seven days you must eat unleavened bread'"* (Leviticus 23:1-6).

Traditional Christianity has tried to do away with this command concerning the seventh-day Sabbath and the annual Sabbaths that are listed here. They find no fault with nine of the ten commandments, but they have tried to "do away with" the fourth commandment that says, "Remember the Sabbath day, to keep it holy" (Exodus 20:8). Either they have sought to do away with the command of the Sabbath or they say the weekly Sabbath is now Sunday, but God said that observing the seventh-day Sabbath is a perpetual covenant! (Exodus 31:15-17).

The Catholic Church has altered this basic commandment in their listing of the Ten Commandments to read, "Remember to keep holy the LORD'S Day." Many in traditional Christianity have adopted this thinking about the Lord's Day which they recognize and teach as being Sunday, which is actually the first day of the week.

It was the Catholic Church in the 300s AD that first began to teach that the command to keep the Sabbath was changed to Sunday (the first day of the week)—the Lord's Day. The Roman Empire at that time even outlawed such an observance on the seventh day of the week. Most all of traditional Christianity since has accepted that change which the Catholic Church states was not a matter of scriptural authority, but of the authority of the Pope who declared it.

The Levitical system, with its laws regarding ceremonies and sacrifices, **was changed** through Joshua the Christ from what is commonly referred to as Old Testament times to New Testament times—the time of the establishment of God's Church. Christ's sacrifice did away with the necessity for observing animal sacrifices. It also did away with the need of this Levitical system that had a priesthood that served in the physical temple in all of its work concerning the service of the temple and in officiating in the sacrificial system.

Christ now serves as High Priest in the spiritual temple of God, and he fulfilled the sacrificial system, thus ending any need for it to continue. But Christ did not do away with the laws of God as many in traditional Christianity claim. He only did away with the laws pertaining to the Levitical system.

The law of God contained in the Ten Commandments has never been changed. The apostles and New Testament church observed the seventh-day Sabbath and annual Sabbaths. The apostle Paul, some thirty years after the death of Joshua the Christ, taught God's people the importance of observing the Sabbath, Passover, and Holy Days.

"For He spoke in a certain place of the seventh day in this way, 'And God did rest the seventh day from all His works'" (Hebrews 4:4).

Paul was explaining that Israel had refused to hear God's instruction and that they were incapable of doing so because they lacked the faith that is made possible only by receiving God's spirit. Paul was explaining that a specific day was set aside for people to hear God's voice—His instruction.

"Again, He limits a certain day [God "designated" or "limited" a specific day—He sanctified the seventh day], *saying through David, 'Today,' after such a long time; as it has been said, 'Today if you will hear His voice, do not harden your hearts'"* (Heb. 4:7).

Paul then got more specific as he explained even more about this to the Church. Traditional Christianity has not understood what Paul was teaching and they have even mistranslated this because they do not recognize the importance of this day that God commands to be kept, and they certainly do not grasp what it pictures.

"For if Joshua [**the Old Testament Joshua who led the children of Israel into the promised land**] *had given them rest, then He* [God]

would not afterward have spoken of another day. There remains therefore a Sabbath [**not the word for "rest" as most translate this, but this is the Greek word "Sabbatismos," which means Sabbath**] *for the people of God. For he who has entered* His rest [**into God's weekly seventh-day Sabbath rest**] *has himself also* ceased from his works [**ceased from his own carnal ways by seeking to live God's ways**] *as God did from His* [**when God rested on the seventh day from His work of creation**]. *Let us therefore be diligent to enter that rest* [**the rest of the Sabbath day**], *lest anyone fall according to the same example of disobedience"* (Heb. 4:8-11).

Paul was explaining that Joshua (who led Israel after Moses' death) was not able to give God's people the kind of rest that the keeping of the Sabbath pictures (foreshadows). After Israel had been in the wilderness for forty years and then led into the **physical promised land** by Joshua, they were not delivered into the time of rest which the seventh-day Sabbath actually pictures. Paul was explaining that God's people had not yet entered into that rest that is pictured in the last 1,000 years (the Millennium) where God's government will reign under the Messiah—the **spiritual rest** that begins during the Millennium that Joshua the Christ will lead God's people into.

Through observing God's weekly Sabbath, one is able to learn what God is teaching through such observance, even as one is taught weekly about God's plan and purpose. It is on the Sabbaths that God teaches His people and leads them into greater and continuing spiritual growth concerning His way of life.

The Sabbaths of God (weekly and annual) are an identification—a sign—of God's people because only His people know them and keep them in spirit and in truth as He commands.

"Sanctify [**set apart for holy use**] *my Sabbaths, and they will be a sign between Me and you, so that you may* **know** *that I am the Eternal your God"* (Ezekiel 20:20).

One must begin to observe God's commanded Sabbaths if one wants to truly come to **know** God.

The seventh day of each week is the day that people are to rest from their normal work routines because it is commanded that there is to be no customary work done on any Sabbath. This is also true with annual Sabbaths (High Days—annual Holy Days). No customary work is to be done on those days.

The weekly Sabbath and the annual Sabbaths are to be kept or set apart for holy use and purpose by those who observe them. That is what is meant when God said to **sanctify** His Sabbaths. Although the weekly Sabbath is always on the seventh day of the week, commanded annual observances can fall on different days of the week, except for one, which is Pentecost.

Sabbaths are set aside for people to focus more on God during those days. They are to come together with others in what God describes as holy convocations. This is time that is set aside for people to listen to what God's ministers teach them during those occasions. It is then that family and friends can spend more time together with others who also have set aside these times to observe.

PASSOVER
The First Annual Observance

It has been shown how the weekly Sabbath foreshadows a basic outline of God's 7,000-year plan for mankind. However, it is the annual commanded observances that fill in the details about that great plan and expound upon it far more fully.

God gave mankind a **weekly** "appointed time" and **annual** "appointed times" for us to keep with Him. The first annual observance is not an annual Sabbath, but it is to be observed first before any of the annual Holy Day Sabbaths. This appointed time that is commanded to be observed is **Passover.**

Passover is a commanded assembly that is observed after sunset at the beginning of the Passover day. It is not a Sabbath, and therefore, not a Holy Day or High Day, and work may be done on that day. It is unique in this regard as an annual observance of a commanded assembly.

God's plan of salvation begins with this day. Without receiving the Passover, Joshua the Christ, one cannot enter into a relationship with God. Accepting Joshua as our Passover and then observing Passover annually, allows one to begin the process of salvation that will produce the blessings God wants for everyone. The annual Holy Days that follow reveal that plan of salvation, but one cannot be included in that plan until the Passover is first received. This is the reason the Passover is the first annual observance.

The proper timing for observing God's Passover has been misunderstood, misrepresented, twisted, and deceitfully changed by many over the centuries. The right time for observing Passover has been attacked much like the timing of the weekly Sabbath has always been under attack.

It has been Satan's desire to deceive mankind into believing anything other than the truth about God's weekly Sabbath and the observance of Passover. The reason for this is that these observances are the basic foundation and the starting point for developing a true and right relationship with God.

It was the newly organized church that falsely called themselves Christian in the Roman Empire under Constantine that changed the weekly Sabbath observance from Saturday to Sunday. They then outlawed Passover, and its observance was replaced by an annual holiday called Easter.

God's Church has literature that gives a very exact and detailed accounting of the proper timing for Passover for any who might want to research this further. It can be found on the Publication page in an article entitled "The Timing of Passover" (www.cog-pkg.org).

The importance of the true timing for the observance of Passover is the primary means by which one can begin to know the true Messiah and to begin recognizing those things that are false. It is by this same means that you can identify false teachers, false religions, and any organization that condones false teachings. It should be noted that even Judaism, which should know better, observes Passover incorrectly by observing incorrect timing and teaching incorrect meaning and symbolism, which changed what God gave.

Leviticus 23 lists all of God's appointed times. The annual observances begin with Passover.

"In the fourteenth day of the first month at even is the Eternal's Passover" (Leviticus 23:5).

Many are familiar with the story of the exodus out of Egypt. It was at this time that God gave the Passover observance to the Israelites.

"The Eternal spoke to Moses and Aaron in the land of Egypt, saying, 'This month shall be unto you the beginning of months [it begins in the spring in the Northern Hemisphere]. *It shall be the first month of the year to you. Speak unto all the congregation of Israel, saying, "In the tenth day of this month they shall take to them every man a lamb, according to the household of their fathers, a lamb for a household… Your lamb shall be without blemish, a male of the first year. You shall take it out from the sheep, or from the goats"'"* (Exodus 12:1-3, 5).

This lamb without blemish was symbolic of Joshua the Christ who was without sin. The apostle Peter explained this to the Church by saying:

"Forasmuch as you know that you were not redeemed with corruptible things like silver and gold from your vain conduct received by tradition from your fathers, but with the precious blood of Christ, as of a lamb without spot" (1 Pet. 1:18-19).

The account in Exodus continues by showing what would symbolize the shed blood of the Messiah until he came to fulfill it. The Israelites were to kill a lamb for their Passover observance. They were to let the blood of the lamb spill out upon the earth and on that first observance in Egypt they were to take some of the blood and put it on the side post and upper doorposts of their homes. Christ's blood would also be spilled on the earth because he would fulfill the symbolism of these lambs, as the true Lamb of God.

"They shall take of the blood and strike it on the two side posts and on the upper door post of the houses, wherein they shall eat it" (Exodus 12:7).

"For I will pass through the land of Egypt this night and will strike all the firstborn in the land of Egypt of both man and animal. Against all

*the gods of Egypt I will execute judgment. I am the Eternal. The blood shall be to you for a token upon the houses where you are, and when I see the blood I will **pass over** you and the plague shall not be upon you to destroy you, when I strike the land of Egypt"* (Verses 12-13).

This pictures what Joshua the Christ would fulfill for mankind. He is our Passover and by His blood we can be saved from the penalty of sin, which is eternal death—a final judgment for all time.

"For the wages of sin is death, but the gift of God is eternal life through Joshua the Christ our Lord" (Romans 6:23).

The penalty for sins that are not forgiven is death—eternal judgment—eternal death from which one can never be resurrected to life again.

Joshua the Christ, the Son of God, the Lamb of God, was God's Passover sacrifice given to mankind whereby we can be saved from death. The penalty of death passes over us. This is where we must begin in God's plan of salvation. It begins with Joshua the Christ. All of us face the death penalty for our sins until we accept the sacrifice of Christ to remove them, as we repent of our sins. Only the blood of Christ, in our stead, can remove that penalty. This is God's Passover sacrifice for us.

"Therefore, just as through one man [Adam] sin entered into the world, and death through sin, and thus death spread to all men, because all have sinned" (Romans 5:12).

We must be forgiven of our sins in order to enter into a relationship with God the Father. Only upon repentance and baptism can we begin the process of being delivered from the pull of our own selfish human nature and the power of Satan that holds mankind in darkness and deception. This is God's plan of deliverance from spiritual Egypt.

"He [God] has delivered us from the power of darkness, and has translated us into the kingdom of His dear Son, in whom we have redemption through his blood, even the forgiveness of sins" (Colossians 1:13-14).

God's Church observes this annual memorial in the very same way Christ did, on Passover night, with his disciples after he had his last supper with them. Nearly 20 years after the death of Christ, the apostle Paul gave instruction to God's Church in Corinth regarding the importance of how to observe the annual Passover.

"For I have received from the Lord that which also I delivered unto you [how to observe Passover], *that the Lord Joshua on the same night* [the Passover night] *in which he was betrayed took bread, and when he had given thanks, he broke it, and said, 'Take and eat. This is my body, which is broken for you. Do this in remembrance of me'* [each year at Passover time]. *After the same manner also he took the cup after supper, saying, 'This cup is the new covenant in my blood. Do this, as often as you drink it, in remembrance of me.' For as often as you eat this bread, and drink this cup, you do show the Lord's death until he comes"* (1 Cor. 11:23- 26).

In this instruction to the Church (the spiritual Israel of God), Joshua the Christ instituted the symbols for Passover on the same night the Passover lamb was killed, roasted, and eaten. On the night of the fourteenth day of the first month, the Israelites were to observe this annual occasion by killing the lamb and eating it. Now the Church of God is to partake annually of the symbols of eating the flesh and drinking the blood of the Lamb of God. The flesh is symbolized by eating a piece of unleavened bread, and the blood is symbolized by drinking a small amount of wine.

As explained earlier, God gave man the means for dividing one day from another by beginning a new day at the very moment the sun sets on the previous day. The nighttime portion of the observance of Passover is at the beginning of that day. The activities that were to follow during the daylight portion of that same Passover day were also fulfilled in Joshua the Christ.

When Israel kept the Passover, the families were to kill and eat the lamb and this is described in scripture as "the sacrifice of the Eternal's Passover." Both the eating of the lamb by the Israelites on the night of the fourteenth, and later, the Church's observance of partaking of the symbols of the bread and wine are symbolic of God giving His Son to be sacrificed for mankind. It also pictures the Messiah's own agreement to give his life as that sacrifice. God the Father and Joshua the Christ willingly gave this sacrifice to mankind, and it was therefore truly "the sacrifice of the Eternal's Passover."

However, the actual time Christ died was in the mid-afternoon on the Passover day. This too fulfilled activities the Israelites were busy carrying out during that same period of time once they began observing Passover and the Feast of Unleavened Bread that followed. During the afternoon portion of Passover, the Israelites were preparing for the first day of the annual observance of the Feast of Unleavened Bread that would follow after sunset on Passover.

The actual killing of the sacrificial animals and their preparation for this feast to follow took place throughout the afternoon of Passover day. But the feasting and the actual offerings upon the altar could not begin until after sunset, once the Holy Day began.

Those animals that were killed during the afternoon of Passover, in preparation for the first day of the Feast of Unleavened Bread, are referred to in scripture as the "Passover offerings." So when scripture spoke of "killing the Passover," it included those things symbolized by the "Eternal's Passover" that was killed and eaten on the night of the fourteenth as well as the symbolism contained in the killing of those animals on the afternoon of the Passover that were to be feasted upon and offered up to God after sunset.

The entirety of Passover in both the night and daytime portions has great meaning in all the symbolism that Joshua the Christ actually fulfilled in his life and death.

THE ANNUAL SABBATHS—ANNUAL HOLY DAYS
THE FEAST OF UNLEAVENED BREAD

Once we have received the Passover sacrifice of Joshua the Christ to pay the penalty for our sins, we can move forward in God's plan for us. The next area of focus is the meaning of the observance of the Feast of Unleavened Bread.

The first day and the seventh day of the Feast of Unleavened Bread are annual Sabbaths, annual Holy Days. The first annual Sabbath, which is the first day of Unleavened Bread, begins immediately after sunset on Passover day.

"On the fifteenth day of the same month is the Feast of Unleavened Bread unto the Eternal. You must eat unleavened bread for seven days. In the first day you shall have a holy convocation [like the weekly Sabbath, this day is also a "commanded assembly"]. *You shall do no customary work* [occupational or regular work] *in it* [it is a Sabbath day]. *But you shall offer an offering made by fire unto the Eternal seven days. In the seventh day is a holy convocation* [Heb.— "commanded assembly"], *and you shall do no customary work in it"* (Leviticus 23:6-8).

This entire "appointed time" is one week in length. During this week we are to eat unleavened bread. We are to have no leavening in our homes during this period and we are to refrain from eating baked products, such as breads and cakes that contain leavening agents.

The symbolism, in this observance, is that leaven "puffs up" just like one's pride puffs up. Leaven is symbolic of sin. Leaven is symbolic of an "expression of pride" against the laws of God. We tend to live as we please rather than express God's will in our lives. Eating unleavened bread symbolizes our desire to obey God and eat of His way of life, the spiritual unleavened bread of life.

This symbolism is also about Joshua the Christ who was without sin—unleavened. The Church pictures this on Passover night when unleavened bread is eaten as a symbol of Christ's broken body. Joshua described much of this process in the Book of John.

With this fundamental understanding of the observance of Passover and the Feast of Unleavened Bread, consider how revealing the following scriptures truly are.

"They then said to him, 'What shall we do, that we might work the works of God?' Joshua answered and said unto them, 'This is the work of God, that you believe on him whom He has sent.' Therefore they said to him, 'What sign do you show then, that we may see, and believe you? What do you work? Our fathers did eat manna in the desert, as it is written, He gave them bread from heaven to eat.'"

"Then Joshua said to them, 'Most assuredly, I say to you, Moses did not give you that bread from heaven, but my Father gives you the true bread from heaven. For the bread of God is he who comes down

from heaven and gives life unto the world.' Then they said to him, 'Lord, evermore give us that bread.' Then Joshua said to them, 'I am the bread of life. He who comes to me shall never hunger, and he who believes on me shall never thirst. But I said to you, that you also have seen me, and do not believe. All whom the Father gives me shall come to me, and he who comes to me I will in no wise cast out. For I came down from out of heaven, not to do my own will, but the will of Him who sent me'" (John 6:28-38).

"Then the Jews murmured about him because he said, 'I am the bread which came down from out of heaven.' So they said, 'Is not this Joshua, the son of Joseph, whose father and mother we know? Then how is it that he says, "I came down from out of heaven?"' Joshua therefore answered and said to them, 'Do not murmur among yourselves. No man can come to me, except the Father which has sent me draw him, and I will raise him up at the last day'" (John 6:41-44).

"'I am that bread of life. Your fathers did eat manna in the wilderness, and are dead. This is the bread which comes down from out of heaven, that a man may eat thereof, and not die. I am the living bread which came down from out of heaven. If any man eat of this bread, he shall live forever. Now the bread that I will give is my flesh, which I will give for the life of the world.' The Jews therefore argued among themselves, saying, 'How can this man give us his flesh to eat?' Then Joshua said to them, 'Most assuredly, I say to you, except you eat the flesh of the son of man, and drink his blood, you have no life in you'" (John 6:48-53).

Joshua the Christ explained that if someone did not receive the Passover ("eat the flesh of the son of man and drink his blood") they could not have the life of God dwelling in them ("you have no life in you") through the power of His spirit. They were yet in sin until this could be a reality in their life. One must first receive the Passover in order to come out of sin and live God's way of life—become unleavened. Only those who become baptized by accepting Joshua as their Passover can themselves then observe the annual Passover.

After we are baptized and our sins are forgiven, we are to begin changing our lives. Contrary to the teaching of traditional Christianity, we are not to remain the way we are by simply accepting grace, but we are to change by becoming a new creature (Gk.– "creation") in God (2 Cor. 5:17). We are not to continue living the same way we did before baptism; however, we will have that same nature in us which we will have to fight against all our lives.

Receiving the Passover, Joshua the Christ, into our lives at baptism is only the beginning of a life-long process of repentance and fight to conquer and overcome our nature. Observing Passover each year is the acknowledgment of our need to continually repent, come out of sin, and to draw closer in unity and oneness with God and His Son.

Paul corrected the Corinthians in a matter that involved two people in their midst who were flaunting their disobedience before the Church. The Church was preparing to observe the Passover season and the Feast of Unleavened Bread, so Paul used this occasion to show them their error.

"Your boasting is not good. Do you not know that a little leaven leavens the whole lump" (1 Corinthians 5:6)?

Paul was addressing their cavalier attitude toward their actions of willingly ignoring sin (their "boasting"). He explained that sin is like a very small amount of leaven (yeast) that can spread throughout dough to make it rise—become puffed up. The lesson was that if sin is not addressed it can quickly grow and spread throughout the Church.

"Therefore purge out [Gk.– cleanse thoroughly] *the old leaven, that you may become a new lump, even as you are unleavened, for even Christ our Passover is sacrificed for us"* (1 Cor. 5:7).

They were being instructed to get rid of the leaven—to get rid of the sin—so that they could become a new lump of bread—a new body—in order to live a new way of life by being renewed in God's way through obedience.

They were not fully working to get rid of the sin in their lives. Humans will always find leaven (sin), but we are to get rid of it when it is revealed to us. This verse is also speaking of the fact that they were spiritually observing the Feast of Unleavened Bread and as part of that observance had removed physical leavening from their homes for this period of time— "as you are unleavened (physically)."

"Therefore let us keep the feast, not with old leaven [sin], neither with the leaven of malice and wickedness, but with the unleavened bread of sincerity and truth" (1 Cor. 5:8).

Traditional Christianity does not teach about these verses that were given long after Christ had died as our Passover, and how they reveal that we are to continue observing God's command to keep the annual Holy Days of the Feast of Unleavened Bread. Paul explained how these days were to be kept in the spirit of what they teach and that our lives are to become unleavened—absent of sin—by living truthfully before God in true obedience to Him in His way of life.

Although those in traditional Christianity teach that the laws of the Old Testament are done away, it should be obvious that they are not. It should be obvious by such verses that the early Church of the New Testament kept the annual Feast of Unleavened Bread. Other scriptures also show how they observed the weekly seventh-day Sabbath and other annual Holy Days as well.

Obedience to God in these matters was just a way of life for the Church. Different accounts throughout scripture reflect that truth. The New Testament is not written in the same way as the Old Testament when Israel was first given the law of God. The period of the New Testament is simply a witness of how the Church sought to live by the law of God that He had given them so long ago. It is not written to convince people of the validity of the law of God; that fact is simply taken for granted.

The Feast of Unleavened Bread teaches us that after baptism and forgiveness of sin through Christ we are to begin a journey out of spiritual Egypt—out of sin and the bondage it holds over our lives. We are to begin a process of change with a new way of living. When scripture speaks of being converted, it means we are to change from our old ways of carnal human nature to the new way of righteousness in God's way of life. Baptism is only the beginning of the process of coming out of sin. It follows with a life-long and continual process of repentance in order to continue in the journey of coming out of sin.

Churches in this world fail to tell this truth. Instead, they teach that we are under grace by the sacrifice of Christ and that the law has been done away. They believe grace means being free from the law of God. But that is not the "grace" that is actually revealed throughout scripture.

"What shall we say then? Shall we continue in sin, that grace may abound? [Paul is asking… if the law is done away through grace, then should we sin even more so that God's grace might be even greater in our lives?] *Certainly not! How shall we,* **who are dead to sin***, live any longer in it? Do you not know that so many of us as were <u>baptized</u>* [Gk.– "fully immersed in water"] *into Joshua the Christ were baptized into his death? Therefore* **we are buried with him by baptism into death:** *that like as Christ was raised up from the dead by the glory of the Father, even so we also should walk in newness of life* [by obedience to God's way of life]. *For if we have been planted together in the likeness of his death, we shall be also in the likeness of his resurrection: knowing this, that our old man* [our previous life before baptism] *is nailed to the pole with him, that the body of sin might be <u>destroyed</u>* [Gk.– "done away with"], *that we should no longer be slaves to sin"* (Romans 6:1-6).

It isn't the law of God that is done away, but it is the "old man of sin" that is to be done away. We are to come out of the watery grave of baptism and begin living a new life as a new creature (Gk.– "creation") in God, just as Paul told the Ephesians "…*that you put off concerning your former conduct the old self, which is corrupt according to the deceitful lusts. But become renewed in the spirit of your mind, and put on the new self, which after God is created in righteousness and true holiness*" (Eph. 4:22-24).

Coming out of spiritual Egypt and becoming unleavened in our lives is a life-long battle. As Paul explained in Romans 7, there is a constant battle against the carnal human mind that is in us, but this phase of God's plan shows us the beginning of a process of becoming free from bondage as we enter into a war of fighting against sin. We have to fight against our carnal human nature and strive to live by God's true way of righteousness. It is through this process, this struggle, that holy righteous character can be developed within us.

Just as God commands us to put leavening out of our homes and to eat only unleavened bread during the seven days of the Feast of Unleavened Bread, He also tells us to put leavening (sin) out of our lives and eat only of the true unleavened bread of life which comes in and through Joshua the Christ

PENTECOST

The next step in God's plan of salvation is pictured by Pentecost, which is also known as the Feast of Firstfruits. Pentecost in Greek means to "count fifty." The date for keeping this appointed time with God can only be known if we understand and observe the Passover and Feast of Unleavened Bread. God very specifically tells when to begin counting, from within a period of time inside the Feast of Unleavened Bread, so one can know when to convene before Him on this third annual Sabbath.

God's plan proceeds forward in an orderly and continuous manner. Each consecutive Holy Day progressively reveals more about the process through which mankind is able to receive salvation and become part of God's spiritual Family. Again, all of God's annual Holy Day observances are listed and commanded in the Book of Leviticus.

*"Speak to the children of Israel, and say to them, 'When you have come into the land which I give to you, and shall reap the harvest of it, then you shall bring a sheaf of the firstfruits **beginning** of your harvest unto the priest.* [Some have incorrectly translated this word from Hebrew as "firstfruits." However, it simply means the "first" or "beginning."] *He shall wave the sheaf before the Eternal, to be accepted for you. On the day after the Sabbath* [the weekly Sabbath] *the priest shall wave it'"* (Leviticus 23:10-11).

One cannot fully know when or how to observe Pentecost unless they understand God's instruction given in these verses that showed the Israelites how they were to observe the Feast of Unleavened Bread.

As these verses continue, one should begin to grasp how God has tied together the importance for what is revealed in the meaning for observing Unleavened Bread with that of observing the Holy Day that follows, which is Pentecost.

The period of time being spoken of in these verses is the Passover season, specifically during the Feast of Unleavened Bread. The smaller early harvest in Israel began in the springtime, but the larger fall harvest, which is also pictured symbolically in God's plan of salvation, will be covered later in a different annual Sabbath.

In Israel, many spring crops are ready to be harvested before Passover. Israel was given very specific instructions regarding the ceremonies concerning this early harvest that they were to observe during the Feast of Unleavened Bread.

"You shall eat no bread, or roasted grain, or green ears, until that very day when you have brought the offering unto your God. This shall be a statute forever throughout your generations in all your dwellings" (Lev. 23:14).

As part of this instruction, the Israelites were told to bring a sheaf of the first (of the beginning) of this harvest. It was to be used later in a ceremony that would take place during the Feast of Unleavened Bread. Although harvesting could begin before this time, they could not eat any of the new harvest until this ceremony was observed. All the symbolism contained in this entire process is awesomely revealing.

This sheaf was to be waved before God as an offering during this ceremony that was always held on the first day of the week (Sunday) during the Feast of Unleavened Bread. The "Wave Sheaf Offering" was symbolic of Joshua the Christ. Christ was to be presented to God to be "accepted" for us, which fulfilled this symbolism when he was received of the Father after his resurrection.

We have already covered the fact that Joshua the Christ was resurrected from the dead at the end of the seventh-day Sabbath. However, Christ did not ascend to God until several hours later on the first day of the week on that following morning. Notice this story as Mary had come to the tomb in the early morning of the first day of the week during the Feast of Unleavened Bread. Mary Magdalene wondered where Joshua's body had been taken, as it was not in the tomb, and she did not know that he already had been resurrected from the dead the previous evening just before sunset on the weekly Sabbath.

"Now Mary stood outside at the tomb weeping, and as she wept, she stooped down, and looked into the tomb. She saw two angels in white sitting there, the one at the head, and the other at the feet, where the body of Joshua had lain. They said to her, 'Woman, why do you weep?' She answered them, 'Because they have taken away my Lord, and I do not know where they have laid him.' When she had said this, she turned around, and saw Joshua standing there, but did not know that it was Joshua. Then Joshua said to her, 'Woman, why do you weep? Whom do you seek?' She thought he was the gardener, and said to him, 'Sir, if you have carried him away, tell me where you have laid him, and I will take him away.' Joshua said unto her, 'Mary.' Then she turned herself and said to him, 'rabboni,' which is to say, teacher. Joshua said to her, 'Do not touch me, for I have not yet ascended unto my Father. Now go to my brethren, and say to them, I ascend unto my Father, and your Father, even to my God, and your God'" (John 20:11-17).

Then the story flow that follows is contained in Matthew's account where he is speaking of what happened next as Mary Magdalene and Mary, the mother of James, were walking back to tell the disciples what Joshua had said to Mary. It is important to note the timing of this and the distinction that is made between this occasion and the previous one when Christ first told the women not to touch him.

"Now as they were on their way to tell his disciples, behold, Joshua met them, saying, 'Greeting.' Now they went and held fast to him by the feet, and worshipped him. Then Joshua said to them, 'Do not be afraid. Go tell my brethren that they are to go into Galilee, and there they shall see me'" (Matthew 28:9-10).

So Mary Magdalene was the first on that Sunday morning to whom Joshua the Christ appeared, and he spoke to her twice: once at the tomb, and then again as she was on her way back to tell the disciples what Christ had told her to say to them.

In the first account, it states that Christ told her not to touch him as he had not yet ascended to God. This was because he first had to fulfill the symbolism of the Wave Sheaf Offering that was always waved by the high priest on this morning of the first day of the week during the Days of Unleavened Bread. After his resurrection, Christ had to first be received and accepted by God as the Wave Sheaf Offering for mankind.

This was a quick ceremony performed by the high priest. It was also a quick fulfillment as Christ had just talked to Mary at the tomb telling her not to touch him, and then as the two Marys were going back to see the disciples, Joshua appeared to them again, and this time, he allowed them to touch him. He did so because he had now fulfilled the symbolism of the Wave Sheaf Offering.

Joshua the Christ perfectly fulfilled all of the symbolism contained in the Passover observance, and he perfectly fulfilled the symbolism of the Wave Sheaf Offering that was presented to God on the first day of the week during the Feast of Unleavened Bread.

Now we can continue with the instructions on how to count Pentecost, as it is given in Leviticus.

"You shall count unto you from the day after the Sabbath, from the day that you brought the sheaf of the wave offering until seven Sabbaths shall be complete. Even unto the day after the seventh Sabbath you shall count fifty days, and you shall offer a new meat offering unto the Eternal" (Leviticus 23:15-16).

The "sheaf of the wave offering," which represented Joshua the Christ, was a specific part of the ceremonies that were to be carried out **during** the Feast of Unleavened Bread. Therefore, this first day of the week has to fall inside these days of observance to start the count of fifty days.

Again, God is very specific as to the timing of this annual Sabbath of Pentecost. This annual Holy Day was to be counted beginning from a specific day (the first day of the week) within the observance of the Feast of Unleavened Bread. Seven weekly Sabbaths, from this day, was forty-nine days. Adding one more day, making it a total of fifty days, would bring us to another period of time on the first day of the week. Pentecost always falls on the first day of the week (Sunday on the Roman Calendar), but that day must always be counted from the first day of the week (Sunday) during the Feast of Unleavened Bread.

Then, in Leviticus, it continues with instruction for the observance of Pentecost.

"From out of your dwellings you shall bring two wave loaves of two-tenths of an ephah [ancient Hebrew dry measurement, approximately equal to a bushel] *that shall be of fine flour. These shall be baked with leaven* [yeast]. *These are the firstfruits unto the Eternal"* (Leviticus 23:17).

"The priest shall wave the bread of the firstfruits for a wave offering before the Eternal, with the two lambs. They shall be holy to the Eternal for the priest" (vs. 20).

On this day of Pentecost, the Israelites were to observe this ceremony. The two loaves were symbolic of the firstfruits (the 144,000) of God's plan. It is about those who will be firstfruits—those first resurrected into the Kingdom of God.

God has a plan of salvation whereby mankind is offered the blessing of becoming a part of His Family—to live in the God Family for all eternity as spirit beings. This Holy Day pictures those whom God called early in His plan to become part of His Family first. As the early spring harvest is referred to in scripture as the "firstfruits of the land," so are these, the firstfruits of God's plan, to become part of His Family earlier than the majority of mankind. The much greater fall harvest of the land pictures salvation for the far larger remainder of mankind, which is represented in the last two annual Holy Days.

These firstfruits are symbolized in the ceremony of these two wave loaves. One wave loaf represented those who lived by faith in the coming of a Messiah through whom God would save mankind. It represents those who were faithful that lived through the time that led up to Christ's first coming as the promised Messiah and our Passover.

The other loaf represents those who have lived faithfully in the acceptance of salvation through our Passover from the time of Christ (after his death) being received as the Wave Sheaf until his second coming.

It was instructed that two lambs be brought along with the wave loaves before God as each lamb represented Christ, a lamb for each of these two periods of time.

As the Wave Sheaf Offering picturing Joshua the Christ is waved to be accepted by God during the Feast of Unleavened Bread, so are the two wave loaves to be waved in an offering to be accepted by God on Pentecost. These firstfruits are pictured as being accepted by God and will become part of the God Family when they are resurrected and given eternal life.

There is also symbolism in the fact that these wave loaves are mixed with leaven. Joshua the Christ is always pictured as "unleavened"—being without sin. But these, although accepted by God, are pictured as being leavened—having been mixed with sin. Christ never sinned and he is therefore pictured as being unleavened. All mankind has sinned, so they are pictured as being leavened.

These wave loaves picture the 144,000 that God has called and chosen out of all mankind in the first 6,000 years of man on earth. They are resurrected to eternal life as spirit beings in the God Family—in the Kingdom of God—when Joshua the Christ returns. God has revealed that the wave loaves are offered up on a Pentecost, and this represents the 144,000 who come with Christ at his return.

Notice how these two loaves of the firstfruits are described in Revelation.

"Then I looked, and behold, a Lamb stood on the Mount Zion, and with him one hundred and forty-four thousand, having his Father's name written in their foreheads. Then I heard a voice from heaven, as the voice of many waters, and as the voice of great thunder, and I heard the voice of harpers with their harps. They sang as it were a new song before the throne, before the four living creatures, and the elders, and no one could learn that song but the hundred and forty-four thousand who were redeemed from the earth. These are they who were not defiled with women; for they are virgins [speaking of that which is spiritual].

These are they who follow the Lamb wherever he goes. These were redeemed from among mankind, being firstfruits unto God and to the Lamb" (Rev. 14:1-4).

These firstfruits are redeemed from among mankind during the first 6,000 years. They were brought out of sin—forgiven of sin—cleansed before God through Joshua the Christ. This 144,000 referred to as "firstfruits" in Revelation 14:4 are the same ones spoken of that have been "redeemed to God" by the blood of Christ (Revelation 5:9) as well as those that "have washed their robes, and made them white in the blood of the Lamb" (Revelation 7:14).

Just as these two loaves are made from a very small amount of the grain from the "firstfruits of the land," so are the 144,000 very small compared to all the billions of people that have lived during this same 6,000-year period of time.

As people come to better understand the plan of God revealed through His Sabbaths, they can begin to understand why so few are spoken of in the Old Testament as having a genuine relationship with God. The Old Testament period covers the first 4,000 years of man up to the time of Christ's first coming as the Passover Lamb of God. This same understanding will also help one see why the Church is spoken of as His little flock over the past 2,000 years. The Church has never been a large organization on earth because God's plan involves redeeming only 144,000 from this 6,000-year period of time.

The story flow of Unleavened Bread and Pentecost in Leviticus 23 is directly tied together. Both involve the early harvest referred to as "the firstfruits of the land." Joshua the Christ is the first of the firstfruits of God's harvest; the 144,000 are pictured as the rest of the "firstfruits of the land."

There is much more to the meaning of Pentecost, but this has given a basic understanding of those who are called firstfruits.

The story of Pentecost is a powerful one. God brought the children of Israel out of Egypt and took them through the wilderness to Mt. Sinai where, on the day of Pentecost, He gave them His law in the form of the Ten Commandments. However, the whole history of the

Israelites is that they could not keep the law. Carnal human beings, of and by themselves, are incapable of keeping the righteousness of God's law. Even to this day, the tribe of Israel known as Judah, generally referred to as the Jewish people, is the epitome of this story. The very best that man can do, on his own ability, is reflected in the life of the Jewish people. None of the other tribes of Israel held to the law of God like the tribe of Judah. All the others rebelled against God, long before Judah.

While man's best example of adherence to God's laws is found in the Jewish people, Christ found himself being attacked by these same people. This revealed that although they had an appearance of holding to the law of the God of the Old Testament, they did not understand Him, His ways, or even the law itself. If they had, then they would have recognized Joshua the Christ as the Messiah. In their blindness, the Jewish people refused the teaching and instruction that came to them from the Son of God.

The witness in their lives, and in the lives of all the Israelites, is that mankind, of and by himself, is incapable of living by the ways and laws of God. Pentecost reveals what is lacking in their lives—why they have not understood the teachings of the Old Testament—and why they did not recognize the Messiah when he came and spoke to them nearly 2,000 years ago.

The book of Acts reveals more about the importance of Pentecost in the plan of God. After Joshua the Christ died and was resurrected, he appeared to the disciples, which is the story in the opening of the book of Acts.

"*In the former account I recorded* [referring back to what he wrote in the Book of Luke], *O Theophilus, of all that Joshua began both to do and teach, until the day in which he was taken up* [taken into heaven] *because after this it would be through the holy spirit that instructions would be given to the apostles whom he had chosen, to whom also he showed himself alive after his suffering by many infallible proofs, being seen of them forty days, and speaking of the things pertaining to the Kingdom of God*" (Acts 1:1-3).

The gospel—good news—that Joshua the Christ taught the disciples was about the Kingdom of God. Although Christ continued with the disciples for forty days after his resurrection, God's purpose was that Christ remain with Him until it became time for him to return in the Kingdom of God as King of kings. Ten days after Christ was taken into the heavens, the disciples observed Pentecost, and from that day forward, the holy spirit is what would lead, guide, and instruct them, as Christ was no longer personally with them in their immediate presence.

"[Christ] *Being assembled together with them, instructed them that they should not depart from Jerusalem, but to wait for the promise of the Father* [referring to receiving the holy spirit], *which, he said, 'You have heard of me, for John truly <u>baptized with</u>* [Gk.- immersed in] *water, but you shall be <u>baptized with</u>* [immersed in] *the holy spirit not many days from now.' When they therefore had come together, they asked of him, saying, 'Lord, will you at this time restore again the kingdom to Israel?'"* (Acts 1:4-6).

The disciples did not understand that Joshua the Christ came the first time to fulfill Passover and that it would be nearly 2,000 years before the Kingdom of God would be established on earth. They thought he might fulfill prophecy by bringing that Kingdom to them at that very time.

"*He said to them, 'It is not for you to know the times or the seasons which the Father has set to be in His own authority. But you shall receive power when the holy spirit has come upon you, and you shall be witness unto me both in Jerusalem, in all Judea, in Samaria, and into the uttermost part of the earth'"* (Acts 1:7-8).

The coming of the Kingdom of God to this earth was not for their time, but it is for our time—now! It is only a very short time away because God has been revealing that all the Seals of Revelation have already been opened. The opening of the Seals has been a major marker for timing in final end-time events. Yes, the sobering reality is that the last Seal—the Seventh Seal—has already been opened and all that remains before WWIII begins is the release of the first four Trumpet events that will be manifest once nuclear weapons begin to be used.

Concerning the day of Pentecost, Joshua was making it very clear to the disciples that they were to stay in Jerusalem until they received the promise of God's spirit. More of this account and the pouring out of God's spirit upon the disciples can be read in Acts 2. Many people who witnessed this great event on the day of Pentecost became convicted of the words they heard from the disciples, so much so that they asked what they needed to do next.

"Then Peter said unto them, 'Repent, and be baptized every one of you in the name of Joshua the Christ for the remission of sins, and you shall receive the gift of the holy spirit" (Acts 2:38).

Although the law of God was given to the Israelites on the day of Pentecost, God revealed to mankind that His way of life cannot be lived through human effort alone, but mankind must also have the power of His holy spirit living in them. That is what was lacking in the children of Israel. It is still lacking in the lives of all who dwell on the earth except for those in the true Church of God whom the Father has called to understand His truth.

God's word and way of life is a matter of the spirit, and one must receive that spirit in order to understand the true will of God. Otherwise, people are limited to their own human reasoning when reading God's words and come up with their own ideas and beliefs about God and Joshua the Christ. That is why there are so many religions on this earth—all conflicting with one another in their teachings. There is only one true Church and one truth—one way of life that comes from God.

Again, mankind is not able to come out of sin on his own. He cannot obey God and come out of sin, as Unleavened Bread pictures, unless God's spirit dwells in him. It is only by acceptance of Joshua the Christ, as our Passover, that we can be forgiven of our sins. As the process of repentance and forgiveness takes place, God is there with the help of His spirit to make salvation possible.

The Book of Acts continues by showing that after baptism we receive the "laying on of hands" through God's ministry, and if we have repented, then we are begotten of God's spirit. It is the actual impregnation of the spirit of God that begets us. This is on a spiritual plane, but it is revealed by the "physical type" of human begettal. At the time a sperm cell impregnates the human egg, a life is begotten. It is not yet born into the world, but it grows in embryo until time for actual birth into the world.

This process, whereby humans are begotten of God's spirit, is likened to the human process. After we are begotten of God's spirit, we begin to grow—spiritually in embryo. As we continue in spiritual growth by conquering and overcoming the way of our selfish human nature, we continue to mature until the time we can be born into God's Family—into the very Kingdom of God. Traditional Christianity does not understand what it actually means to be "born again."

The expression "born again" is seen by most to mean a kind of "religious experience" leading to the acceptance of the one they call "Jesus" Christ. Though such people often do experience an emotional change accompanied by a life-changing focus, it is not what God reveals to be true.

Nicodemus, who was recognized as a great religious leader of his time, came to Joshua and asked him about the Kingdom of God. But Nicodemus could not understand what he heard. Joshua had told him, "Truly, truly, I say to you, except a person be born again, they cannot see the kingdom of God" (John 3:3). Nicodemus could only think physically about what Christ said and asked him, "How can a person be born when they are old? Can they enter a second time into their mother's womb and be born?" (Verse 4). Notice Joshua's response:

"Joshua answered, 'Assuredly, I say to you, except a person be born of water and of the spirit, they cannot enter into the kingdom of God. That which is born of the flesh is flesh, and that which is born of the spirit is spirit'" (John 3:5-6).

Joshua made it very clear. He said that which is born physically can only be produced by something physical. In human life when a physical sperm cell impregnates a physical egg, a physical embryo is produced. It is all physical. The physical process of an embryo growing in a mother's womb produces a child at birth.

God has given man a human spirit that makes us different from animals. It gives us individuality. We are not pre-programmed to respond to nature as God made the animal kingdom. With this "spirit essence" in the human mind, we have the God-like capacity of thought, creativity, and memory. This ability makes us individually unique. We have freedom of choice; we are free moral agents.

God cannot create perfect righteous character in others; it can only be accomplished as a matter of free choice. Otherwise, we would have to be programmed to respond "robotically" in matters of morality to live perfectly in accordance with God's law. But God wants us to choose on our own; we must choose between our own selfish ways or the ways of God. Again, the opportunity to choose comes in God's own time. Before this time comes to mankind—before God can give this opportunity to people—the witness of mankind is that it will always reject God! So in God's perfect timing, He will give people the best opportunity possible to be able to receive Him and His way of life.

Paul shared this knowledge of the human mind with the Corinthians. Paul explained that those in the Church could understand the mysteries of God. These "mysteries" cannot be understood without God's spirit and, therefore, His ways remain hidden—a mystery to mankind.

"But God has revealed them unto us by His spirit, for the spirit searches all things, yes, the deep things of God. For what man knows the things of a man, save the spirit of the man which is in him? Even so the things of God knows no man, but the spirit of God" (1 Corinthians 2:10-11).

Paul is clearly showing that without God's holy spirit a person is unable to know the truths and ways of God because He must reveal them. Mankind can only understand those things that are on a physical plane and cannot understand things that are on a spiritual plane. That is why Nicodemus could not understand what Christ was saying. He was not being drawn by God's holy spirit.

The spirit is the power of God. It is not a "being" as traditional Christianity teaches. The teaching of a trinity is false! There is no being called the Holy Spirit.

"Now we have not received [speaking to the Church], *the spirit of the world, but the spirit which is of God so that we might know the things that are freely given to us of God. Which things we also speak, not in words which mankind's wisdom teaches, but which the holy spirit teaches, by comparing spiritual things with spiritual. But the natural man* [physical human being] *does not receive the things of the spirit of God, because they are foolishness to him, and neither can he know them, because they are spiritually discerned"* (1 Corinthians 2:12-14).

So mankind of itself is unable to know God and His ways unless He reveals them. This is the reason mankind has continually rejected God and His ways. The pride in selfish human reasoning rejects the truth of God. Instead, mankind has formulated its own religious ideas and concepts of God that are more to its liking. The witness of mankind over 6,000 years is that it rejects God. That is why there are people who will hate what is written in this book. They cannot get past their own pride! That is also the reason why this world must be humbled before Joshua the Christ returns as King of kings.

If you are understanding these things, then there is only one way that is possible! God is giving you that opportunity and ability now. You are being drawn by God's spirit. If that is the case, then the choice is yours. Will you accept what is true? Some will have to go through more humbling by experiencing catastrophic events that can work to turn a mind to look to God for help and answers. The longer people reject God, the less likely they will be to receive His help and favor to live through those things that are coming.

God is going to begin to call the whole world! Yet most will not humble themselves to receive the Kingdom of God that is coming.

Let's return to the story flow of Pentecost. The physical process for human birth can only produce that which is physical, and the same is true of spiritual birth. A human being must be begotten of God's spirit. This is accomplished by the impregnation of God's spirit with the "human spirit" God has given all mankind. After the baptism in water by being totally immersed, one comes up out of the water and is from that point forward to walk in newness of life. It is immediately after baptism that the "laying on of hands" is performed by the ministry and the impregnation of God's holy spirit can beget us.

Once begotten of God's holy spirit, one can begin to grow spiritually, but only "in embryo" within the Church. We live in a physical body that is impregnated with God's holy spirit. We begin living a life of conquering the flesh—the pulls of human nature—thereby developing holy, righteous character. This process eventually allows us to be "born" into the Kingdom of God—the God Family—as spirit beings, fully "born of the spirit."

Joshua the Christ explained to Nicodemus that, "that which is born of the flesh is flesh." He was explaining that flesh (that which is physical) can only produce something that is flesh—physical. Human physical begettal leads only to human physical birth. But Christ went on to explain: "that which is born of the Spirit is spirit." Only when one is impregnated with the holy spirit of God can one, through time, be born into—enter—the Kingdom of God.

It is through this process that all the firstfruits will enter the Kingdom of God. When Joshua the Christ returns, they will be resurrected into spirit life, as spirit beings, composed of spirit in God's Family.

Pentecost pictures the "means" by which a person can understand and live God's ways. Through spiritual maturity and time, one can be changed from mortal to immortal—from physical to spiritual—born into God's spiritual Family. Pentecost also pictures the firstfruits of God's Family, those who will be resurrected first, out of all mankind, at the end of the first 6,000 years of mankind on earth. But all those who follow will also go through the same process of being drawn by and then begotten of God's holy spirit which can lead to their being born into the very God Family.

During this final period of the end-time, it was in 2008 that God revealed an additional truth to His Church about Pentecost. It is about the actual timing for when Christ will return to establish the Kingdom of God on earth.

Joshua the Christ is called the first of the firstfruits and he is pictured by the Wave-Sheaf offering that was waved before God to be accepted by Him as the first to be received into His Kingdom—His Family—in spirit life. Christ perfectly fulfilled this Wave-Sheaf offering when he was accepted by God on the Sunday morning after his resurrection. To fulfill this, Christ had to be accepted by God on the exact morning of the day the Wave-Sheaf was commanded to be observed.

The Wave-Sheaf offering always occurred on a Sunday morning during the Feast of Unleavened Bread. It was from this point that people were to count forward by 50 days to know when to observe the annual Holy Day of Pentecost.

God has revealed that in like manner, the rest of the firstfruits that are pictured by the wave loaves that are to be accepted by Him, must also occur on this Holy Day in order to fulfill its meaning. This means that the 144,000 represented by the wave loaves are to be resurrected and accepted by God to be received into His Kingdom—His Family—in spirit life just as Christ was when he fulfilled the Wave-Sheaf offering. The Wave-Sheaf offering and the Wave Loaves offering are uniquely tied together in timing and purpose.

God has now revealed that it will be on a day of Pentecost that Christ will return. It is then that he will be united with the 144,000 who are at that time resurrected into God's Kingdom. They will then come with Christ as a great spirit army who will put an end to WWIII and after that will establish the Kingdom of God to reign over mankind in the Millennium.

FEAST OF TRUMPETS

As one moves forward from one annual Holy Day to the next, more continues to be revealed about God's plan and purpose for mankind. Next, we come to the fourth annual Holy Day that occurs in the fall in the Northern Hemisphere. This day is known in Judaism as Rosh

Hashanah, and although Judaism has lost the true meaning and purpose of God's Holy Days, they do know the correct day for its observance.

The correct time for the Feast of Trumpets is generally listed on the Roman Calendar in September or early October.

"Then the Eternal spoke to Moses, saying, 'Speak to the children of Israel, saying, "In the seventh month [of God's calendar], *in the first day of the month, you shall have a Sabbath, a memorial* [a yearly observance] *of blowing of trumpets, a holy convocation"'"* (Lev. 23:23-24).

The Feast of Trumpets primarily focuses on events that lead up to and include Christ's coming to establish the Kingdom of God—His government on earth. Although there is meaning in Pentecost that foreshadows Christ's actual return and the resurrected 144,000 that will return with him, the Feast of Trumpets also includes this event (within the 7th Trumpet) by announcing it and the events that follow. This last Trumpet also includes events that work to establish God's government after Christ returns with the 144,000. These events tie in the meaning of Pentecost with the Feast of Tabernacles which pictures the establishment of the Millennium.

Some of the greatest meaning in the fulfillment of the Feast of Trumpets is the final heralding (trumpeting) that proclaims the coming of the King of kings who is to reign over mankind as the prophesied Messiah.

In his first letter to the Thessalonians, Paul talks about trumpets, and their meaning is also contained in the fulfillment of the Feast of Trumpets.

"But I do not want you to be ignorant, brethren [this is addressing the Church—those who are called to be among the 144,000], *concerning those who have fallen asleep* [speaking of those who were called and have died in the faith over the past 6,000 years], *so that you do not sorrow, even as others who have no hope. For if we believe that Joshua died and rose again, even so God also will bring* [send] *those who sleep in Joshua with him* [God will resurrect them to return with Joshua when he comes]*"* (1 Thessalonians 4:13-14).

"For this we say to you by the word of the Lord, that we who are alive and remain until the coming of the Lord [speaking of those still living who have been called to be firstfruits among the 144,000] *in no way precede those who are asleep* [dead in Christ]. *For the Lord himself shall descend from heaven with a shout, with the voice of the archangel, and with the **trumpet** of God, and the dead in Christ shall rise first. Then we who are alive and remain* [those few called to be firstfruits who are still alive in the Church at the time of Christ's coming] *shall be caught up together with them in the clouds to meet the Lord in the air, and so shall we ever be with the Lord"* (1 Thessalonians 4:15-17).

Paul described this same event to the Corinthian church.

*"In a moment, in the blinking of the eye, at **the last trump**: for the **trumpet** shall sound, and the dead shall be raised incorruptible* [given spirit life], *and we shall be changed"* (1 Corinthians 15:52).

Paul explained this event of God's plan that will take place when the last trumpet—**the Seventh Trumpet**—begins to be fulfilled. When this Trumpet event begins, the 144,000 will be resurrected. Those who are dead are resurrected first, then immediately following that, those who are yet alive who are part of that count of the 144,000 are changed to spirit life and no longer physical.

Most all who have been sealed as the firstfruits—the 144,000—are dead, but they will be resurrected at this time to immortal life, once this **last trumpet** event becomes fulfilled. Those few firstfruits who are alive at this time will be changed in an instant from mortal physical life to immortal spirit beings to become part of the God Family—the Kingdom of God.

"The seventh angel sounded, and there came to pass great voices in heaven, saying, 'The kingdoms of this world have become the kingdoms of our Lord, and of His Christ, and He shall reign for ever and ever'" (Revelation 11:15).

All the firstfruits called over the past 6,000 years will be resurrected on the day of this **last Trumpet event**, the first event of the **Seventh Trumpet** of the Seventh Seal. Yet the actual time of Christ's return with the 144,000 is what the Holy Day of Pentecost reveals.

However, it is the announcement **from all Seven Trumpets** that leads up to this great fulfillment. The primary fulfillment in the meaning of the Feast of Trumpets is contained in the announcement from all Seven Trumpets.

God's Holy Days focus on specific segments of His overall plan for mankind. These often overlap and are intertwined in meaning and purpose because these all work together through a complete process that concerns salvation that is spread over 7,100 years.

The first six Trumpets concern events that are about WWIII. These Trumpet events that precede the Seventh Trumpet are all part of what makes the fulfillment of the beginning of the Seventh Trumpet possible.

The announcement of the Seventh Trumpet begins with the declaration that "the kingdoms of this world have become the kingdoms of our Lord, and of His Christ, and He shall reign for ever and ever." Once this portion contained in the meaning of Pentecost is fulfilled, with Christ returning with the 144,000, there is yet more that becomes fulfilled in the meaning of Trumpets that goes beyond this event which then establishes Christ as the King of kings.

As trumpets are used in the announcement of Christ coming as King, he does not become fully established as King over all the earth until he and the 144,000 take control of it. The first 6 trumpet announcements are used as alarms of war before Christ's coming. The 7th Trumpet not only announces Christ's return with the 144,000, but it also announces a war that will continue after that return. That war is for the purpose of firmly establishing the government of God's Kingdom over the nations.

"Now I saw heaven opened, and behold, a white horse. He who sat on him was called Faithful and True, and in righteousness he judges and makes war [Gk. – **wages war**]. *His eyes are like a flame of fire, and on his head many crowns* [figuratively—**now ruling over all nations**]. *He had a name written that no one knew except himself, and he was clothed with a robe dipped in blood, and his name is called The Word of God* [**who is Joshua the Christ**]. *The armies* [**the 144,000**] *in heaven* [**the heaven of the atmosphere above the earth (in the sky)**], *clothed in fine linen,*

white and pure, followed him on white horses. Now out of his mouth goes a sharp sword, that with it he should strike the nations, and he will rule them with a rod of iron. He treads the winepress of the fierceness and wrath of Almighty God, and he has on a robe and on his thigh a name written: King of kings and Lord of lords" (Revelation 19:11-16).

So this final fulfillment that is pictured in the Trumpets that lead up to Christ's coming continues to be fulfilled even after his return. That is for the purpose of establishing his reign in the Kingdom of God that will now rule over the earth. It has also been quoted earlier that at this time Christ and the 144,000 will begin to destroy those who are destroying the earth.

In this manner, the meaning of the Feast of Trumpets ties in the meaning of Pentecost through Trumpets in order to establish the Millennium, which is pictured by the Feast of Tabernacles.

The blowing of trumpets had great meaning to the Israelites after they had been freed from Egypt. As the Israelites moved through the wilderness for forty years, trumpets were used to signal instructions, especially for movement from one encampment to another. Trumpets were also used as a warning of alarm and war. It should be clear how the physical use of these trumpets by the Israelites bears meaning in the fulfillment of God's plan and purpose contained in the meaning of the Feast of Trumpets.

THE DAY OF ATONEMENT

The fifth annual Sabbath is the Day of Atonement. Judaism calls this time Yom Kippur, and the correct day for its observance is generally recorded on the Roman Calendar by that same name.

"The Eternal spoke to Moses, saying, 'Also on the tenth day of this seventh month there shall be a Day of Atonement. It shall be a holy convocation [commanded assembly] *unto you, and you shall afflict your souls* [accomplished by a total fast from food and drink], *and offer an offering made by fire unto the Eternal. You shall do no work in that same day for it is a Day of Atonement, to make an atonement for you before the Eternal your God'"* (Leviticus 23:26-28).

"'You shall do no manner of work. This shall be a statute forever throughout your generations in all your dwellings. It shall be unto you a Sabbath of rest [an annual Sabbath], *and you shall afflict your souls in the ninth day of the month at even* [beginning from sundown of the ninth day], *from even unto even* [observed until sundown of the next day], *you shall keep your Sabbath'"* (Leviticus 23:31-32).

This annual Sabbath pictures the entire process covered from Passover to the Feast of Trumpets. Much of that process will have been fulfilled when Christ returns and Satan has been removed from the presence of mankind.

This day pictures the atoning process—the process whereby mankind can be reconciled to God. The firstfruits of God, after Trumpets has been fulfilled, are now fully atoned—reconciled—to God. The entire process (revealed through Passover, Unleavened Bread, Pentecost, and Trumpets) shows how the firstfruits were able to be born into God's Family—becoming part of the Kingdom of God.

Although the complete process will have been accomplished in the firstfruits, billions remain who are yet to be atoned—reconciled—to God. Every human being must still go through the same process as those called in the first 6,000 years who are among the 144,000. The Day of Atonement pictures that entire process. Everyone must come into unity and oneness with God–to become **at one** with Him.

Being reconciled to God the Father by the blood of Joshua the Christ begins with Passover. We must repent, come out of spiritual Egypt (sin), which is pictured by the Feast of Unleavened Bread, be baptized, and receive the impregnation of God's spirit (pictured through Pentecost).

As we grow spiritually and overcome our nature, God can begin to transform the very way we think and bring us into unity and harmony with His one true way of life. After someone has successfully gone through this entire process, they will be able to be made fully **at one** with God by a change from mortal to immortal, from physical to spiritual, into the Kingdom of God.

"I therefore implore you, brethren, by the mercies of God, that you

present your bodies a living sacrifice, holy, acceptable unto God, as your reasonable service. Do not become conformed to this world, but become transformed by the renewing of your mind so that you may prove what is that good, acceptable, and perfect will of God" (Romans 12:1-2).

The Kingdom of God is the Family of God. It will be composed of spirit beings who were once physical. They will be **at one** with God for all eternity.

The Fate of Satan and the Demonic Realm

Although this day pictures the entire process of reconciliation, of being fully atoned to God, it also pictures the fulfillment of another great event which pictures the primary influence of sin being completely removed from mankind.

When the Kingdom of God comes to this earth, everyone from that point forward will be offered the ability to enter into this process of atonement to God, as opposed to only a few who were offered this during the first 6,000 years. This time of a greater salvation for mankind will flourish in large part because of the fate of Satan and the demonic realm.

When God's Kingdom comes mankind will have been delivered from its own destructive ways. Now, Joshua the Christ will rule over all the earth with the 144,000 that were resurrected at his return. The ways of God will govern the course of mankind. Justice will be swift. The knowledge of God will fill the earth. People will learn to live in peace and harmony with others.

During that time, there will be only one religion on earth. There will be only one government ruling the earth. Everyone will be given the opportunity to keep the seventh-day Sabbath and the annual Holy Days. Great harmony, peace, and genuine love will fill the lives of families, communities, and businesses—in all who choose to live God's way.

False religions, politics, lobbyists, cumbersome and bureaucratic governments, corporate greed, drug smuggling, human trafficking, and so many other evils in today's world will not be allowed to exist. The way of competitive greed will be replaced by the way of cooperation geared toward benefitting others and the planet.

But even with all the awesome improvements that will take place for mankind in that time, one great obstacle still stands in the way of total peace, harmony, and prosperity for mankind. That obstacle is Satan and his demons (the angels who rebelled with him). The Day of Atonement also pictures the removal of Satan and his demons from the presence of mankind.

Lucifer was one of the archangels of God. He and a third of the angelic realm were given the responsibility of caring for the earth. The government of God was administered through this great archangel. His story is one of pride and rebellion toward God. Isaiah 14:12-14 and Ezekiel 28:12-17 give a general outline of this being, yet much more of the story is contained in fragmented areas throughout scripture.

God has not revealed the duration of timing for these various events. However, the evidence in our immediate solar system, as well as the earth itself, reveal a great deal when combined with the true accounts of scripture. Millions of years ago, God created the universe and our earth. But, again, God has not revealed the exact timing or the complete order of these events anywhere in scripture.

Before the creation of the physical universe and earth, God created the angelic realm. God is spirit and those beings He created are spirit. Nothing existed except the spirit world. The limited capacity of the human mind can only deal with the physical world around us, but our ability to grasp a spirit world is limited to physical concepts. God revealed that He did create a physical universe that included this earth. It is recorded that the angels rejoiced in God's physical creation.

God revealed to the angelic realm portions of His plan to create His own Family through human beings. The Book of Hebrews reveals that the angelic realm—the angelic kingdom—was created to minister, in time, to those who would live physical lives and eventually be born into God's very Family.

THE FALL OF THE UNITED STATES   241

At some point in time, Lucifer began to desire more for himself. He did not agree with God's plans or the purpose for the physical creation. He rebelled against God, and nearly a third of the angelic realm eventually rebelled with him. As a result, a great angelic war was fought; it extended into the physical creation.

God declared that the original creation of earth was made perfect and beautiful. Life was on the earth, but it was not the life that would exist when man would eventually be created. The earth had early forms of life on the land, in the sky, and in the sea. Skeletal remains of many of these creatures can be seen in museums and are evident throughout the earth.

What happened? Scientists try to give their "intellectual" interpretations of these matters, but the simple reality is that everything was swiftly destroyed at the time of Lucifer's rebellion. All life on earth was destroyed suddenly. That was hundreds of thousands of years ago. The story beginning in Genesis is speaking of mankind's creation, along with appropriate plant and animal life to complement mankind. It is not the actual original creation of the earth itself—that happened so very long before mankind's creation.

"In the beginning [There is no definite article in Hebrew. It should read, 'in a beginning...'] *God created the heaven and the earth.* [In a beginning, God did create the earth and the entire universe over much time—millions upon millions of years ago. There was no evolution, but simply a vast amount of time in creation.] *And the earth was* [Heb.— "became"] *without form, and void; and darkness was upon the face of the deep. And the spirit of God moved upon the face of the waters"* (Genesis 1:1-2).

In this account, the earth already existed. It had been initially created millions of years earlier. However, it had come to be in a state of waste and disorder. Darkness shrouded the entire earth. As it states, the power of God's spirit began to move over the waters of the earth, as the waters already existed. Then, God began to work on the entire earth—to bring back life. The entire picture here was one of chaos, as God began to renew the face of the earth as described in

Psalms. Yes, the earth is millions of years old, but mankind has only been here for nearly 6,000 years.

Due to God's plan to create His own Family, Elohim, that would be much greater than that of the angelic realm, Satan began to turn against God. He loathed God's plan to create beings that, with time, would become greater than him. Once he had turned a third of the angelic realm to his own jealous thinking, they were determined to destroy all life on earth. They did just that as the first creation of life was destroyed in an instant. God has not yet revealed to mankind how all this occurred, but only that it did.

When Satan's rebellion took place, God changed Lucifer's name to Satan, and those angels who followed him became known as demons. God confined them to this earth. Their presence and influence on mankind would serve as a part of God's plan to reveal the destructiveness and evil of all that resists His righteous ways.

When Lucifer rebelled, the government of God on earth had ceased. It is now, in our time, that the government of God is going to once again be restored. Joshua the Christ will usher in the Kingdom of God—the government of God over the earth.

Yes, this Day of Atonement also pictures the removal of Satan and his demons from the presence of God and mankind. They will no longer be able to influence and deceive mankind, except for a very short time at the very end of the 1,100-year reign of the Kingdom of God. At that time, this Day of Atonement will have even more meaning when Satan and the demons are once again removed, and this time—for all time—for all eternity.

The Day of Atonement pictures a time when Satan and the demons will have no part in God's future plans and purpose of continuing life. Instead, this annual Sabbath wonderfully pictures this world becoming fully atoned to God.

THE FEAST OF TABERNACLES
This period of time has great meaning, but we will only cover a condensed version of this Holy Day season. Leviticus 23 continues with

the annual Holy Days and describes a final observance that lasts for eight days. The first seven days is called the **Feast of Tabernacles** with the first day being an annual Sabbath. This period of seven days is followed by an eighth-day observance, which is also an annual Sabbath, the last day in the revelation of the plan of God. It is called the **Last Great Day.**

This Feast of Tabernacles pictures the time when the Kingdom of God will come to rule mankind for 1,000 years. Much has already been said about the coming Messiah and his reign on the earth. This festive observance pictures the time that is about to be ushered in on this earth. It will come once Christ and the 144,000 intervene to stop WWIII.

As it has been stated, the weekly Sabbath pictures the last 1,000 years in the 7,000-year plan of God. The Feast of Tabernacles focuses mostly on this same period of time and pictures that final 1,000 years when the Kingdom of God will rule all nations.

This seven-day Feast has also been referred to as the Feast of Booths in Old Testament observance because God had told the Israelites to build a kind of booth (open-air hut) which was to be a small temporary structure that was made of branches, twigs, and leaves and/or palms. One was to sit inside this booth for a small portion of time each day of the Feast and to specifically remember and think upon how God had delivered them from captivity in Egypt and then led them into a prosperous promised land. They were to remember how the children of Israel dwelt in temporary dwellings (tabernacles) for 40 years as they journeyed through the wilderness until God brought them into the promised land.

The Feast was to be observed in this manner until the Church of God was formed in 31 AD. Just as Christ changed how the Passover was to be observed differently once the Church began, the way the Feast of Tabernacles was observed had also been changed. The Israelites were to focus in a physical sense upon how God had delivered them from Egypt and led them to a land that He gave to them.

However, for the Church, God revealed the manner in which

the Feast of Tabernacles is to be observed that carries the spiritual meaning of what the Israelites had observed physically.

God's plan and purpose through what is revealed in this Holy Day season is about how He is leading mankind into a kind of spiritual promised land or spiritual inheritance. As physical human beings, we are given temporary dwellings—our physical human bodies—to live out our physical lives. However, God's purpose is to offer mankind, in His timing, the opportunity to be delivered from the bondage of selfish carnal human nature and the ways of mankind that are likened spiritually to being in spiritual captivity in Egypt.

Although mankind has only a temporary time for dwelling in a physical human body, God's purpose is to lead it into age-lasting life in spirit bodies—no longer in temporary dwellings, but spirit dwellings forever in the God Family of Elohim.

As with the physical Israelites, mankind can be delivered out of the corruption and bondage of living in temporary dwellings as they move through the wilderness of a carnal life. With the help and power of God's holy spirit, mankind can grow spiritually until a time that it can be delivered into a spiritual promised land—an incorruptible inheritance into the Kingdom of God as Elohim.

The Millennial rule of Christ and the 144,000 pictures a time when mankind will have no more wars, no more rulership from manmade governments, and no more religious confusion that has existed over the past 6,000 years. Mankind will be able to enjoy a prosperity, richness of life, and peace of the likes that it has never experienced before. The Feast of Tabernacles pictures this incredible age that is now about to be ushered in.

This Holy Day period pictures this new era of great salvation that mankind will be able to experience under the rule of Joshua the Christ and the 144,000 who are established to rule with him. This festive season not only reflects that righteous rule over mankind, but it pictures God's Church becoming established as the only true form of worship on earth.

THE LAST GREAT DAY
An additional day (eighth day) that follows the Feast of Tabernacles is traditionally referred to in God's Church by either of two names: the Last Great Day or the Great White Throne Judgment. It is the seventh and last of the annual Sabbaths of God. It is an exciting revelation in the plan of God. As the early spring harvest of firstfruits is pictured in Pentecost, so is the larger fall harvest pictured in the Feast of Tabernacles that focuses on the Millennium and the Last Great Day that concludes the final 100 years.

The Last Great Day pictures a time of great judgment that follows the 7,000-year portion of God's plan. It is a judgment period that covers a span of 100 years. This is the time spoken of earlier in this book when there will be no more birth of human life. The process of human begettal and birth will come to an end once the 7,000 years is over and the last hundred years begins.

Since this final period of human existence during this last hundred years has already been spoken of earlier in this book, it is not necessary to repeat everything here, but one needs to simply understand that this is what this seventh Holy Day is all about.

This is the time when billions will be resurrected to a second physical life. It is during this 100-year period that all who are given a second physical life to live will have the opportunity to choose and live God's way of life. In making such a choice, they can become part of the Family of God—the Kingdom of God—born as spirit beings, just as the 144,000 were.

Those who refuse will die a second time—a second death—never to receive life again. God's judgment on those who do not want to be part of His Family is not eternal torment. It is a punishment that will last for all time. It is death—never to be resurrected to life again—an eternal punishment.

It is during this last 100 years that billions will be resurrected. Those who have lived and died, young and old alike, will be given life again in physical human bodies that are filled with vibrant health—

whole and complete. It is then they can choose to become part of God's eternal Family. That is the story of the Last Great Day and the completed creation of Elohim!

It is during this period that billions of people who have lived and died within some period of time during the first 6,000 years will now be given the opportunity to know and choose God's true way of life. Everyone will be given 100 years in this second physical life in order to decide for themselves if they truly want God's way of life or not.

Although many will choose God, there will still be many who will not. They will want to hold on to some other way and many of them will simply want what they knew and lived in their first physical life.

This last annual Holy Day also pictures what will happen at the end of this hundred years. It is at the end that millions upon millions will have chosen God's way and grown spiritually to a level that they can then be accounted to be changed from physical life to spirit life in God's Family—Elohim.

It is also toward the end of this hundred years that those who have not chosen God's way of life will be judged to receive a second death. They will be put to death in this final moment of judgment. This is an eternal punishment that the world of traditional Christianity has twisted to mean being eternally punished. That is a sick and perverted concept and is blasphemous toward God. God does not have the kind of mind that would do such a sick thing. Instead, this concept reveals the kind of sick mind that is in Satan's thinking toward mankind.

An eternal punishment of a second death given to all who refuse God's way of life is simply a punishment that is everlasting in which they will never be resurrected to life again.

So at the end of 7,100 years of mankind dwelling upon the earth, there is an end to God's plan for mankind as there will be no such existence ever again. Those who have been redeemed from among mankind over the previous 7,100 years are those who have freely chosen God's way of life. When the Last Great Day comes to an end, there will be no more existence of mankind and those who continue on are those who will have been resurrected—changed from mortal to immortal—into everlasting spirit life as spirit beings in the God Family—Elohim.

This has always been God's desire and plan for the creation of mankind. The creation and purpose of the existence of mankind is for the greater purpose of the creation of God's own spirit Family. His Family is being created within human life that covers a span of 7,100 years. God's Holy Days reveal that great plan and the process that is required to enter His Family—a Family that He loves beyond what mankind can comprehend.

Printed in Great Britain
by Amazon